NEWSPAPERWOMAN OF THE OZARKS

Ozarks Studies

EDITED BY BROOKS BLEVINS

OTHER TITLES IN THIS SERIES

Twenty Acres:
A Seventies Childhood in the Woods

Hipbillies:
Deep Revolution in the Arkansas Ozarks

The Literature of the Ozarks:
An Anthology

Down on Mahans Creek:
A History of an Ozarks Neighborhood

Newspaper-woman of the OZARKS

THE LIFE AND TIMES OF LUCILE MORRIS UPTON

SUSAN CROCE KELLY

The University of Arkansas Press
Fayetteville
2023

978-1-68226-236-8 (paper)
978-1-61075-801-7 (electronic)

27 26 25 24 23 5 4 3 2 1

Manufactured in the United States of America

Designed by Daniel Bertalotto

♾ The paper used in this publication meets the minimum requirements of the American National Standard for Permanence of Paper for Printed Library Materials Z39.48–1984

Library of Congress Cataloging-in-Publication Data

Names: Kelly, Susan Croce, 1947- author.
Title: Newspaperwoman of the Ozarks: the life and times of Lucile Morris Upton / Susan Croce Kelly.
Description: Fayetteville: The University of Arkansas Press, [2023] | Includes bibliographical references and index. | Summary: "Newspaperwoman of the Ozarks is a long-overdue study of Lucile Morris Upton, one of the region's best-known reporters and local historians. A longtime reporter and columnist at Springfield Newspapers during a time when the remote Ozarks was reshaped from backcountry into a national vacation hub and the role of women in the United States shifted drastically, Upton not only reported on these rapidly changing times but also personified them in her own life. In this significant contribution to the historical research of Ozarkers' daily lives, author Susan Croce Kelly traces Upton's life, from teaching school to covering the news to governing her city and raising awareness for historic preservation, and paints a vivid picture of Ozarks culture over nearly a century of change"—Provided by publisher.
Identifiers: LCCN 2022061277 (print) | LCCN 2022061278 (ebook) | ISBN 9781682262368 (paperback) | ISBN 9781610758017 (ebook)
Subjects: LCSH: Upton, Lucile Morris. | Women journalists—Arkansas—Biography. | Women journalists—United States—Biography. | Ozark Mountains—History.
Classification: LCC PN4874.U68 K45 2023 (print) | LCC PN4874.U68 (ebook) | DDC 070.92 [B]—dc23/eng/20230117
LC record available at https://lccn.loc.gov/2022061277
LC ebook record available at https://lccn.loc.gov/2022061278

FOR JANE AND SHARON

There is a story of a certain editor who was asked to define the difference between a "newspaper man" and a "journalist."

He replied that a newspaper man was one who had worked for years on the press, writing editorials, criticisms, literary articles, and everything else that goes to make up a great paper; while a journalist was a young man fresh from college, with no experience of his own and usually too conceited to profit by that of others. After he has worked a few years, gets some of this self-esteem rubbed off, and learns to estimate himself at something like his true value, he becomes a plain, ordinary newspaper man.

The same definition will apply to women with equal force. It is the young girl fresh from school who insists upon her title of journalist; the woman who has labored side by side with men for years and whose work will stand the strain of comparison is content to be a "newspaper woman."

—**Helen M. Winslow**, "Some Newspaper Women," *Arena Magazine* 17, no. 1, December 1896

CONTENTS

ACKNOWLEDGMENTS

Some things just take time. This book has been in the works for at least twenty-five years, and during that time an almost uncountable number of people have helped me make it happen.

Lucile died in 1992; in 1995, I had the good sense to interview a number of people who had known her as friends, newspaper colleagues, or fellow history buffs. John Hulston, Ann Fair Dodson, Elizabeth McCain, and Gordon McCann set me on the right path to understanding Lucile's value to the region. Almost a decade later, when I moved back to the Ozarks and renewed many old friendships, I was able to talk to others who had worked with Lucile or Betty Love, including several of my own colleagues from the *Springfield News and Leader*: Dale Freeman, Mike O'Brien, Bob Linder, and Barbara Clauser. Others who remembered Lucile to me were the wonderful folks at Wilson's Creek: battlefield curator Jeffrey Patrick, and curator Alan Chilton, who shared memories of Lucile and treasures from the Battlefield library.

Brooks Blevins, the Noel Boyd Professor of Ozarks Studies at Missouri State University, encouraged my interest in Lucile, and ultimately accepted my manuscript for the University of Arkansas Press.

I have taken the time, imagination, and help of librarians and archivists all over central and southwest Missouri, especially Anne Baker, Tracie Gieselman-Holthaus, Shannon Mawhiney, and others at Missouri State University Special Collections, and Brian Grubbs and his local history crew at the Springfield-Greene County Library Center. Connie Yen at the Greene County Archives, all the wonderful librarians at the State Historical Society of Missouri, Gwen Simmons at the College of the Ozarks' Lyons Library, and members of the Ralph Foster Museum staff also have skin in this game. I even pulled together a small roundtable of former colleagues at the *St. Louis Globe-Democrat*: Anita Buie Lamont, Karen Marshall, and Margaret Sheppard, to share their memories of Life-As-Newspaperwomen.

The book simply couldn't have happened without Pam Morris Jones, Lucile's grandniece, a meticulous researcher and record keeper, and my cousin. Pam was the person who cleaned out Lucile's office and saved many of her papers that otherwise would have been discarded. Pam has also offered insights from the time she spent with Lucile growing up and later, when she regularly visited Lucile in the nursing home where she spent her last few years.

Another remarkable bit of luck for me—and for Lucile—has been my acquaintance with Lynn Morrow, the father of Ozarks history and a patient adviser and reader who listened to me and set me straight innumerable times.

Finally, but not least, are my many friends and fellow writers who seemed to think enough of this project to drop everything many times to read, and reread, all or parts of the manuscript and answer dozens of "Is this all right?" questions. This vast army of wonderful people is led by Jeanne Kern, whom I can never repay, along with John and Gina Hess, Mike O'Brien, Tom Peters, Pam Morris, Everett Kennell, and members of my family.

Mostly, because he has had to live with Lucile—and practically without me—for the past two years, I want to thank my husband, Joel.

NEWSPAPERWOMAN OF THE OZARKS

INTRODUCTION

Many people have written about the Ozarks, but often the ones who achieved the most popular and/or financial success with their tales were not Ozarkers. They were men and women who chanced into the region early in the twentieth century, added their imagination to what they saw and heard, and wrote novels, poetry, "studies," and nonfiction commentaries about the curious "hillbilly" people and marvelous scenery of this remote area. Many, but not all, of these people were self-styled anthropologists, bent on describing a way of life that was changing as fast as automobiles were taking over Ozarks roads. While those outsiders attracted a lot of attention, it was left up to the local Ozarks newspapermen and newspaperwomen to tell the real story of their world as they covered the daily doings of their neighbors and their communities. These people and their newspapers played a significant role in what was happening across the region, yet, for the most part, the local press was seen as simply part of the background and, apparently, not worth investigating and writing about. It was an unfortunate oversight.

More than a century has passed since the Ozarks became a tourist mecca, thanks in large part to the publication of Harold Bell Wright's novel *The Shepherd of the Hills* in 1907 and the construction of Powersite Dam in 1912. Readers still revel in that historic novel, in folklorist Vance Randolph's collections of folk songs, folktales, and bawdy stories; and they look into geographer Milton Rafferty's discussions of how the landscape and the people interacted to create the Ozarks culture. Millions of tourists regularly find their way to our hills, lakes, and rivers.

In recent years, historians have provided readers with a variety of new works on the Ozarks' past, and a new *Literature of the Ozarks* has highlighted writing by Ozarkers over the past century and a half. Yet there has been little to no examination of the newspapers and newspaper people that informed much of that historical research and provided the background to Ozarks daily life. Ironically, while scholars recognize that newspapers offer a window into a community's history and culture, the reporting and reporters of local news in remote regions have not been studied in the detail afforded to large city dailies, and certainly not in relation to other aspects of the Ozarks.

Today, the newspaper universe is changing and disappearing every bit as fast as the old Ozarks changed a century ago. The company once known as Springfield Newspapers, Inc., because of its morning, evening,

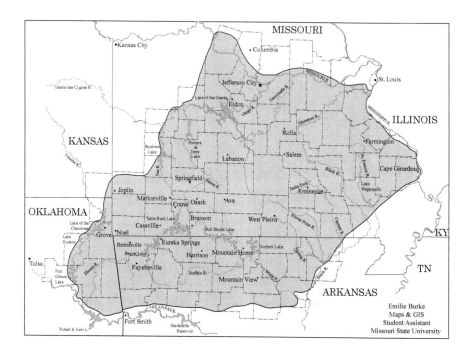

The Ozarks: Fifty-five thousand square miles of sparsely populated green hills, deep valleys, small towns, limestone caverns, high bluffs, and miles of translucent waters flowing across rocky riverbeds. *Map by Emilie Burke and Jim Coombs, Map & GIS Unit, Missouri State University.*

and Sunday publications now has only a single product. In 2020 an announcement came from faraway owners Gannett Inc. that the company's giant press would cease, the building would be sold, and the daily *Springfield News-Leader* would be printed 160 miles away. Nationally, between 2004 and 2020, more than two thousand newspapers in the US closed, the vast majority being rural and weekly. In almost that same time period (2008 to 2020), the number of newspaper newsroom employees in the US diminished by more than half, from 71,070 in 2008 to 31,000 in 2020. In 2019, of those reporters and editors left behind, forty-one percent were women. As of this writing, Springfield Newspapers has only thirteen full-time reporters in a newsroom that once welcomed more than fifty. And while we have seen biographies and memoirs of newspaper journalists, they tend to be journalists from big city dailies, like Gail Collins of the *New York Times*, Celestine Sibley of the *Atlanta Journal*, foreign correspondent Martha Gellhorn, Texas newspaper columnist and author Molly Ivins, investigative journalist Ida B. Wells, and the like. As far as books about newspaperwomen in the Ozarks, a search showed only one: a biography of Roberta Fulbright, who owned and published the *Northwest Arkansas Times*.[1]

Into that mix I offer a look at the life and times of Lucile Morris Upton, a longtime reporter and columnist at Springfield Newspapers. Born in rural Dadeville, Missouri, two years before the twentieth century, and coming of age just as the Nineteenth Amendment was passed, Lucile was neither a suffragist nor an equal rights activist, but part of a broad movement of independent women who took advantage of doors that opened to them and lived life on their own terms. When writers suggested that the West was a good place for an independent woman to live, or at least to find herself, Lucile took herself off to New Mexico to teach school. After the end of the school term, having determined to trade her life's work from teaching for journalism, she managed to secure a newspaper job at the *Denver Express*. By the time she returned to Missouri two years later, she had been a "sob sister" in Denver and a city desk reporter for the *El Paso Times*. As a reporter for, variously, the Springfield *Leader*, *Leader and Press*, *Daily News*, *News-Leader*, and *News-Leader and Press*, she charted the growth of the Ozarks as a tourist region, became the first woman in town to cover the jail and justice at the courthouse, and edited an Ozarks-wide column that made her a pen pal and friend to historians, poets, and other writers all over the region. Her passion for Ozarks history led her to write a critically acclaimed book on the 1880s vigilante group known as the Bald Knobbers and, ultimately, to convince Springfield and Greene County to pay attention to important artifacts of the past. Through her many contacts—and, after her retirement, a seat on Springfield's city council—she became a key player in encouraging civic leaders to push for Wilson's Creek Civil War battlefield to become part of the National Park System and to make the Nathan Boone homestead a Missouri state park. Both were accomplished, the first established in 1960 and the second purchased by the state in 1991 but not opened to the public until after her death.[2]

During her years as a Springfield reporter—many of those before the advent of television—Springfield's newspaper was the largest daily for a hundred miles in any direction. There is value in recording important aspects of an institution like that, and the way it affected the lives of the community and the people who worked there. Newspapers were also changing in those days, from political or philosophical mouthpieces like the memorably named *Unterrified Democrat* on the northern edge of the Missouri Ozarks, to become more objective in their coverage of the news. Although Lucile was hired by a newspaper before she could save enough money to attend there, the University of Missouri had opened a coeducational school of journalism in 1908, the nation's first. The new school's goal was to teach students to be professional journalists through both classroom instruction and the hands-on experience of producing a community newspaper. Elsewhere, other journalism schools and departments of journalism were opening, notably at Columbia University in New York and Northwestern University near Chicago. Despite not having attended journalism school, Lucile's professionalism was never in doubt.[3]

Before she died in 1992 at the age of ninety-four, Lucile had become a much-lauded regional celebrity as a role model for young women, a cheerleader for aspiring writers, and a dogged proponent of historic preservation. Lucile never finished college—and certainly was never considered a professional historian—but almost every part of her life and a great deal of her newspaper reporting were inspired and guided by her lifelong passion for stories about the Ozarks and Ozarks history. Similarly, this book, while not a formal academic or anthropological study, offers a look at Lucile Morris Upton's life and her work at a regionally influential newspaper, in large part through her own words. For a region as place-proud and history-focused as the Ozarks, it is past time to study one of the region's best-known newspaperwomen as well as the publications where she spent forty years.

Lucile was my great-aunt. She was a highly respected—and sometimes feared—retiree of the Springfield *News and Leader* when I joined that newsroom staff. I was twenty-six years old at the time, about the same age as she had been when she became a Springfield reporter a half century before. During the few years I lived in Springfield, I was privileged to spend many evenings and afternoons in Lucile's living room listening to her talk about her newspaper days, her family, and her love of local and regional history. She fascinated me, but it was not until I also retired and had an opportunity—and the perspective—to study her personal papers that I realized just what a pioneer she had been and how her life exemplified the lives of so many early twentieth-century women. Like the historic sites she loved and sought to preserve, her story is one that deserves to be told and remembered.

| 1 |

GROWING UP OZARK

On June 23, 1923, when Lucile Morris walked past the crowd outside Denver's First Baptist Church and presented her brand-new press card to the security guards at the door, they immediately ushered her to a pew directly in front of the spot where US President Warren Harding and Mrs. Harding would be seated.[1]

Lucile was twenty-five years old, new to Denver, new to the newspaper business, and suddenly she was on assignment from the *Denver Express* to cover the president of the United States. Granted, it was only a Sunday morning church service, and she would not be doing an in-depth interview, but it was heady stuff nonetheless.

Not many careers begin like hers did. But then, not many Ozarks girls have lives like Lucile's.

In the early 1900s, when the population of the US had reached 76,212,168 and Missouri's population had passed the three million mark, the small but well-to-do farming community of Dadeville boasted several churches, a telephone exchange, a bandstand for the town band, and the Morris Hardware & Undertaking business. Despite a lack of paved streets, the town also was home to a hotel, two banks, a dry goods store, movie theater, grocer, several doctors, and a blacksmith. On one side of the blacksmith's shop, near the bottom of the big Bull Durham Tobacco sign, someone had scrawled: "Madstone at the Morris Farm."[2]

In the days before rabies treatments were readily available, the location of a madstone was vitally important to people in the rural US. If a dog started frothing at the mouth or acting strange, it was an almost sure thing that the dog had contracted rabies, and it had to be killed. If the dog had bitten anyone anywhere near Dadeville, there was only one known treatment—the Morris madstone. Madstones were fibrous calcified substances about the size of small eggs, found in the stomachs of white deer.

People believed that when one was soaked in warm milk and placed on the bite from a rabid animal, it would suck the poison from the wound. Needless to say, a good number of people sought help at the big farm at the edge of town. It wasn't at all unusual for someone to knock wildly on the door in the middle of the night or interrupt the family on their way out to call on friends. The frantic visitor would be greeted by a gentleman with the odd, old name of Mount Etna and his wife, Ella. One of them would always go with the desperate caller to administer the madstone.[3]

Lucile was the couple's granddaughter. She may or may not have overheard her grandmother question the madstone's effectiveness—after all, not all dogs who "acted funny" had rabies—but she certainly understood that the odd-looking object set her family apart. She probably also knew that by the early 1900s, not everyone believed in madstones. Even in small rural towns on the edge of the Ozarks, people were beginning to see automobiles, use Brownie cameras, listen to phonographs, and read news of Dr. Louis Pasteur's 1885 treatment for rabies. On the other hand, the Ozarks was a region steeped in the past, and many people did believe in the power of madstones, just as they believed that growing a mustache strengthened weak eyesight or that a poultice of chicken manure mixed with lard was a successful treatment for pneumonia. Those Ozarks superstitions were not part of Lucile's childhood but, like her grandmother, she understood that some people believed in them and, therefore, they needed the security of the Morris madstone. Especially since the Pasteur treatment was not readily available in the Ozarks.[4]

Lucile lived with her widowed mother and two brothers in a small house on the edge of her grandparents' farm and watched the comings and goings at the big house with great interest. Her father, Albert, had been the old couple's only son. When he died in 1908 from a long illness, he left his wife, Veda Wilson Morris, nine-year-old Lucile, eight-year-old Mount Etna, who was named after his grandfather, and two-year-old George. Albert had been the successful proprietor of the town's hardware and undertaking busines. After he died, Veda sold the stock in the store to Fred Hulston for $6,000, but she kept the building, and the monthly rent payment of twenty dollars provided a basic income for the small family. Veda and the three siblings continued to live in the little house near Albert's parents, and very near Albert's grave, which could be reached through a gate not far from the front door. Because Albert had worried that his children wouldn't remember him, one of his dying wishes was to be buried in their front yard. Rather than just plunking his casket down in the farmyard, the elder Morris honored his son's wish by donating a small tract of land to the local Masonic Lodge for a Dadeville Masonic Cemetery. Lucile remembered that "three of Papa's closest Masonic friends chose the acre from his farm where the lodge would start a cemetery. When that was done, the three selected the lot that was to be reserved for our family. . . . nearest our home. Very important to us in those days was the fact that when the cemetery was fenced, the Masons allowed Mother to buy a gate through which we children could walk directly to Papa's grave." Before he "took sick," Albert had been a Mason. To Lucile, "A Mason, particularly a Mason in the Mellville Lodge of Dadeville, I thought, was a person on whom a widow and her children could rely."[5]

GROWING UP

Even though Lucile and her brothers lost their father, and their mother never remarried, they certainly didn't grow up alone. Both their grandfather and grandmother Morris came from sizable families, and Veda was the youngest of fifteen. Veda's father, Solomon Wilson, had come to Missouri from Tennessee just before the Civil War and was a successful merchant in the county seat town of Greenfield. Her closest brother, the

Grandfather and Grandmother Morris and Old Moll in front of the small house at the Dadeville farm where Lucile grew up. *Morris family photos.*

The three Morris siblings: Etna (standing), Lucile, and George. Note the wad of gum in George's left hand. *Morris family photos.*

three siblings' uncle George, was a banker and businessman in nearby Everton. The rolling prairie land of Dade County was full of well-to-do Wilson aunts and uncles to look after the three Morris youngsters, as well as plenty of cousins to play with during long summer days and at many family gatherings.

Lucile, Etna, and George were all tall and slim, with dark hair and almond eyes inherited from Grandmother Ella's family. Their mother saw to it that they were educated, dressed well (especially Lucile), knew how to act in polite company, and were prepared to take charge of their own futures. Quite aware that as an adult she would have to fend for herself, Lucile planned to become a teacher. "I didn't know of anything else," she recalled years later, after her long career as a newspaper reporter and writer. She was also tough—in the way any girl with two brothers grows up to be tough enough to hold her own even against high odds.[6]

She was close to her two younger brothers when they were growing up, and the three would remain close throughout their lives. Etna was nearest to Lucile in age and outlook. A ringleader among his peers, Etna grew up to be a banker—thanks to their uncle George—and a politician. Little brother George was an outdoorsman. For some time, Veda paid him a penny for every mouse he trapped, which he would skin and mount on a board to prove his catch. Most days, he took his shotgun with him to school, and on the way home, he would hunt small animals that came across his path. As an adult, George supervised the state of Missouri's fish hatcheries and made a national name for himself in the science of fish culture.[7]

STORIES

The big farm at the edge of Dadeville was a good place to grow up. Most of the time, the three siblings attended school and helped out on the farm, but there were also times when they would sit with their grandparents and listen to stories. Those stories were about their world: the family, their town, and the green Ozarks foothills where they lived. Lucile was mesmerized by tales of how her family fared during the Civil War, which had ended only thirty-three years before she was born. Given the nature of the war in Missouri, many of the combatants knew, or were related to, each other. Kinch (Kincheon) West, leader of a vicious guerrilla gang that burned Dadeville during the war, was born and grew up in Dade County. The story of a chance meeting between West and her grandfather Wilson probably gave Lucile the shivers. Reportedly, West said, "Sol, I could have killed you plenty of times during the war. I saw you hiding out in a ditch in your fields more than once." She also heard the story of how Grandmother

Wilson's brother, Confederate Captain Silas Bell, was killed in 1861 during the terrible Battle of Wilson's Creek just outside of Springfield.[8]

Of especial interest to Lucile, though, was the true story of Grandfather Morris's two oldest brothers, Will and Ed. To her, their story was more evidence of her family's distinctiveness. "Grandfather Mount Etna was twelve years old at the outbreak of the war," she said later. "I was always sorry he had been too young to fight. His older brothers were of divided opinions." Will (William H.), about twenty-eight, had left the farm to become a businessman in St. Louis, where he became wealthy. Tradition was that he outfitted a regiment for the Confederacy and was made a captain. Ed (Edmond J.), about twenty-six when the war commenced, was a Dadeville farmer who owned the 180-acre farm that her grandfather later purchased and where Lucile grew up. Ed became captain of a local unit that became Company E of the 15th Regiment, Missouri Cavalry, Missouri Volunteers, in the Federal Army. According to family lore, Captain Will took his Confederate company to Texas so as not to fight his brother, and he remained in the South following the war. The two brothers never saw each other again.[9]

The stories about her family's past gave Lucile's world another dimension and instilled in her a lifelong interest in how things came to be. They also helped her understand that what seemed obvious was not necessarily true. "When I was a child, dozens of old men who had fought during the Civil War were still living in our section of Dade County," she said. "They told hair-raising stories of encounters with bushwhackers . . . and often pointed out to me the one house that was left standing after Kinch West burned the town. Vaguely I recall stories the old-timers related about that fire, but I couldn't begin to repeat an authentic account of it."[10]

On the other hand, Lucile did eventually learn the true story of the Dade County regiment organized by Captain Ed. In the years after the war, Captain Ed "took down with rheumatism" and drew a pension until his death in 1891 or 1892. When a family friend commented that Ed must have been badly hurt in the war to get "such a sizable pension," Lucile's grandfather told her otherwise and said that Ed "never smelled powder except when they went hunting or shot up a dance . . . None of them!" She was shocked to learn that, yet she wanted to know more: "I found, by asking questions once in a while, that he was right. Not more than a dozen Melville (Dadeville) men were in the war. Two or three were in the Wilson Creek ruckus and one or two at Pea Ridge and that's about all. They would blow and cuss the Rebs and tell about where they were in the war, but they were not. They didn't go. I must say this version of the Dadeville fighting men was a blow to my childhood memories of venerable oldsters who whiled away long hours on store porches rehashing heroic

Civil War deeds." For ever after, Lucile would seek out people who could tell her—truthfully—about the past.[11]

Besides tales of the Civil War, Lucile and her brothers loved hearing stories from their grandparents that were more personal and closer to home. A favorite was about the ancestor who earned that very strange name, Mount Etna. Grandfather Morris told them the name came from a Welsh ship captain lost at sea somewhere south of Italy in the midst of a fierce storm. Just as the captain was about to lose hope, a volcano erupted on the nearby island of Sicily, spewing fire and ash into the sky. The captain recovered his bearings, steered his ship to safety, and when he returned home, he was so grateful for being saved from shipwreck he named his next-born son Mount Etna, after the volcano. Mount Etna became a family name, handed down for many generations and across two continents. Lucile well knew the little Morris Cemetery just a few miles from Dadeville where she and her brothers could find a number of tombstones chiseled with the names of their Mount Etna Morris forebears.[12]

Lucile also liked to hear her grandmother tell the story of her own name. A traveling preacher was staying with Mount Etna and Ella in the big farmhouse on the July night in 1898 when she was born in the little house next door. As was the custom in those days, her grandparents asked the reverend if he would like to name the baby. He suggested Winnie Davis, after the daughter of Confederate President Jefferson Davis. Out of politeness, the new parents accepted Winnie for the baby's first name, but they would not burden their daughter with Davis. Veda added Lucile as the second name, after the beautiful and wise heroine in Owen Meredith's popular book-length poem, *Lucile*, which had been published a decade before. Lucile she became, and she made her first newspaper appearance the following week: the editor of the local *Dade County Advocate* reported, "Born to Mr. and Mrs. Albert Morris, of Dadeville, on Wednesday night of last week, a daughter, of the usual age, weight, and degree of fineness . . ."[13]

As she was growing up, carrying the name of the Confederate president's daughter probably wasn't too much of a burden as Lucile was never called Winnie, but being part of a Democrat family in heavily Republican southwest Missouri did require a certain amount of grit even for a small child. "So overwhelmingly Republican was the Dadeville of my youth it was difficult to get representation from the Democratic party to man the election booth," she remembered. Besides her father, "a close friend who lived on a farm near town and the postmaster were the only Democrats I knew. Every election day I bled and died for the Democratic party. All the other school kids, including my erstwhile best friends, jeered at me and chanted, 'Black cats and pickled rats, are good enuff for Dimmicrats!'"

Lucile survived, but she never forgot. She was a Democrat the same way she was a girl with curly brown hair named Morris—she was born that way. Later, a friend described her as "a strong Democrat and a liberal for her time." She remained a member of the Democratic Party all her life and, after Etna began running for office, the proud sister of a Democratic politician. She herself was never a political activist, not even a campaigner for the right to vote—and she did not campaign years later when she won a seat on the Springfield City Council.

Politics aside, Lucile continued to revel in stories of her family, her town, and her Ozarks world, especially stories of how things came to be the way they were. "I think I was born with an interest in history," Lucile later told an interviewer. "I don't know why I'm always so interested in the background of all these places, but I am, and that's what got me started." All those stories she heard added extra dimensions to life in Dadeville and were a promise that there was more to the world than what she saw every day.[14]

THE WIDE WORLD

Lucile had a first chance to experience the larger world at the age of six, when her father and grandmother Morris took her to the St. Louis World's Fair. They rode the train to St. Louis and stayed in a hotel. Eighty years afterward, she still regarded it as a highlight of her life. "The main thing I remember was the Ferris wheel. I don't think I rode on it, but it was there every time you looked up." One thing she did not remember was the state of Maine's giant pine lodge, although she would make its acquaintance several years later.[15]

Not long after that trip to St. Louis, Lucile learned that she lived in the Ozarks. "Our Dade County home was on one of the infrequent Ozarks prairies—called Crisp Prairie—and I didn't think the hills around there amounted to much," she related. However, one year, a schoolmate returned from a summer in Taney County's White River country and bragged that she had been to the mountains. "Any sort of trip impressed us, for we lived ten miles from where the railroad trains whistled," said Lucile, "but somehow I doubted that my school friend had been to any mountains." So she asked her mother: "To my astonishment, mother explained that I also had seen mountains—the Ozarks mountains, and in fact, I lived in them. She added, however, that our section of the range might more accurately be called the foothills."[16]

Lucile completed grammar school in Dadeville, growing up with chil-dren of families much like hers, people whose ancestors had come from the British Isles and who had moved west over the generations, finally settling in southwest Missouri. High school, though, was a different story. In those days, not everyone attended, much less finished, high school. And for those who did, it was often a complicated process. For Lucile, coming from a self-described "bookish family," there was little question about her education. Thanks to her very determined mother and the support and encouragement of her many aunts, uncles, and cousins, Lucile would later tell people that she graduated from high school three times. Dadeville High School only went through tenth grade and the term lasted only seven months, so after she graduated from Dadeville, she had to finish her studies elsewhere. She spent the following year about sixty miles away in Conway, a railroad town organized just after the Civil War. One of the many Morris cousins was teaching in Conway, and Lucile boarded with her and two other teachers that year, in a woman's home. Conway's high school was just three years, so after a successful year there, Lucile graduated again, then moved with a friend to Greenfield, the Dade County seat, to live with the friend's grandparents and attend Greenfield High School. That fourth and final year of high school, Lucile was busy. Besides doing her part as a forward on the girls' basketball team, writing stories, and acting in the senior play, she attended parties, fell in and out of love, went on outings, and was elected secretary of the senior class. She was bookish, but not at the expense of having a good time.[17]

When Lucile's Greenfield's class of 1915 developed its list of future roles for the graduates, Lucile was voted most likely to be a suffragist. The idea that the independent, spirited girl would make a career of promoting women's rights certainly fit. She was the perfect age to become involved, and she had the example of Emily Newell Blair, a writer and serious suffragist living about seventy miles away in Carthage. When Lucile was in her teens, Blair's name appeared from time to time in the Dade County newspapers, and about the time Lucile was finishing high school, Blair was named publicity chair for the Missouri Equal Suffrage Association and the first editor of its monthly publication, *Missouri Woman*. If a woman wanted to be a suffragist, there wasn't a much better role model than Emily Newell Blair. Lucile, however, wasn't interested. What probably appealed to Lucile far more than Blair's push for the vote was seeing Blair's name as the author of articles in national magazines like *Good Housekeeping*, *Cosmopolitan*, and *Harper's Bazaar*—and possibly hearing in 1915 that Blair was a founding member of a group called the Missouri Writers Guild. Thirty years later, Lucile would preside over that organization. Future suffragist or not, on May 21, 1915, at 7:30 in the evening, with her mother and brothers in the audience, Lucile walked across the stage of the Greenfield Opera House and received her third—and final—high school diploma.[18]

WHITE RIVER COUNTRY

Shortly after her graduation, Lucile had her first chance to see the Ozarks mountains her grade school friend had bragged about all those years before. Her uncle George built a house in a fashionable White River development south of Branson, and he purchased the lot next door for Lucile. She and her brothers built a little frame cabin on the property, painted it yellow, named it Wayside Lodge, and spent most of the next several summers there, often with visiting friends. That particular section of the White River country was very popular—and not just with Ozarkers. During the years when Lucile, Etna, and George were growing up and learning about how life used to be, the rest of the world was learning about the Ozarks. There had been a scattering of unpleasant—but widely read—publicity about the Ozarks in the late 1880s concerning the vigilante doings of a group called the Bald Knobbers. Then, a quarter century later, after a preacher in Lebanon, Missouri, camped on a ridge above the White River and became acquainted with some of the local people, he penned a romantic novel that became an instant, and worldwide, bestseller. Harold Bell Wright's *The Shepherd of the Hills* introduced the world to the rivers, caves, and wild landscapes of the Ozarks mountains, along with a memorable cast of characters. Over time, beautiful Sammy Lane, handsome Young Matt, no-good Wash Gibbs, Young Matt's heart-of-gold parents, Old Matt and Aunt Molly, plus Uncle Ike, the postmaster at Notch, Missouri, and the only real identifiable character in the book, would become archetypes for the way the outside world thought about Ozarks hill people.

Almost immediately after *The Shepherd of the Hills* was published in 1907, tourists began swarming into the region. Fishermen and hunters from the big cities had long found their way to the Ozarks' teeming streams and quiet woodlands, but the book, which was reprinted in several languages, attracted a whole new group of people. Coincidentally, several newly built railroad spurs made the Ozarks of southwest Missouri and northwestern Arkansas more easily accessible to vacationers. In the midst of this boom, the Ozark Power and Water Company received congressional authorization to build a hydroelectric dam on the White River near Forsyth. The construction project brought about a thousand jobs to Taney County and plunked down more than $2 million into the local economy. Development followed. A few miles upstream from the new Powersite Dam that had created an even newer Lake Taneycomo, the small community around what had been Reuben Branson's general store and post office was incorporated as the town of Branson. Across the river and a little way upstream from Branson, Springfield real estate developer W. H. Johnson cast his sights on a Missouri Pacific Railroad stop at Hollister, another small village and post office. Johnson platted a town and, with his son, built twelve buildings in the English Tudor Revival style. The stucco buildings with their steeply pitched roofs and half-timber trim were eye-catching. When Johnson named the street out in front Downing Street, his "English village" of Hollister became a tourist attraction. Almost simultaneously, Ozarkers like Uncle George—and his niece—began building their vacation homes on a steep hill nearby. Since there was a Presbyterian church, auditorium, and campground at the top of the hill, the hillside development quickly became known as Presbyterian Hill.[19]

Very near Presbyterian Hill was the big log structure that had been the State of Maine building and one of the most popular exhibits at the 1904 St. Louis World's Fair. After the fair, the Maine building was taken apart and relocated to a bluff above the White River in Hollister, where it served as headquarters for the St. Louis Hunting and Fishing Club for several years. In 1915 the Maine building changed hands and became the new home of the School of the Ozarks, a Southern Presbyterian Mission school for Ozarks children who had no other chance at an education. Lucile and her pals loved to go to the grand old building. She remembered it as being "just lovely with beautiful pictures of birds and things. We used to go over there from Presbyterian Hill and get lemonade and cake they served in the dining room. They always had that for tourists and people who stopped in."[20]

During her summer visits to Presbyterian Hill, Lucile made the acquaintance of a number of local people, one of whom was poet John G. Neihardt. Neihardt hired her to teach his children to type, and they became friends. Later Neihardt became a national figure with his epic poetry and his book *Black Elk Speaks*, about conversations with an Oglala Sioux holy man. In those summers, Lucile also got to know old-timers who told her stories of the Ozarks. She learned about Henry Schoolcraft, who had explored the region a century earlier. She heard about Civil War skirmishes, about robber Alf Bolin, who menaced the area during the great conflict, and about the night-riding Bald Knobbers, a vigilante group organized after the war to bring law and order to the still-conflicted Ozarks. She also became interested in Nathan, the youngest son of Daniel Boone, who had surveyed the country around Springfield, and who lived the latter part of his life on a farm only a few miles from Dadeville.[21]

COLLEGE

In the meantime, at the end of Lucile's first summer in the yellow cabin on Presbyterian Hill, she headed to Springfield, thirty-five miles southwest of Dadeville, to attend Drury College and become a teacher. By Dadeville standards, Springfield was a big city. It was home to nearly forty thousand residents and was not quite one hundred years old when Lucile arrived. It was a hub for the St. Louis–San Francisco (Frisco) Railway and—reflecting its industrial growth—a strong union town. Downtown boasted a couple of hotels and three skyscrapers, the first of which was the ten-story Woodruff Building. The Woodruff Building housed a drugstore, barbershop, pool hall, and two elevators, along with a good number of business offices. A few blocks away, the new Heer's Department Store offered upscale shopping and a popular ladies' tearoom. Lucile already knew about the Civil War Battle of Wilson's Creek that was fought near Springfield, but she learned that Springfield's vivid history didn't stop there. The first western shoot-out—when Wild Bill Hickok shot and killed Dave Tutt—took place on the city's central square in 1865, and, also on the square, three Black men were lynched in 1906.[22]

Drury College, part of Springfield since 1873, was the town's upscale institution of learning. Founded by Congregationalist Home Missionaries, Drury was patterned after Congregationalist liberal arts colleges like Oberlin, Carleton, Dartmouth, Yale, and Harvard. Probably more significant to Lucile, Drury's first graduating class in 1875 was all women. At Drury, Lucile studied chemistry, history, English, math, and German—noting, "None of these are favorite" in a scrapbook she kept at the time. She also made the acquaintance of at least two people who would figure large in the future of Springfield. One was Lester Cox, a member of her freshman class from nearby Republic, who would become a leading area businessman and a backer of Springfield's first commercial radio and television stations, and who would give his name and substantial effort to refurbishing Springfield's Burge-Protestant Hospital into a sprawling CoxMedical complex. The other person she met at Drury was Dr. L. E. Meador, her history teacher. Meador, who was an economist and political scientist, became an important civic leader in the state, a mentor to Lucile, and a good friend. Later, both Cox and Meador, who shared Lucile's passion for local history, turned their considerable energies to one of her favorite causes: seeing Wilson's Creek Battlefield recognized as a national park.[23]

At the end of Lucile's first year at Drury, the family bought an automobile—an Overland Model 83B Touring Car. Lucile was so proud of that car that she pasted a picture of it in her scrapbook, noting, "This is my new Overland 83B Touring Car. Bought May 22, 1916." Dadeville also took note: a county history reported that "Mrs. Morris [Veda] . . . drives an Overland car, is a good roads booster and is a splendid specimen of the up-to-date, Twentieth Century woman who takes a lively interest in public affairs and presides over an ideal home." The other twentieth-century woman who drove that car, of course, was Lucile.[24]

| 2 |

EXPANDING HORIZONS

Maybe it was the new automobile; maybe, as she said years afterward, it was trouble with her eyes; whatever the reason, Lucile did not return to college that fall. Instead, thanks to education courses she had taken at Greenfield High and her studies at Drury, eighteen-year-old Lucile was hired by her own Dadeville school to teach in the primary grades. She was already acquainted with the families of most of her students, and knew many, but not all, of her fellow faculty members. Among those she did not know was a young man about three years her senior named Homer Y. Garland, known as Hy. A graduate of the Normal School in Warrensburg (today University of Central Missouri), Garland was beginning his second year at the Dadeville school and his first as principal of the high school, which was located in the same building where Lucile taught elementary students.

It probably came as no surprise to anyone in that little town that Lucile and Garland began keeping company. Her varied high school experiences and even her early trip to the St. Louis World's Fair had given her a taste for the world away from Dadeville. And there weren't many fellows around as worldly, never mind charming, and fun to talk with as Homer Garland. Or as tall. Add the fact that he was ambitious, with no intention of remaining in Dade County or teaching for the rest of his life, and Lucile was smitten. Likewise, the willowy brunette with the amazing brown eyes and a taste for literature and history would have certainly been an object of interest for Garland.

The two kept company the way young people did in those days. They attended Sunday concerts performed by the enthusiastic town band in which Etna was a tuba player. They fished in the nearby Sac River and took long drives in the countryside. They went to see silent movies at Dadeville's movie theater and perhaps thrilled to films like *The Girl Reporter* or *The Perils of Pauline*, both starring Springfield native Pearl White. No doubt Lucile told Garland about her young father, who was a leading citizen of the town—despite being a Democrat—when he became fatally ill. She related stories about pioneering ancestors and probably told him about the madstone.

Garland, in his turn, told her about his father's career as editor of a union publication in Springfield, owner of a printshop, and then publisher of the *Otterville Mail* newspaper in a small town about 130 miles north of Dadeville. He told of his own plans to save his money and become a newspaperman Out West. Lucile disclosed her hopes of one day teaching school in Kansas City and making a success of her life. Over time, they began to talk about a future together. When the weather was nice, she invited Garland to the siblings' cabin on Presbyterian Hill. That was a good time for Lucile. She discovered she could be a successful teacher, and she was in love.[1]

Lucile and Homer Garland in Branson. *Morris family photos.*

Then things changed. Congress declared war on Germany April 6, 1917, and passed the Selective Service Act seven weeks later. Daily life was totally disrupted as the country geared up for war, and young men all over the Ozarks left to join the military. Lucile's cousin Norman Quarles, a fellow teacher, joined the army and was sent to France. Within weeks, Garland decided to enlist. He announced he would not return to the Dadeville school in the fall, went home, and applied for officer training. He also began to write to Lucile, a correspondence that lasted through the end of the world war and beyond. Although none of her letters remain, she kept a great many of his, and they pretty much tell the story of their romance. In one of his first letters he referred to a long talk they had just before he left Dadeville: "You said, and your voice was troubled, 'I don't know whether a girl of my age knows her mind.' . . . I wonder."[2]

Lucile may not have "known her own mind" or been deeply in love, but she did care for Garland, and she was keen on hearing about his plans to be a newspaperman. Being a writer, he was glad to oblige her interest in the world of journalism and, it being wartime with so many jobs going vacant, he was able to step into a temporary reporting job. Following his discharge from basic training at Fort Riley in July 1917, and while he was waiting on the army to call him up for Officer Candidate School, Garland found a position at the *Daily Drovers Telegram*, a farm publication that covered news of the Kansas City Stockyards. He referred to it as "one of the corn belt dailies" and advised Lucile that, dull as it was to report on feed prices, he enjoyed working on a publication. "I intend to stay in the newspaper game," he wrote.[3]

Within a few months, Lucile heard from him that he had moved up and on, to the city desk of the Parsons, Kansas, *Daily Sun* newspaper, covering day-to-day happenings in that small town. Along with reading his continued protestations of undying love, Lucile learned that his new job had two perks: it paid three dollars a week more money, and it was much closer to Dadeville than the Kansas City Stockyards. Garland was acquiring his journalism experience the way most reporters did in those days, beginning at a small publication, then moving on to larger ones, earning more pay and better assignments with each new job. That kind of training generally involved moves across the country before the journeyman reporter could settle in for the rest of his career. To Lucile, it must have sounded far more interesting than teaching. When the Thanksgiving holiday rolled around that fall, she, along with Etna and two friends, traveled to Parsons to see just what a newspaper reporter's life was like. Their visit to an "exceedingly tall reporter who wanted to forget there was such a thing as a newspaper while he entertained a party of out-of-town guests, including one particular " 'friend'?" made the *Sun*'s gossip columns the following week.[4]

MURDER AT THE MOVIES

Garland's love letters to Lucile were full of his experiences covering mostly unexciting agricultural and small-town news, but not all small-town news was dull. Lucile and her brother George learned that one evening when they found themselves caught up in a big-time news event that made the papers across southwest Missouri. Life in rural small towns like Dadeville was good, but it could also be rough. People kept guns—and madstones—to protect themselves and, in those pre-Prohibition days, liquor was everywhere. When she was about nineteen, Lucile and some of her teacher friends were at the local movie theater, the Skydome, when the manager shot and killed a local citizen. On that particular night, Lucile and her chums were sitting in the main part of the theater, and George was with some of his buddies in the balcony, known as the "pigeon roost."

Years afterward, George remembered the event vividly. "I was just a little old kid," he said, "Here comes this guy, Chess (Chester) Pyle, and he was drunk. He stayed drunk most of the time. He came up in the Pigeon Roost and sat down and began passing around a big bag of peanuts. Naturally, we got as close to him as we could. Well, Chess would eat peanuts a while, then he'd holler real loud . . . The manager of the show, Thee (L. T.) Dunaway, he come back and told Chess to shut up, and Chess stood up and called him everything in the world. He disturbed everybody in the show—of course it wasn't a show-you-could-hear because they had words on the screen. Dunaway made another trip up and tried to make Chess shut up and he didn't do it. Then here come Thee's wife and she tried to make him shut up. (We heard Chess was having an affair with her.) Then Thee come back. I was still right there eating peanuts. Chess stood up, threw his hands out and said, 'See, you haven't got guts enough to shoot me!' I saw Thee pull out a gun, and brother, I disappeared right down off the Pigeon Roost as fast as I could. Thee shot him twice while Chess was standing up there, then Chess fell down into the aisle and Thee shot his gun three more times." George hustled down to the projection room, where he found Lucile and her friends. "All of 'em were in there, scared to death. I stayed a bit outside the door then I started home. I ran in and put my pajamas on and started to get in bed, and Mama was there and she asked, 'Did anything happen tonight?' "[5]

As with Kinch West a half century before, both Pyle and Dunaway lived in Dade County and were well-known to the local people. Pyle, who was married, came from a prominent Dadeville family. Dunaway was a former postmaster. The local newspaper, the *Greenfield Vedette*, described Pyle as "aside from the occasional times when he was in his cups, a most likeable young man." However, the article went on to say that "when drinking he became abusive and it had been felt even by his friends that sooner or later he would encounter serious trouble." The murder was picked up by other newspapers, including the *Springfield Leader*, where Lucile would later be a reporter. Lucile wrote to Garland about the evening and he wrote back immediately sympathetic that "you girls had to see it all . . ."[6]

Five months after the shooting, a Dade County jury found movie theater manager Dunaway not guilty of murder. The *Dade County Advocate* had this to say about the trial:

> This was a case which grew out of a killing at Dadeville, a full and impartial account of which was given in *The Advocate* at the time and which it is not necessary now to repeat. Raking up skeletons and shaking moulding bones is not news. Suffice it to say that after hearing all the testimony, the jury before whom the case was tried returned a verdict of acquittal [then it listed the names of the jurors].[7]

Pointed newspaper commentary like this was prevalent in those days and was one of the reasons for a nationwide move to make newspaper reporting "more professional." That was the goal of the country's first school of journalism, which opened on the campus of the University of Missouri in 1908. Even today, however, there are those who lament the personal touch provided by some old-time editors. One in particular was Arthur Aull at the Lamar, Missouri, *Democrat*, who kept the nation entertained for years in the early-to-mid-twentieth century by reporting on details of marital disputes, city council squabbles, and business dealings in his hometown, which was not too far north of Dadeville.[8]

WAR AND PESTILENCE

That fall, as Lucile readied herself for her second year as a Dadeville schoolmarm, Garland wrote to ask, "Are you glad it [school] is beginning or do you rather dread it? Poor child! All those dirty brat kids in that hot dirty room—your patience astonishes me." Yet a few days later, he followed up on a more positive note: "When a teacher has the ability to make children love her, and at the same time is able to teach them something, she is bound to make good." Both letters must have contained truths, because at the end of that school year, Lucile resigned so that she could continue her college studies, and the parents of her students organized a gala dinner in her honor.[9]

When Lucile moved back to Springfield in the fall of 1918, three things were different. Instead of returning to Drury, she enrolled at the Fourth District Normal School, the local teachers college and today's Missouri State University. The war in Europe was affecting life at home: even in Missouri farm country, the food supply was an issue. In Springfield, restaurants were making victory bread almost without flour, and everywhere the US Food Administration warned, "The food supply of the world is short and getting shorter. You cannot take eighteen million men out of production and put them into destruction of human products and expect things to go on as before."[10]

Besides the war news, though, the newspapers were also full of disturbing articles about an influenza epidemic. So bad was the epidemic in southwest Missouri that all of Springfield's public schools, theaters, and other public meeting places closed on October 1. Within weeks, both Drury and the teachers college closed. As the epidemic spread into smaller Ozarks towns like Dadeville, Everton, and Greenfield, public gatherings were canceled and local schools shut down as well. Forty miles south of Springfield, the School of the Ozarks at Point Lookout reported that the pestilence "settled on the students and faculty like a pall." More than half the school was infected, and the place was shut down with no outside help, so the healthy members of the school community took care of the sick ones. Springfield reopened fairly quickly, and Lucile stayed well, but Etna, who was at the University of Missouri in Columbia, was downed by the flu, luckily a relatively mild case.[11]

While Lucile was balancing her studies against the local threats of influenza and worry that eighteen-year-old Etna might be drafted, she received a letter from Garland, who announced he was leaving the Parsons *Sun* behind for Officer Candidate School at Camp MacArthur in Waco, Texas. It turned out that he was in Waco only a few months; the war ended that November, before his company could be sent to Europe. Soon after he was mustered out, Garland landed yet another newspaper job, this time as a reporter for the *Tulsa Democrat*, a big step up from the small-town *Parsons Sun*. A few months after he joined the *Democrat*, he even crowed to Lucile that he had gotten a scoop on the more respected *Tulsa World*. From the *Democrat*, Garland's letters waxed eloquent—and a bit cynical —about his new reporting job. "We're having it very dull now insofar as big local news is concerned," he wrote. "—a few deaths, conventions, minor accidents, and that sort of thing makes up the entire roster. But one of these days, or nights, there will be a suicide and a train wreck and a killing all at once. Then business will pick up." Since Lucile had been close-up at a killing that made the news, it is questionable whether she was terribly impressed.[12]

NEW PLACES AND NEW FACES

As the year progressed, Lucile visited Garland in Tulsa when she could, he visited her in Springfield, and once they even spent a weekend in the romantic Missouri spa town of Excelsior Springs. Yet, when the school term ended that spring of 1919, Lucile was restless. Fortunately, she had a chance to travel and was able to spend the summer visiting her cousin Ingalls and her mother's closest sister, Tori (Victoria) Wilson Giles, in Hereford, Texas, located in the far western part of that state. While she was in Hereford, a local newspaper wrote of her visit, calling her "a popular . . . Society girl." This was her first taste of the West, and during that summer, she and Ingalls traveled around a bit, visiting friends in other small Texas and nearby New Mexico towns.[13]

The fact was, Lucile not only expanded her geographic horizons by visiting Hereford but her emotional ones as well, and she learned even more about newspapering in the process. That summer, she met Bob Stewart, a traveling salesman from New Mexico, who was smitten by the "brown eyed beauty from Missouri," and with whom she would be in and out of contact for a number of years. Another time, when she went with Ingalls to visit friends in Clovis, New Mexico, she made the acquaintance of Jack Hull, the publisher and editor of the Clovis *News Journal*. A decade her senior, Hull had newspaper stories to tell that made Garland's life as a Tulsa reporter sound pretty dull. Hull's experiences were the stuff of novels and movies. Lucile heard about gunfights, including one between the Clovis fire chief and a local saloonkeeper. Hull had witnessed murders, watched an exchange of bullets on top of a freight car, and took part in a chase after two bank robbers, barely missing a bullet in his windshield. In later years, Hull described "those eventful days in Clovis history that made my newspaper career something never to be forgotten" and called it "the hey-day of newspaper work here."[14]

Garland's deeply earnest letters, on the other hand, included his news of a police strike and pending Tulsa visit by the Prince of Wales, but he also shared his high-minded thinking about journalism careers. "You'll think the sole aim of a newspaper is to wait for a misfortune to cover, but that really isn't so," he wrote to her. "Did you ever consider what would happen if we were without newspapers—even for a day? Business would be partially paralyzed and the whole country would be as greatly upset as if there were no bread. The spreading of knowledge about the daily happenings of the world—that's our mission and it cannot be said to be minor or unnecessary." Garland's dispatches about the nobility of newspaper work, and probably her chance meeting with Hull and his electrifying stories, emboldened Lucile to consider the possibility of a newspaper career for herself. She told Stewart as much, but was vague as to how she would make that happen.[15]

Later that summer, after Lucile returned to Missouri, Garland visited her at the cottage on Presbyterian Hill, following up with an amorous letter about "dark paths on a quiet hill" and "canoe rides over black water to my sweetheart." It may have been a romantic visit, but as far as Lucile was concerned, something was off. He was pushing for a deeper commitment, yet told her he wasn't prepared to support a wife. Over the next few months, Lucile allowed their relationship to deteriorate. Late the following spring, after several highly emotional letters on Garland's part, she cut it off. Ultimately, Homer Garland was probably the most important man in Lucile's life. He was her first lover, but more than that, it was Garland who planted the seeds for her future. He taught her about the newspaper world, and the more she learned, the more interested she became. If it weren't for Garland, Lucile's life would most probably have followed a different path.[16]

As she mulled over thoughts about journalism, Lucile came back home to teach school. This time her classes were in the Wilson family's hometown of Everton, a small town ten miles south of Dadeville. When Lucile arrived, her mother and youngest brother were already there; Veda had moved to Everton a year earlier to keep house for Lucile's uncle George, who had been widowed, and to give her brother George a chance to attend all four years of high school in one place.

Lucile taught in Everton for two years, spending the summer months at Wayside Lodge on Presbyterian Hill. There, she was busy with canoeing, swimming, and enjoying the tourist sites, often in the company of Etna and his college friends. More important, she took a step toward becoming a journalist: she wrote and sold her first newspaper article, and won an honorable mention in a contest to promote floor wax. The article, which appeared in the old *Kansas City Post*, was just a small feature about Presbyterian Hill and the curious names of some of the cottages there, but she had the satisfaction of seeing her work in print for the first time. The *Post* paid her the princely sum of one dollar for her submission.[17]

OUT WEST

After her second year of teaching elementary school in Everton, Lucile opted for an adventure: she decided she would find a teaching job Out West. After all, she had good memories of her summer in Texas and, apparently, there was a lot of opportunity for women in that part of the country. She also had a few contacts: out of Lucile's small high school class, a number of her classmates had moved to California and several more had started their adult lives in the Rocky Mountain West.[18]

Since the turn of the century, the American West had become "the place to go" for travelers, for people seeking adventure, even for presidents, as well as for independent young women in search of relaxation or challenges in the outdoors. Western promoters with their "See America

First" campaign, the railroads with their Harvey House partnerships, and a growing number of national parks and resorts had lured countless thousands to view the West through romantic eyes and to see it as a place to cure everything from tuberculosis to nervous prostrations. Writers and artists, especially female writers and artists, played a big role in touting a place where a twentieth-century woman would want to be, and where she could successfully be independent. Writers like Mary Roberts Rinehart, a wildly popular and prosperous mystery author, wrote dozens of articles and a 1918 book, *Tenting Tonight*, about her western adventures—exactly the kind of material a young woman like Lucile would grab up and devour.

Lucile surely heard stories about exciting automobile trips over virtually impossible mountain roads, health cures in El Paso, and romantic rail journeys to places like Colorado, Santa Fe, or Glacier National Park. As someone who had been living away from home on and off since she was a young teenager and who was needing a change, a teaching job Out West was the perfect answer. A New Mexico travel guide urged, "Come out in the open! Let us fill your lungs with the purest of sun-laden, balsam-charged air. Let us induce you to . . . free the spirit, and give new life, vim, ambition, activity to the will!" Lucile was ready, and once she began looking, she heard that the small town of Roswell, New Mexico, regularly hired teachers from eastern places like Missouri. It didn't take long before she was one of them.[19]

Yet in September 1922, when the young woman stepped off what was known in Roswell as "the teacher train," she probably didn't find as much of the Wild West as she had hoped. Despite the fabled Chisum ranch nearby, and tales of a cattle baron war that involved Billy the Kid, what she found was a fast-growing farm town in the Pecos River Valley that prided itself on being an agricultural and industrial center—a very different place from old and storied Santa Fe, fewer than two hundred miles away. In some ways, Roswell in the 1920s, with a few more than seven thousand people, was not unlike the large towns of her Middle Western childhood, and very much like the towns in west Texas she had seen on her summer in Hereford. That part of eastern New Mexico was not particularly popular with the rest of the state. Because of its flat land, oil economy, conservative social leanings, and its significant white Protestant population, the area was even known as Little Texas.[20]

Roswell's first settlers had actually been a group of Missourians. The Missourians didn't stay long, but soon after they left the area, a Van C. Smith, variously referred to as an Omaha businessman or a gentleman gambler, and his partner built two buildings near the failed settlement, opened a store and post office, and put rooms upstairs for paying travelers. Smith named the post office location after his father, Roswell Smith.

In 1877, another Missourian, Captain Joseph Lea, and an associate bought out the two partners, entered into the cattle business, and worked to bring more settlers—mostly Protestant midwesterners and west Texas farmers—to Roswell. After artesian wells were discovered in the area in 1890, and the railroads arrived in 1893, Roswell became one of the fastest-growing towns in the American Southwest. Lea, who died in 1904, came to be considered the Father of Roswell.[21]

Lucile spent a successful year in Roswell. Instead of living with a local family, as most young teachers did, she moved into a boardinghouse, the Hotel Gilkeson, and raised a few eyebrows in the process. Once she began to meet people and was comfortable in her classroom, she took time to investigate southern New Mexico and southwest Texas. There were jaunts around the region with Stewart, and regular weekend trips with teacher chums to nearby places like Carlsbad Caverns and the Guadalupe Mountains. At Christmastime, she and another teacher traveled two hundred miles southwest of Roswell to El Paso to see friends from the Midwest and venture across the border into Ciudad Juarez. They had a fine time, and on her return, she wrote about the trip, describing fast-growing El Paso, nearby Fort Bliss, the large number of tuberculosis sanitariums, and their cross-border trip to Juarez. "We had to go across the bridge over the Rio Grande," she wrote, "and then we were out of the US. In going over this bridge, though, you first pass a man who sells you a pass, costs a quarter for a car I think, then two other men stationed farther along on the bridge look you over and motion you to go on . . ."

In Juarez, the friends visited the old Franciscan Mission, the market, and a cabaret. About the cabaret, where customers had to ante up a nickel to dance, she noted, "It was all very thrilling. When we went in, a Mexican beauty was singing 'Silent Night.' After she had finished they yelled 'Everybody dance' and they did . . . Then the next number was a male quartet after which everybody danced some more, then they had their special Christmas number. It was real cute . . . It all looked like a cabaret scene in a picture show."[22]

CHANGE OF PLANS

Meanwhile, as the winter of 1923 turned into spring in New Mexico, Lucile decided not to return to Roswell. She had managed to secure her dream teaching job in Kansas City and needed to get back to Missouri to save some money. Saving money was crucial: during her time in Roswell, she had made up her mind that dream teaching job or not, she was going to attend the University of Missouri's school of journalism as soon as she could afford it.

Missouri's journalism school was not only the first one in the country, it was also a leader in the movement toward professionalizing the newspaper business. Founder Walter Williams, a longtime newspaperman himself, was famous for writing the Journalist's Creed, which became a backbone to the school's instruction and outlook. The creed emphasized public trust, fairness, accuracy, responsibility, independence, and, especially, public service. In accordance with that philosophy, the new school curriculum offered students classroom instruction that focused on high ethical standards and professionalism, plus practical experience gained in producing *The Missourian*, a student-run community newspaper.[23]

In 1910, the first graduating class of the new school included one female, Mary Gentry Paxton. After graduation, Paxton went to work at the *Kansas City Post*—the same newspaper that had published Lucile's first article. Paxton was a pioneer as an early journalism student, but in the larger world women had been involved in producing newspapers since colonial days, and in the late 1880s and 1890s, there were some women journalists who were making the news as well as covering it. Those were the days of activist female writers and editors like muckraker Ida Tarbell, who exposed the wrongdoings of the Standard Oil Company, and African American journalist Ida B. Wells, who worked to document lynchings and crusaded for equal rights. It was also an era when a variety of women "stunt reporters" actually put themselves in harm's way to expose social ills—and sometimes make a difference. The most famous of these women was Elizabeth Cochran, who took the pen name of Nellie Bly. In 1888, Bly talked her way into a job at Joseph Pulitzer's New York *World* when she agreed to spend a week in New York's insane asylum for women and write about it. Her series, "Inside the Madhouse," attracted national attention but, even better, Bly was asked to testify before a grand jury, three female doctors were hired to treat the women, and the institution received increased funding. Other female reporters managed to expose various societal shortcomings, both with Nellie Bly–type stunts or simply by focusing attention on issues. Similarly, later generation newspaperwomen on the often-despised women's pages used their observations and talents to write about changes happening in women's lives and to crusade for social reform.[24]

By the time Lucile decided to enroll in Missouri's journalism school, many smaller newspapers counted on women for their day-to-day reporting. In 1920, women made up sixteen percent of all working journalists and were beginning, here and there, to work shoulder to shoulder with men, filling front pages with stories on politics, crime, and business. In Arkansas, Lessie Stringfellow Read, a reporter for the *Fayetteville Democrat*, moved up to become that newspaper's editor in 1918, working for female owner Roberta Fulbright. In St. Louis, Marguerite Martyn, whose family hailed from Springfield, had joined the St. Louis *Post-Dispatch* around 1900 as a staff artist. Martyn was a talented sketch artist and, as it turned out, equally talented at interviewing and writing about her subjects. Many of her illustrated interviews appeared in newspapers across the country. Eventually she became so popular that the *Post* would print her byline as big as the story headline, and her fame was such that she interviewed presidents William Howard Taft and Woodrow Wilson, plus people like Lillian Russell, Andrew Carnegie, William Jennings Bryan, and a host of suffragists.[25]

During her year in Roswell, Lucile may also have heard of Isabel Worrell Ball, a journalist hired by the *Albuquerque Journal* a generation earlier to follow and report on the construction, labor unrest, and Indian raids that befell the hapless Atlantic and Pacific Railroad. Later, Ball was a literary editor for the *Kansas City Times*, reporter for the *Kansas City Star*, a Washington correspondent for the *Topeka Journal*, and one of the first woman reporters to be seated in the US Senate's press gallery. Her presence in the press gallery, Ball reflected, was greeted "with the enthusiasm of a case of smallpox" by the male reporters. In other words, newspaper work wasn't always easy for women, but it was doable.[26]

So the idea of becoming a newspaperwoman was not out of the question at all when Lucile packed up her belongings in Roswell and accepted a ride home from a fellow teacher from Missouri who owned an automobile. When Lucile learned the journey would include a side trip to Denver, she readily agreed. No matter how they went, Lucile knew, the ride home was going to be an adventure. Driving an automobile cross-country in 1923 was a challenge even for the most seasoned automobilists. Most roads had yet to be paved, breakdowns were almost inevitable, and if their timing didn't put them to arrive in towns with hotels, the young women probably would find themselves camping alongside the road or in one of the new community campgrounds that were springing up to serve intrepid automobile travelers.

It must have been an arduous journey, given the topography of the land and the nature of the roads they had to travel, but the two young women took their time and made the best of it, stopping to explore Santa Fe and other sights along the way. Once they reached Denver, they spent several more days looking around—long enough for Lucile's friend to decide she would spend the summer in Colorado and not return to Missouri's heat and humidity. At that point, Lucile could easily have boarded a train for home, but with journalism on her mind and nothing to lose, she applied for a job at the *Denver Post*. The *Post* couldn't use her, but the editor kindly suggested she try the smaller afternoon paper, the *Denver Express*. At the

Express, when she told the editor she had neither a journalism degree nor newspaper experience, he assured her he would rather train his own people. He hired her on the spot.[27]

| 3 |

NEWSPAPER GAL

Immediately after joining the staff of the *Denver Express*, Lucile wrote to her mother, "My first day at the newspaper is over. I guess I'll learn if I don't get fired in the process." She also urged her mother to visit: "I'm crazy for you to come out and all of us get settled . . . I like Denver. You will like it better than Kansas City."[1]

Veda did, in fact, visit Denver within a few weeks and agreed that Denver was, indeed, a fine place. Etna had married the year before, but Veda brought George along, and when she left, George stayed behind, moved in with Lucile, enrolled at the University of Denver, and worked part-time as a city streetcar conductor.

In the 1920s, everybody liked Denver. It was the financial capital of the Mountain West and, as a rail hub, the Mile High City was mecca for travelers from the East Coast and Midwest. The city's climate not only brought people there for their health, but they also came seeking adventure in the Rocky Mountains. In other words, it was a totally different sort of place from Protestant, agrarian Roswell. Or the Ozarks.

Because Denver was a relatively new city, it had a population more accepting of new ideas and reforms than places farther east. Colorado was the first state (after the Territory of Wyoming) to extend suffrage to women (1893). In 1916, Denver opened the free Edith Griffith Opportunity School to teach men and women basic trades, and even offered free elementary education to those who needed it. The city was a regular stopping place for leaders in the women's movement and the suffragist-organized National Woman's Party. At the same time, Denver had borne the booms and busts of the silver market. It was a hotbed of crime, drugs, illegal liquor, and labor unrest. It had the largest African American population in the West, a significant number of Chinese residents, a growing Hispanic community, European immigrants who had come to work in the mines—and a powerful contingent of the Ku Klux Klan.

During the unsettled years after World War I, Klan power was at its height all over the US. In Denver, partly because of rampant crime, the Klan had no trouble settling in. Imperial Wizard William Simmons made a scouting visit to Denver in 1920. Within a year, the Klan was ubiquitous in Colorado.

By offering brotherhood and the kind of lodge organization that Denver's midwestern Protestants had missed when they came west, plus uncontroversial special events like auto races and picnics, the Klan easily gained members and support. Initially, it positioned itself as a civic group, backing education projects, relief for the poor, the community chest, and other social welfare enterprises. However, it didn't take long for the Klan's dark side to surface. Besides being anti-Black, the new post-1915 Klan was anti-Jewish, anti-labor, anti-immigrant, and anti-Colorado's Roman Catholic population. Very quickly, as it was doing across the country in those years, the Klan moved into politics. By 1923 it garnered enough members and influence to elect Klan member Ben Stapleton as Denver

Not long after Lucile joined the staff of the *Denver Express*, Veda came to visit. *Morris family photos.*

mayor and, by 1925, to fill most statewide offices, including that of governor. The two largest newspapers, the *Denver Post* and the *Rocky Mountain News*, ran hot and cold on support for the Klan and Klan candidates, but Lucile's smaller, prolabor *Denver Express* was opposed to the Klan and never vacillated. Despite Klan threats to boycott *Express* advertisers, Lucile's editor, Sidney Whipple, kept up a vicious attack, week by week, on the Klan's activities and its growing influence in both Denver's and the state's government.[2]

Even though Lucile's job never required her to report on Klan doings, as a member of the *Express* staff, she had a not-always-pleasant front-row seat for the rancorous—and potentially dangerous—political newspaper battle. On the other hand, she was fortunate that she had come to a place where newspaperwomen had been on the job for a half century. As historian Sherilyn Cox Bennion points out, the West had long been a good place for women journalists, in part because of a general sense that women and the press both sought to bring the trappings of civilization to the frontier. In 1900, for example, already seven percent of the journalists in the thirteen western states were women. Some of those pioneering women were still around when Lucile came on the scene; others, like native Missourian Helen Laverty, whom Lucile would work with on another newspaper, had made their mark and then moved on, but all of them contributed to what it meant to be a newspaperwoman in Denver.[3]

DENVER NEWSPAPERWOMEN

One of Denver's earliest newswomen was Caroline Churchill, a travel writer who extolled the joys of being an unaccompanied woman in the Rocky Mountain and Pacific West. Churchill settled in Denver in 1879 and founded a feminist newspaper, which she first named the *Antelope*, then later changed to the *Queen Bee*. Churchill used the *Bee* to crusade for equal rights and especially for women's suffrage. A couple of years after Colorado women secured the right to vote, the *Bee* ceased publication.[4]

Another Denver feminist, Helen Ring Robinson, wrote articles for the Denver newspapers, including interviews with prominent authors and politicians, and when the Democratic National Convention came to Denver in 1908, she covered it. In 1912, she was the first woman elected to the Colorado State Senate. Robinson was a member of the fabled Denver Woman's Press Club, an important anchor for newspaperwomen and leading feminists that still exists today.[5]

The story of the press club is also the story of probably the city's best-known early woman journalist. Minnie Reynolds joined the *Rocky Mountain News* in 1891 by accident: she signed her letter of application

"M. J. Reynolds" and was hired under the assumption that she was a man. When she arrived at the newspaper, they took her, but assigned her to the society page. That didn't last: before long, she moved to head of the women's page and, from there, she went on to become a leading political writer. Reynolds was another of the organizers of the push to secure the vote for women in 1893: during the campaign, she persuaded a good number of the Colorado newspapers to make space for suffrage news and editorials. She helped establish several local women's clubs and was part of a drive to open libraries, including a traveling library for the State Federation of Woman's Clubs. However, she is probably best remembered for her role in founding the Denver Woman's Press Club.

In 1898, when the General Federation of Women's Clubs was planning to hold its national meeting in Denver, Reynolds received queries asking whether Denver had a club for newspaperwomen. At the time it didn't, but she and a few female colleagues got together to organize one. She drew up a constitution and bylaws, and the women were so enthusiastic, especially about her membership requirements, that they adopted them immediately. To wit:

> No woman shall be admitted to the club who is . . .
> a. A bore
> b. Who holds out on news reporters
> c. Who has not a proper respect for the power of the press
> d. Who does not read your paper
> e. Who cannot do something to drive dull care away.
> Copy readers and proof readers are forever barred from membership in this club.[6]

During her time in Denver, Lucile participated in the press club's activities and even served on committees for one of the city's "largest and most spectacular" social functions, the club's annual Pageant and Ball. Originally held to raise money to pay for a permanent press club home, the ball eventually became a fundraiser for the city's charities. Even in Denver, most newspaperwomen wrote society news, so the event was always high-lighted in the newspapers, thereby attracting attention and support from Denver's social and financial elite.

By the mid-1920s, thanks to the Nineteenth Amendment, Lucile had cast votes in two national elections, but in Denver and elsewhere, feminists were fomenting for the next step: passage of the Equal Rights Amendment (still not passed as of this writing). Because of women like Reynolds, Robinson, and Churchill, as mentioned earlier, Denver remained a regular stop for leading feminists and speakers on the equal rights circuit.

Lucile was enthusiastic about her many assignments to cover progressive woman newsmakers, but to her chagrin, interviewing nationally prominent women was only a secondary part of her job. Her primary responsibility at the *Express* was the advice column, which she authored under the newspaper's trademarked name, Cynthia Grey. In the parlance of the time, she was a sob sister.

The term "sob sister" was coined around 1910, during the sensational murder trial of wealthy New York playboy Harry Kendall Thaw, who had killed Stanford White to salvage the reputation of his chorus-girl wife. Four newspaperwomen—Winifred Black, Dorothy Dix, Nixola Greeley-Smith, and Ada Patterson—were among the dozens of reporters covering the titillating trial, and before it was over, they were receiving almost as much publicity for their passion-filled articles as the trial itself, never mind that many of the male reporters' accounts were equally dramatic. (Interestingly, it wasn't the fact that women were covering a trial; even then, that was not unusual. It was the fact that *four* women were covering the trial, and apparently were doing it well enough to capture the public's imagination.) Later, Dix became a household name when she penned the first newspaper advice column. The combination of the scandalous subject matter and lovelorn advice probably was the origin of the sob sister sobriquet. And the position of sob sister—writing emotionally charged stories that targeted women's heartstrings and authoring an advice-to-the-lovelorn column—was where many newspaperwomen began.[7]

Years later, when Lucile gave a talk about her career, she told her audience, "I started in as the greenest cub. I had written only one newspaper article in my life. I told the editor frankly that I had no training, except such general information as two years of college and five years of teaching had given me. They started me out on the lovelorn column and I sat up most every night for a week reading such columns in other newspapers and trying to improve mine."[8]

During her first couple of weeks on the job, Lucile reported the following:

- Prices of dairy products and produce were stationary (June 13)
- The YWCA was beginning summer programs for girls (June 15)
- Nurses were giving school children basic physical exams (June 15) and
- A five-year-old who had been dragged by a tram car was "bravely bearing his suffering ... from ... an accident that may leave him maimed for life." (June 19)

Then on June 25, 1923, the editor looked around the newsroom, called her up, and sent her to the First Baptist Church, where President and Mrs. Harding would attend services. Later, she told a group of listeners, "I never have before or since felt so proud as I did that Sunday morning when I walked up to a burly policeman who was helping keep back the crowd from a roped-off enclosure around the church door. I presented my card, which announced that I was a newspaper reporter, was passed through the church door and seated directly in front of the space where the president and his wife sat in a few moments. That was a thrill that comes once in a lifetime."[9]

Her article wasn't exactly breaking news. She described Mrs. Harding's attire ("brown and henna colored costume"), the church décor ("pink and white peonies, palms and American flags"), the crowd's enthusiasm, and the pastor's sermon ("The Light of the World—Jesus").[10] Yet, covering the president of the United States was something that informed the rest of her newspaper career. The editor also gave her a byline. Despite the fact that he misspelled Lucile as "Lucille," it was a generous gesture; identifying the author of an article (or a photograph) has always been entirely at the discretion of the editor, and this was not a particularly important story.[11]

As Lucile gained experience, she began to assist or fill in for the *Express* general assignment reporters covering what she considered "hard news." From time to time, she was sent to cover the Denver courts and the statehouse, and she even wrote the occasional obituary when a leading citizen died. She learned on the job, but she also had support from one of the city's leading journalists. Her first newspaper heroine, she remembered, was Frances Wayne of the *Denver Post*, whom she described as "decidedly the big shot among newspaperwomen. I began hearing stories about how she lorded it over the other women reporters. Then one day I was sent to get an interview at the city jail. It was my first time to step inside a jail. I was to interview a woman forger and it was my first time to talk to a woman criminal . . . close to being my first time to write a newspaper story of any importance. I went on into the cell with the woman forger, got my feeble interview and started back out to the jail office . . . to my surprise the matron introduced me to Frances Wayne . . . Perhaps Mrs. Wayne took pity on so unsophisticated a girl reporter, or maybe she was just big-hearted, but anyway she did many lovely things for me while I was in Denver. She and her friend, the former Polly Pry [the *Denver Post*'s first female reporter], sponsored me in the Woman's Press Club before I really had enough experience to merit membership."[12]

Everything she did at the *Express* confirmed the merit of her decision to become a reporter. She wrote to Veda that "I feel like the original bonehead around here, but I suppose I will eventually get over that . . . I may not hold down this job, but begorra it has taught me one thing. I was right when I decided I would like newspaper work and if I get kicked out here I am going to try another one. I don't much mind the hours I have to work.

Eight o'clock is a little early of course, but I get off at five and . . . never work on Saturday afternoon," concluding that "it's lots of fun."[13]

SOB SISTER

During that year, Lucile did have some time to explore the area, sometimes with George or, perhaps in her early months there, with tire salesman Bob Stewart, whose travels periodically brought him through Denver and who was a loyal correspondent, even though she wrote to Veda shortly after she settled into her hotel lodgings, "I am not going to waste stationery on him, not even this fine office copy paper [i.e., newsprint] I am using on you." Most of her time, however, was devoted to being Cynthia Grey, the lovelorn columnist. She advised girls whether to kiss their boyfriends good night and told boys what to do when their sweethearts fell for better-looking men. In one case, she received several letters from an older married woman who wanted advice on winning back a wandering husband. "I answered them personally, giving her detailed and solemn advice," she recalled later. "It sounded so impressive she decided she would come into the office and talk it over with me. You can imagine her dismay when she saw that Cynthia Grey was an inexperienced youngster who never even had got herself a husband, much less managed one." It must have been useful information, though, because the woman wrote back later, asking for more advice. When one young woman wrote, "I'm just friends with a married man . . ." her answer was: "It is a very great injustice to yourself in many ways . . ."[14]

Lucile not only gave advice as Cynthia Grey but also often turned the letters back to her readers, asking what they would do under those circumstances, or what guidance they would give the letter writer. Sometimes she consulted with legal authorities, as in the case when the letter writer wanted to know if a marriage would be valid if a person under the legal age married in Colorado and lied about his or her age. She learned, and passed on to readers, that it was not illegal unless the parents wanted to contest the marriage and have it annulled. She advised young women on applying for jobs: know what you want, talk in a straightforward manner during your interview. She encouraged one to dress well and use cosmetics wisely, and she advised another to burn old love letters (something she never did).[15]

The column also served as a forum. She received and ran letters with pro and con opinions on Prohibition and a variety of other subjects; she printed one letter from a woman whose temper had destroyed her own marriage and wanted to warn others to learn to hold their tongues. She provided one letter writer with a recipe for dill pickles, answered questions on grammar, and relayed information on how to get in touch with the state superintendent of schools in Wyoming. One reader asked what kind of letter to write to a music publisher when sending an original score. Another reader wanted to know where to get eagle or turkey tail feathers—difficult at that time of year, but "in a few weeks most any wholesale produce company will have them." Her column also functioned as a local trading site: Does someone have a baby buggy you don't need? Old children's clothes would be appreciated. Anyone want a five-week-old Mexican sheepdog?

As the year progressed, her answers became less conservative and her advice to young women more pointed, suggesting they become more independent and make more decisions themselves, probably reflecting her own growing individualism and sense of self. When asked what career a young woman should pursue, her answer was: the one for which you are best adapted. "You must be interested and capable," she wrote, but urged the girl not to limit herself: "We have famous women writers, artists, actresses, teachers, nurses, lecturers, executives." In short, she exhorted, get an education, and "when you find the work in which you can best express your real self and can get the most pleasure, it will take only honest hard work for you to attain whatever degree of fame you covet." Cynthia Grey also discussed equal rights. "The question today includes much more than it did when our grandmothers began first to timidly suggest it," she wrote. She went on to enumerate key issues: equal pay, equal inheritance rights, equal opportunities in education, and, again, whether girls who have worked before marriage should or could keep their positions after marrying.[16]

COVERING THE FEMINISTS

To give her respite from the lovelorn and helpless, the *Express* did send Lucile to cover other kinds of women's stories. She went to church and wrote about faith healing, and she wrote about the Free Opportunity School. She told people to take broken-but-repairable toys to firemen so Santa could take them to poor children. If a leading feminist came to the area, Lucile was often the reporter who wrote the story. When Margaret Sanger visited Denver, Lucile wrote about birth control. When the National Woman's Party staged a huge event in Colorado Springs to recognize the seventy-fifth anniversary of the first Equal Rights Convention (in Seneca Falls, New York)—and to arouse interest in the Equal Rights Amendment—the *Express* sent her to cover that event and send back stories on what was happening.

Alice Paul, a leader in the women's suffrage movement, had proposed the Equal Rights Amendment in 1923. When she and socialite Alva

Belmont, a leading supporter of the movement, came through Denver in 1924 on their way to Colorado Springs, Lucile interviewed the two women and accepted their invitation to cover the event—on their condition that she become a member of the movement. Lucile joined; her editor sent her to the convention; she wrote a number of stories about it—and then ended her paid membership. Throughout her life she professed to not being an equal rights activist, but about this particular event she later said, "Actually as a reporter I had no business in any kind of movement. I believe that it is the business of a newspaper reporter to give unbiased reports of happenings and not to be involved in the mechanics of it."[17]

Lucile worked hard throughout her life to remain unbiased, and she definitely was not an equal rights activist, except insofar as she set an example for other women to follow. She was, as historians Wilda M. Smith and Eleanor A. Bogart suggest, "typical of a large group of women achievers who enjoyed the fruits of the struggle for equal rights but did not directly involve themselves in that struggle . . . [with the] rationalization that . . . when she succeeded it helped all women, . . . typical . . . of a large segment of the working woman population then as it is even today."[18]

About Belmont, Lucile remembered, "I was quite impressed by Mrs. Belmont—the wealthy woman from the East who was out to educate the West. However, I had difficulty interviewing her, for she kept wanting to interview me. She kept wanting to know if I faced discrimination in my work. I was so deliriously happy to have a newspaper job I couldn't complain about anything."[19]

Her article about Alice Paul discussed issues of equal pay, women's rights in marriage, and other feminist matters. When she interviewed Sue White, another leader in the equal rights movement, she noted White's observation that out of 531 members of Congress in 1923, only one was a woman. "English women have a slogan," White told Lucile. " 'Three hundred women in parliament.' " White, and probably Lucile as well, would have been appalled to learn that the US Congress would not have one hundred female members serving at the same time until 2013, ninety years in the future.[20]

Toward the end of the year, Lucile became discouraged and tired of being Cynthia Grey. When someone pointed out the old adage that "nothing in the world is so unpopular as advice," she took it personally, then wrote a column to that effect and asked the opinion of one of her male newspaper colleagues. He reminded her that she regularly encouraged her readers to "dodge joy-killers" and that she should take her own advice. "After that," she wrote, "I felt all encouraged—over my OWN advice—and I wasn't one bit unpopular with myself because I had given it."[21]

Lucile and George, who lived with her in Denver,
enjoy a day off together. *Morris family photos.*

Years afterward, in a talk to a businesswomen's group, she said, "Sometimes I pick up a lovelorn column and read it. I always smile at the thought that most persons think the letters are faked. I wouldn't go so far as to say that I never did fake a letter for my column, but when I did it was to start a discussion or to get my correspondents off of some argument they were on. The best letters never were published, for they were such intimate personal problems that it would have been an injustice to have risked some reader guessing the identity of the writer."[22]

Nonetheless, the business of giving advice hung heavy on her. That, and the *Express* vendetta against the Klan. "Gradually," she later recalled, "I became weary of being so serious minded. I decided that I was through with lovelorn columns for life. No matter what other assignments I had on *The Denver Express*, I had to keep that column. So I quit and went to El Paso, Texas. Rather, I went to El Paso and after I found out I could get a job there, I quit." Lucile was tired of "being so serious minded," but there was another issue as well. George told her he couldn't handle the

Mile High City's altitude, so they agreed to see if she could get a job in El Paso. The two made a quick trip to El Paso, where Lucile did, indeed, get a job with the *El Paso Times*. George went back to Missouri, and Lucile returned to Denver, quit her job with the *Express*, and moved south: "Those were the good old days," she remembered, "when reporters could go from one paper to another without difficulty. That's how they moved up the ladder."[23]

EL PASO

Lucile was on her way. And she couldn't have landed her second newspaper job in a more interesting place. She arrived in El Paso in early fall of 1924. Her new home was a very different place from high-flying Denver, smaller and younger as an American city, but it offered a way across the Rio Grande and a year-around pass through the southern tip of the Rocky Mountains, which had seen travelers for hundreds of years as they followed the trail between Santa Fe and Chihuahua, Mexico, and later across the American Southwest. Zebulon Pike is generally credited with being the first Anglo to spend time in the area (one story had him at the home of the captain of the garrison in nearby San Elizario, playing cards with the captain's wife and sister in 1807), but Anglo settlers didn't really begin to trickle into what is now El Paso until after the Mexican War. The treaty signaling the war's end in 1848 settled the Texas-Mexico border at the deepest channel of the Rio Grande, and the Compromise of 1850 placed the village of El Paso squarely on the American side of the great river, across from much older and much larger Ciudad Juarez. Four years after that, the Gadsden Purchase finalized the US-Mexico boundary from El Paso to the west.[24]

The village grew slowly over the next few decades, then changed spectacularly after the Southern Pacific and Santa Fe railroads chugged into town almost simultaneously in the late spring of 1881. The trickle of frontier settlers into the little border community became a flood. Before the railroads arrived, El Paso was a rowdy settlement full of bars, bordellos, gambling houses, and dance halls. After the railroads came, it kept many characteristics of a border town, but it also began a climb to respectability. The culture, of course, was Mexican and the population largely Mexican and Pueblo people, but there were also Anglos, Chinese who had come with the railroads, and others from all over the world. Two newspapers, the *El Paso Times* and the *El Paso Herald*, were founded in the wake of the railroads' arrival in the 1880s.

In 1923, a popular historian and native son, Owen P. White, described the way El Paso changed from wild and woolly frontier village to a forward-looking city. When he was growing up, he said, El Paso "had been small, tough, vivid, beautiful, and honest, and naturally I resented the thought that when I wasn't looking, Civic Pride and Reform and Social Consciousness had sneaked in . . . and cut down my grand old cotton-woods, and paved my streets, and abolished my saloons and gambling houses and bordellos and dance halls, and had thus turned my town, with its glorious personality, into a town for everybody." Although White later moved to New York City, where he hobnobbed with literary and journalistic stars of the times, he was still in residence when Lucile arrived in El Paso and still writing on occasion for the *El Paso Herald*.[25]

White was correct. By the time Lucile joined the staff of the rival *Times*, El Paso was a business center for the many mines in the area; home to the world's largest smelter and, because of the climate, a large center for health seekers, especially those suffering from tuberculosis; and a multi-ethnic city of seventy-seven thousand. One key to the change, as White had suggested, was that the railroads brought newspapers, families, and especially American women to El Paso. As happened in so many western towns, the ladies took the place in hand. Members of the El Paso Woman's Club, which was organized in 1894, individually and together launched the first children's library in the US (and the El Paso Public Library); established the first public kindergarten in Texas; started a public school in 1891; organized the Ladies Benevolent Association, which opened the city's first hospital; promoted sanitation; and worked for welfare reform.[26]

EL PASO TIMES

Thanks to her journalism experience in Denver, Lucile was welcomed to the *El Paso Times* as a veteran reporter and assigned to the city desk. As a woman, she still came in for her share of heart-wrenching stories, but as she later recalled, "I seemed to lose the sob sister designation and had such challenging assignments as city hall and a convention of the American Federation of Labor." Her story about Samuel Gompers and the AF of L was eerily reminiscent of her story about President Harding: Gompers died less than a month later.[27]

At the *Times* Lucile joined a staff that had seen a generation of woman reporters covering the news and, history buff that she was, she ate up accounts of some of those women. One of them, Peggy Hull, had been at the *Times* only a few years earlier, covering General John Pershing's battles against Mexican bandit Pancho Villa. During World War I, Hull talked the *Times* editor into sending her—unaccredited—to France with El Paso–area troops, where she didn't actually cover the war itself but wrote highly popular articles about the military men, life in an artillery training camp, and Paris during wartime. Her "chatty little stories" of war appeared in El Paso, and they also attracted the attention of editors across the US, much to the displeasure of the accredited male correspondents. When she returned to El Paso after a few months, she was a national celebrity and was welcomed home by a big crowd, a red carpet, city dignitaries, and a band. She didn't stay long; after a few months, Hull talked the Newspaper Enterprise Association and her contacts in military leadership to support a this-time successful application, and she became the first accredited female war correspondent. With credentials in hand, she accompanied the US Army to Siberia and later reported from the Pacific during World War II.[28]

When Lucile arrived at the *Times*, she found a group of dedicated journalists who were, as she was, and as Hull had been, on their way somewhere else. "Those were the good old days, when reporters would start in California, go to Phoenix or Tucson, work until they got a pay check ahead, then drift to El Paso for a few months," she later recalled. "From there, they usually went to New Orleans, then they would get together the fare on to New York. It worked the same way on the westward trail. We had some crack reporters out of New York offices who were working toward California."[29]

Two itinerant reporters who arrived at the *Times* about the same time as Lucile were Kenneth Stewart and Evelyn Seeley, who later married. Seeley, an Illinois native, started her career at the *San Francisco News*, where, as Lucile said, "She talked the editor . . . into letting her work as a cub reporter at a low salary until she got experience. . . . She later went to New York and spent many months working at any sort of writing she could get until she finally landed a job on the *World*, [where] she became the principal woman feature writer on that paper, and was assigned to help cover the story of the kidnapping of the Lindbergh baby." Stewart, who was born in California, worked his way east via the *Fresno Bee*, *El Paso Times*, and several other newspapers to the vaunted *New York Times*. From reporter, he moved on to university professor and later wrote a book, *News Is What We Make It*, about his newspaper career.[30]

"Newspapermen were on the move in the mid-twenties," Stewart wrote in his book. "El Paso was a crossroads . . . The clear air of the high desert land along the Rio Grande restored lungs racked by tuberculosis, and newspapermen exiled from the humid East went there to carry on their work in surroundings that helped to counteract the effect of long and irregular hours in smoke-filled city rooms. When my broken journey eastward brought me to the telegraph desk of the *El Paso Times* in the fall of 1924, fully half the staff could be counted in various stages of convalescence." It didn't hurt, either, during those Prohibition years that El Paso had easy access to the cantinas in Ciudad Juarez.[31]

Another *Times* notable who was, in fact, convalescing in El Paso, was Duncan Aikman, book editor of the *Times* when Lucile was on the staff. Aikman, an East Coast intellectual who came west, was a native of Indiana and a Yale graduate who had written for a number of eastern newspapers before landing in El Paso and eventually moving on to Los Angeles. In the 1930s he became a freelance writer, selling articles to H. L. Mencken's *American Mercury*, among other publications, and was the author of several books about the West.[32]

REPORTER AT WORK

As for Lucile, when she became a member of the *Times*'s news staff, she was dismayed to learn that not only her newspaper training but also some of the KKK baggage of her last job had followed her to Texas: "When I got to El Paso, they were just getting over a similar [KKK] fight there. A story they told about that is one that still haunts me. The editor there had been so bitter in the Klan fight that threats were made against his life. Some of his friends begged him to seek protection from the Klan, and at their insistence he finally asked that two policemen accompany him home from the office each night. Later he found out the policemen both were Klansmen." Unlike what happened in Denver, however, El Pasoans minimized the Klan's importance after only a small setback. The Klan arrived in El Paso promising to do civic good and won all seats in the school board election. Shortly thereafter, the city leaders realized that there was more to be lost in multinational, heavily Catholic El Paso than to be gained by overtly preaching white Protestant supremacy. The Klan lost control of the school board in 1923 and never again was of much importance in El Paso.[33]

With no worries of having to walk a fine line around Klan activities or Klan leaders, Lucile threw herself into her new job. She was assigned to the regular beat of covering city hall. She interviewed successful women, as she had in Denver, but she also had an opportunity to do much more. Her first bylined article for the *Times* concerned the pending visit of the military zeppelin *Shenandoah*. Given El Paso's location around the corner from Fort Bliss, she wrote regularly about various goings on of the military. She covered a speech by El Paso Congressman Claude Hudspeth, in town to talk about the iron fence that the government was erecting on the Mexican border. She interviewed Hamilton Holt, president of the League of Nations Non-Partisan Association, on the group's push for the US to join the league, which Congress had rejected. When nationally known humorist George Ade came to El Paso for a short visit, she interviewed him and later told friends he was the most unfunny person she had ever tried to interview.[34]

When Lucile wasn't covering visiting dignitaries, the military, or city hall, she wrote a variety of stories about the local scene. One was about a couple that offered citizenship classes to non-Americans. She covered school and library news, reporting that *Tom Sawyer* and *Little Women* were the most desired books in the children's library. But she also did her share of heavy lifting, writing about the Victorio Apaches of New Mexico seeking a return of their ancestral lands, and authoring an exposé series about an elementary school whipping that led to criminal charges against a principal. She covered crime stories from time to time and wrote an article on the difficulties one family had in bringing the body of a dead relative across the border from Ciudad Juarez for burial in the US.

Additionally, the *Times* gave her opportunities to write feature stories, which she loved doing. As an example, a notice in the local health bulletin led her to write about superstitions surrounding healing, perhaps with a thought to her grandmother's madstone. She reported that brain fever did not come from excitement, that mosquitoes did not come from decomposed leaves, and that tuberculosis was not hereditary. She also related that despite the city health department warnings, a former prize-fighter-turned-local-detective assured her that raw meat was, in fact, a "true and tried remedy" for black eyes. In March 1925, she interviewed another successful woman, a native El Pasoan named Clara Hawkins who was in town visiting from London. According to Hawkins, who was a corporate advertising executive, "it doesn't matter where one starts when she takes up a career . . . the only thing is to start somewhere," a sentiment with which Lucile no doubt concurred.[35]

After about a year at the *El Paso Times*, Lucile had found her niche. She was well respected, productive, resourceful—and she loved being a journalist. But the "niche" didn't mean she wanted to stay in El Paso. Through Aikman, who was a veteran of the International News Service (INS) and had worked in Europe during World War I, she applied for and received a job offer from INS in London. In April 1925 she left the *Times*, bid adieu to her friends and the old border town, and headed for Missouri to see her family for a few weeks before embarking on her new assignment in Europe.

| 4 |

BACK IN THE OZARKS

When Lucile arrived back home, she couldn't help but have recognized the massive contrast between El Paso and the Ozarks. El Paso, a busy border city in the Chihuahua Desert, was an exciting crossroads. People of all kinds bumped elbows in El Paso—because their road led that way; because the dry air and desert climate were good for their health; because they were part of the international community of Pueblo Indians, Anglo-Americans, Europeans, Chinese, South Americans, and, mostly, Mexicans; or simply because they were on their way somewhere else and either ran out of money or needed a place to stop.

The Ozarks, on the other hand, was fifty-five thousand square miles of sparsely populated green hills, deep valleys, small towns, limestone caverns, high bluffs, and miles of translucent waters flowing across rocky riverbeds. In many ways more isolated and certainly with a far less diverse population than El Paso, the Ozarks had been settled over the prior 150 years largely by pioneer descendants of wayfarers from the British Isles. It was a place where, according to one Ozarks historian, "Vast stretches of rocky, infertile ridges and hollows, or hollers, provided little more than bare subsistence for generations of families . . . some of the nation's most concentrated districts of white poverty and poorest counties west of the Mississippi."[1]

Poor, perhaps, but what that meant to Lucile, and others who were rapidly transplanting themselves into that rocky terrain to live and write, was that they found, on the small farms and homesteads that dotted the Ozarks, people who even yet depended on oral history. Those were people who identified more with the creek or hill or valley where they lived than they did with the community down the road, and who often persisted in the old ways of living. Many of them still retained and delighted in some of the stories and songs that their forebears had brought with them as they migrated west and south into the Missouri and Arkansas and Oklahoma hills.[2]

"It was not until I had left the Ozarks and seen considerable of other states with which to make comparisons, that I began to realize what a rich heritage in folklore, tradition, and history we possess," Lucile observed.

She had grown up reveling in what she believed were true stories of her own ancestors and localized versions of the great drama of America—Spanish gold left by the conquistadors or brought by members of short-lived Mexican Emperor Maximilian's loyalists, encounters with vestiges of the Delaware and Osage peoples, who had been pushed out as white settlers arrived. She was mesmerized by Daniel Boone's son Nathan, who helped open the Missouri Ozarks to roads and settlers, and whose large log home was still standing near Ash Grove. And she had listened with horror to bloody and confusing accounts of the Civil War, which had splintered towns and families alike—including hers—and of harmony not returned even after several generations.[3]

When Lucile returned home to the Ozarks, the White River communities of Branson and Hollister were high on the list of places she wanted to learn more about. Conveniently, both of her brothers were living in Branson at the time, temporarily running a bankrupt hardware store for their banker-uncle George Wilson. Etna was a family man—he and his wife, Helen, had a baby daughter, June—and George was continuing his studies through a correspondence course with Quincy College in Illinois. Visiting them and having a chance to play with baby June was a perfect excuse for Lucile to seek out elderly Ozarkers with long memories. "I liked to talk to the old timers," she later told a television interviewer. "I was just fascinated by the stories I had heard about the Bald Knobbers and I talked to all the old timers I could." In the 1920s, more than a few Civil War veterans were still around, and stories of those Ozarks vigilantes who had initially organized to bring order to the postwar chaos were still fresh in many people's minds.

WRITING OZARKS STORIES

Experienced newspaperwoman that she was, Lucile almost immediately turned her nosing around into articles for the large newspapers in St. Louis and Kansas City. She sold a few feature articles to the *Post-Dispatch* that fall, one on a memorial for characters out of Harold Bell Wright's novel, *The Shepherd of the Hills*, and a second on the School of the Ozarks. Her first piece revolved around a ceremony to unveil a monument to the likely—but deceased—models for the stalwart and heart-of-gold "Old Matt and Aunt Molly" characters from the famous tale. A "thank you" letter from the *Post*'s editor verified that the St. Louis reading public relished news of the quirky, clannish, isolated hill country.[4]

Writing the article gave Lucile a chance to renew her acquaintance with poet John G. Neihardt, who spoke at the memorial ceremony. In that talk, Neihardt lauded the "pioneer virtues" displayed by the real-life couple, J. K. and Anna Ross, in life and in the book:

I have known them under other names and other places, and the memory of such people warms the heart in a hustling world where far too many hearts seem cold; for it is a memory of old-fashioned human kindness—old fashioned and yet the need of it can never be outlived however much the self-mad world may try . . . in a time when most men must labor under the pitiful illusion that somehow it is better to be envied than to be loved; in a time when more than plenty for oneself seems better than a great heart giving freely from a little hoard.[5]

In his reflections, Neihardt was advancing the popular image of the purehearted and noble Ozarker that was drawing so many tourists to the region (as opposed to the shiftless, ignorant hillbilly image that existed next to it and perhaps drew just as many visitors). Lucile just took it a step further by selling it to the *Post-Dispatch*. Over the years, she would remain friends with Neihardt, asking him to review her first unpublished novel, and more than once inviting him to be a guest speaker in writing seminars she was organizing.

For the *Kansas City Times* and also the *Post-Dispatch*, Lucile interviewed another character out of *The Shepherd of the Hills*. Levi Morrill, Wright's "Uncle Ike," was the only identifiable real person in the novel. Morill, the ninety-year-old postmaster in tiny Notch, Missouri, had come to the Ozarks for his health. His past was somewhat irregular, but so was the past of more than a few other Ozarks hillfolk. Morrill had been born into a Quaker family on the East Coast. He graduated from Bowdoin College at the age of fifteen, studied law, worked as a printer's devil at a New York newspaper, then went west to the Kansas frontier. When his health broke, a doctor recommended he might live a few months longer if he relocated to the Ozarks hill country. In the Ozarks he regained his health, opened a store, became the local postmaster, and, along the way, met Wright. Morrill's brother, incidentally, was elected governor of Kansas, and an uncle was President Grant's treasury secretary—but a person would never guess those things from seeing Lucile's newspaper photo of the stooped old man in overalls with long white hair and a fuzzy white beard. Lucile also took another photo that day: one of Uncle Ike holding the hand of a small girl, her two-year-old niece, June, whom she had brought with her to the interview. She later had the picture enlarged and framed to hang over her desk.[6]

Another article she wrote for the *Post* further embellished the Ozarks image. The School of the Ozarks in Hollister was already well-known to area visitors, and stories about the unique Ozarks school were popular. Founded by the Southern Presbyterians to provide an education for students from places that didn't have high schools, the School of the Ozarks

When Lucile interviewed Levi Morrill, who was the "Uncle Ike" character in *The Shepherd of the Hills*, she took along her niece, June. She hung this photo of the two over her desk, where it remained for the rest of her life.

Author's photos.

required young people to "pay" their way by working on campus. Student work crews erected buildings, cooked and served meals, landscaped the grounds, and, after the school became a college, even built a runway to serve an aircraft maintenance program. A printshop, canning factory, dairy barn, machine shop, and, in later years, a holiday fruitcake kitchen all gave students useful skills, provided the school with a large and productive staff, and brought additional income as well.

While the school existed to educate needy young people, so did other missionary schools in the region. However, as historian Brooks Blevins points out, the school's canny marketing, which featured pictures of Ozarks poverty and "forlorn children," generated huge sums of money and a great deal of interest from wealthy donors—far more than the other mission schools or even area colleges. Lucile's piece for the *Post* was to announce that the School of the Ozarks' curriculum was expanding to a full four years of high school. (About thirty years later, the school would become a junior college, then a four-year college in 1965. The name was changed to College of the Ozarks in 1990.)[7]

A third article for the *Post* featured Branson's taxi driver extraordinaire, Pearl Spurlock. When Spurlock's husband, who owned a garage, needed someone to drive groups of tourists, she acquired a chauffeur's license, settled herself behind the wheel of a six-passenger taxi, and began piloting vacationers through the White River country. As it turned out, she enjoyed the tourists, and she loved to tell stories of the Ozarks. Before the end of her thirty-year career, Spurlock had driven and entertained vacationers who had come to see *The Shepherd of the Hills* country from as far away as Japan, Australia, Turkey, and Persia. Those people, of course, were in addition to the thousands of passengers who came from Canada, Europe, and the US.[8]

JOB HUNT

When Lucile began writing feature stories for the Kansas City and St. Louis newspapers, she had expected her visit to the Ozarks would be a short one before she went on to her job in London. However, things didn't quite work out that way. "When I came home," she explained later, "Mother was sick, so I stayed here for a while." Yet the longer Lucile tarried in the Ozarks, the more curious she became about the region's past, and the less she wanted to push on to the press job in London. Ultimately, an emergency appendectomy helped make her decision: her future would be better spent at home. Since she was already in contact with newspapers in Kansas City and St. Louis—sizable papers that would appreciate her Denver and El Paso credentials—she set out to get a job with one of them.

She secured a letter of recommendation from Alden Evans, her old city editor and friend at the *El Paso Times*. About Lucile, he wrote, "She writes a good story and makes friends wherever she goes . . . we hope to have her back sometime. She had the city hall run while here, most of the time, and it is one of the hardest at the paper." Evans also wrote a chatty, personal letter to Lucile about who was still on the staff and who had moved on. He noted that "Hal Kelly is covering courts. He has been here a week and has been sober all the time . . ." Despite Evans's high recommendation, as well as an endorsement from Denver *Express* managing editor Josh Wilson, both the *Star* and the *Post-Dispatch* turned Lucile down. "I applied to the *Kansas City Star* and they said, 'Oh, we don't take women reporters,' " she told friends. Of course, at that time they did have women in their society department, but that was not something Lucile had any interest in doing. "Then I applied with the *Post-Dispatch* in St. Louis. They said, 'Oh, we don't have women reporters.' So I came back home."[9]

Many editors in those days still didn't like the thought of women in the newsroom. Yet, the 1920 US census reported that 5,730 of the country's 34,197 editors and reporters—more than fifteen percent—were women. Granted, most were not on the news desks, but as historian Kathleen Cairns points out, "The largest number of women journalists were young with nearly half between the ages of twenty and thirty-four." Cairns says this suggests that young women on the verge of choosing life paths saw journalism as a viable option.[10]

The thing was, both the *Star* and the *Post* had hired women in the past, and still did. The *Post*'s Marguerite Martyn was very popular. But that, apparently, was not the same as having a woman covering the so-called "hard news." Already-famous novelist Edna Ferber had begun her career at the Appleton, Wisconsin, *Daily Crescent*. About that, she wrote, "I wouldn't swap that year and a half of small-town newspaper reporting for any four years of college education." Later, Ferber worked at the *Milwaukee Journal* and covered both the 1920 Democratic and Republican national conventions for the United Press Associations.[11]

The sob sisters at the *Chicago Tribune* and the two Hearst newspapers in that city covered Chicago's criminal courts and the women's jail—and produced lurid and highly popular stories of love, lust, betrayal, and murder. In 1923, a minister's daughter from a small Indiana town talked her way into joining them as a crime reporter for the *Tribune*. Maurine Watkins was at the *Tribune* for less than a year, but those few months made her famous. After spending time meeting and writing about women who, among other deeds, had murdered their husbands and/or their boyfriends, she left Chicago abruptly for the drama department at

Yale. There, she turned her stories from the *Tribune* into a scathing, funny, satirical play, which she titled *Chicago*. The melodrama of a dance hall girl who shot her lover, was forgiven by her rich husband, turned herself into a media star when she was put on trial, and was eventually exonerated became a Broadway hit. It ran for six months, then toured the country, playing in both Kansas City and St. Louis. In 1927, Cecil B. DeMille turned *Chicago* into a popular silent film starring Phyllis Haver. Springfieldians had a chance to see the *Chicago* movie at the Gillioz Theatre in the fall of 1928, and there's a fair chance that Lucile, who later became a courthouse reporter herself, saw the film and learned Watkins's story. It was no secret that *Chicago* had been written by a girl reporter.[12]

Ironically, even though they weren't accepted in Kansas City or St. Louis, Lucile quickly learned that women were holding down a variety of jobs in newspapers across the Ozarks. Three of the most well-known were the Williams sisters, who published the West Plains (Missouri) *Quill* about one hundred miles southeast of Springfield. The sisters—Cleora, Ella, and Fritze—had literally grown up in the office of the newspaper that their father, Mills Williams, founded in 1885. They began their tenure when Cleora (1881–1967), the oldest, stood on a box in the printshop and helped fold newspapers. By the time their father died in 1930, they were jointly listed on the masthead as editors and business managers. There was also a younger brother in the family, but he left West Plains for the big city and became an advertising man on the East Coast. The sisters ran the newspaper until 1946, when it was sold.[13]

To the south, Maud Duncan, editor and publisher of the Winslow, Arkansas, *American*, played an important role in educating Arkansas's small-town newspaper publishers when she provided hands-on support to the fledgling journalism department at the University of Arkansas. The school had no printing press, and Duncan helped out by bringing students over to Winslow to teach them typesetting and printing and, coincidentally, to help her put out her *American*. In 1925, Duncan gained nationwide attention when she successfully ran for mayor and backed an all-female city council slate.[14]

Rebuffed by the big city papers, Lucile considered her options. Life as periodic contributor to various journals and magazines didn't really appeal, nor did the idea of going back into teaching to support her freelance writing. As *New York Times* columnist Margaret H. Welch had written a generation before, "newspaper work seems incomparably easier than teaching, notwithstanding the three months' vacation of the school-mistress. Life with a copy-pad or wielding a blue pencil can never, to my mind, touch the routine drudgery of over and over drilling of the young . . ."[15]

NEWSPAPERWOMAN—AGAIN

So Lucile did the obvious; she applied for a newspaper job in Springfield. Before the end of 1926, she was welcomed at the *Leader*, Springfield's oldest newspaper, and she wasn't even the first woman reporter in town. Lucille Anderson of nearby Ozark been hired by the competing *Springfield Republican* in 1917. Similarly, Lucile was not the first woman hired by the *Leader*. When she arrived at the *Leader*, the editor saw that she had worked in Denver and asked if she knew a woman named Helen Laverty. Laverty had left Denver before Lucile arrived, but she had taken Laverty's job and knew Laverty's brother plus many of her friends. Then the *Leader* editor told Lucile that Laverty would soon be coming to Springfield. After Laverty arrived, the two women covered the Ozarks together for most of two decades and became fast friends for the rest of their lives.[16]

At the *Leader*, Lucile was assigned to the city desk covering the regular news, but she was also occasionally sent to write first-person stories about something new or different happening in the Ozarks. One of her first "stunt stories" took place in October 1929, when she was assigned to join the Ford Air Tour for a day. Held annually between 1925 and 1931, the Ford Tours were a series of multiday air races designed to highlight the importance and reliability of aviation in the day-to-day US and sponsored in part by the aircraft division of the Ford Motor Company. Since flying was still such a novelty, the planes always attracted huge crowds and a lot of press attention. On that mid-October day, twenty-seven planes were competing in the St. Louis–Springfield lap of that year's five-thousand-mile, thirty-two city race. Lucile had taken a train to St. Louis the day before so she could be one of dozens of reporters from all over the country participating as passengers.

Her first-person article about the trip made the *Leader*'s front page: "It is 10:30 a.m. as the checker quickly dips his white signal flag and our neat little red and white seven-passenger cabin ship mounts above the starting line in the takeoff from Lambert Field," she wrote. "To say I am thrilled to be riding in one of the racing planes is putting it mildly. It's my first airplane ride." Lucile loved the bumpy ride in the Lockheed Vega, loved telling readers how the tour was helping to show Americans that flying could be part of the country's everyday transportation system, and really loved the fact that her plane won that day's leg of the race, touching down on Springfield's grass airfield in front of twenty thousand cheering people one hour and nineteen minutes after taking off in St. Louis. In one of those particularly satisfying story twists, Lucile also wrote about her plane's pilot, whom she found to be "pleasant and friendly as we chatted beside the plane before the takeoff." The pilot's name: Wiley Post. At that time, Post was just beginning to attract national attention, but within

In 1929, Lucile reported on the Ford Air Tour from her seat in a plane piloted by Wiley Post. She is shown here with two fellow passengers, Lockheed factory representative T. Foye Shoemaker and Mrs. Stanley Stanton, a bride on her honeymoon with one of the other pilots. *Morris family photos.*

the next seven years he would shoot to international fame as the first pilot to fly solo around the world, and he would set a number of other aviation records.[17]

Lucile's experience in Denver and especially in El Paso had taught her that journalism was a fluid profession. What she may not have known was that the fluidity extended beyond reporters. Not long after she joined the *Leader*, owner Harry S. Jewell announced his retirement and sold the newspaper to a couple of East Coast investors. Only a few weeks later, the two investors sold the paper again, this time to Edson and Joel Bixby, whose family published newspapers in Muskogee, Oklahoma, and who already owned Springfield's morning paper, the *News*. After the purchase, Lucile moved over to the *News*.

During her first day on the job for editor Edson Bixby, he told her she needed to choose a pseudonym. Even fifty years later, she still sniffed at the idea: "When they asked me to write under a pseudonym, I said, 'Why I've always written under my own name, except when I worked for a paper in Denver. There, I used their copyright name for their lovelorn column, but I never wrote under a pseudonym for my feature stories—ever.' And he said, 'Well all our reporters do.' "He said, 'What's your nickname?' And I said, 'Celia,' and he said, 'Celia—Celia. 'Ray for Celia! Celia Ray!' So I became Celia Ray and I wrote under that name for five or six years, and then they let us go back to our real names, which is much better." When Laverty came to town, she also took a pseudonym. As Docia Karell, her work was so popular, and she was so pleased with the name, that she kept it permanently, even as her career sent her overseas to Japan with the US Army Information Service and later as an editor for Japan Air Lines.[18]

GETTING ACQUAINTED

At the *News*, Docia Karell was a star feature writer and a columnist. Lucile was a general assignment reporter, covering everything from the occasional murder to chamber of commerce events, to pieces on Ozarks history and culture. She also had a weekly music column and, later, a book column. It was the stories about the history of the Ozarks that Lucile relished, and given the growing recognition of the area as a tourist destination, they were plentiful and important. In 1919, thirteen tourism-minded counties in southwest Missouri and northwestern Arkansas had joined together and organized the Ozarks Playground Association to attract more visitors to the area. By 1926, thirty-three counties, including several in northeast Oklahoma, were involved in promoting "The Land of a Million Smiles." Their target was automobile owners. The arrival of Henry Ford's Model T in 1908 had pushed Congress to get involved in highway building and by the 1920s, the technology was in place to pave roads, the federal government was providing matching funds for road paving, and Missouri had gotten behind good roads with the passage of the 1921 Centennial Highway Act. The Ozarks saw a surge of visitors as people propelled their automobiles into the region.[19]

Typically, the press joined with community leaders and tourism people to show off the area's wonders. Key among those wonders were the caves, especially Marvel Cave. In 1889, William Henry Lynch, a Canadian dairyman and miner, had purchased the cave then known as Marble Cave. He opened it as a tourist attraction in 1894. In 1913, he built a road to the cave from the White River Railway's nearest flag stop. A dozen years later he paid to improve the road between his cave and Branson, and he started a bus service between the two. Lynch died in 1927, and his daughters, Miriam and Genevieve, shouldered the job of managing—and promoting—the cave, which they renamed Marvel Cave.[20]

In July 1929, the sisters threw a party. They invited members of the press and local dignitaries to their home in Branson for lunch followed by a tour of the cave. Docia wrote the story about the afternoon for the *Springfield Leader.* Lucile and other newspaper colleagues attended, but they were only part of the guest list. Among other journalists were two editors from the nearby town of Ozark—Emmitt Reid of the *Ozark Democrat* and John M. Pile of the *Christian County Republican.* Local celebrity May Kennedy McCord, who was well on her way to fame as a promoter of Ozarks folkways, was also a guest. Emcee for the afternoon was newly elected Congressman Dewey Short, who hailed from the nearby Stone County town of Galena. Short took the floor, Docia wrote, "to tell stories—recite poetry—'kid' those gathered there—philosophize and even preach a little—then to wise-crack and set everybody laughing." Short always put on a good show no matter the occasion. He would go on to serve a total of twelve terms in Congress, become a widely quoted Ozarks character in his own right, and a prominent promoter of the region. Stalwart Ozarker that he was, the Republican Congressman later became nationally known for his vocal and vituperous opposition to Franklin Roosevelt and the New Deal.[21]

Events like that afternoon with the Lynch sisters, plus her newspaper assignments and her own curiosity, introduced Lucile to many of the larger-than-life people who made the Ozarks such a draw for tourists—and for a growing cadre of others, both natives and outsiders, who were lured to the region by the folklore, the pioneer ways of the hill people, the music, and the beauty of the area. These were men and women who were doing what they could to collect and preserve what they saw and heard in the region—and to share it with the wider world.

May Kennedy McCord was one of the most prominent. Although her parents were well-educated midwesterners and not native Ozarkers, she grew up in Short's hometown of Galena, where she absorbed the old ballads, folk stories, dialect, superstitions, and ways of life—and learned to play the guitar. Unlike most of the "authentic Ozarkers" who captured the nation's imagination, McCord was relatively well educated. In 1918, when she was thirty-eight, she and her traveling-salesman husband, Charlie, moved from rural Stone County to Springfield, where she became a popular folk singer and raconteur. In 1929, she began writing a widely read magazine-turned-newspaper column called "Hillbilly Heartbeats." Later, she had a radio program in the big city of St. Louis, followed by another on station KWTO in Springfield. She became active on a national level as a speaker and director of the National Folklore Federation, and she collaborated with local preservationists to save knowledge of the ways of the old Ozarks. According to historian Brooks Blevins, McCord's background gave her a "unique insider/outsider perspective on the region and its culture. It was extremely rare for a true rural Ozarks native with deep roots in the region to join the group of Ozarks chroniclers and watchers, especially before WWII."[22]

As Blevins points out, by the late 1920s the Ozarks was becoming home to a good number of "Ozarks chroniclers and watchers"—outsiders who devoted themselves to telling the rest of the world about the wonders of the Ozarks and Ozarks people. Vance Randolph was one of the best known of these outsiders. A native of Pittsburg, Kansas, with two college degrees, Randolph moved to Pineville, Missouri, in the southwest corner of the state, initially aiming to do scholarly research on the Ozarks mountain people. It wasn't long, however, before he began writing books and magazine articles about Ozarkers and the Ozarks for the general public, thereby doing as much as anyone to promote the backwoods hillbilly image of the region.[23]

Not long after he arrived in Pineville, Randolph penned a column in the weekly *Pineville Democrat*, in which he asked for, and then began collecting, traditional Ozarks music and paying attention to backwoods Ozarks folkways. This interest ultimately turned into nearly two dozen studies of Ozarks language and folklore, and a highly respected four-volume collection of Ozarks folk music published by the State Historical Society of Missouri between 1946 and 1950. Lucile, whose music column for the newspaper also made her the recipient of old folk songs from her readers, was often sought out by Randolph to share her contacts and materials. This led to a good bit of resentment on her part, and an on-again, off-again friendship between the two.

Another Kansan who fell in love with the Ozarks was Otto Ernest Rayburn. Rayburn found his way to the hills in 1917, first to teach school and, soon after, to publish a series of magazines. The first was *Ozark Life: The Mirror of the Ozarks*, which he published from Kingston, Arkansas, with the help of another Ozarks romantic, Ted Richmond.[24]

Rayburn's *Ozark Life* magazine was the first home for McCord's "Hillbilly Heartbeats" column. From the beginning, she used her bully pulpit as a place to promote the hillbilly, whom she described as "stout hearted, rock-ribbed brother to toil." Over time, the column and McCord became important to many Ozarkers. They wrote to her, and sent their verse and observations; she, in turn, printed their work and made her column as much a conversation as something to simply read.[25]

Newspaper people, of course, became Lucile's friends. Besides Docia, there was Beth Campbell, who was at the *Leader* in the late 1920s. Fern Shumate was a reporter at the *Springfield Press*, writing, as she said, "everything from the children's page to murder stories" under the name Nancy Nance. Over time, Shumate became a friend of Randolph's; later, at Randolph's suggestion, Shumate left the newspaper business and became a freelance writer and Ozarks novelist.[26]

Lucile also made the acquaintance of another group of very influential and often underestimated Ozarks journalists. These were the rural correspondents for the small community newspapers that flourished across the region. Mostly women, these contributors wrote about the goings-on in their home neighborhoods: who came to dinner, the sermon preached at church on Sunday, the weather, maybe a description of the nest of baby rabbits out near the barn. Sometimes, some of them wrote poetry. Other times, they would take on more serious matters—the economy, suffrage, or even an upcoming election. Mary Elizabeth Mahnkey was one of those country correspondents. Daughter of Alonzo Prather, a popular state legislator who had been a leader in the original Bald Knobber organization, she grew up loving books and writing verse almost as soon as she could read. Beginning when she was a teen, she shared her thoughts and poetry in the *Taney County Republican*, reporting on the doings of her small community, clouds, chickens, ball games, and what was blooming in her garden. She later contributed a monthly column, "In the Hills," to the Springfield Newspapers' "The Waste Basket" (later "Over the Ozarks") section for eighteen years, had a book of her poetry published, and wrote for a number of regional and national magazines. Born in 1877, she was a generation older than Lucile, yet she became a friend and a resource in Lucile's research on the Ozarks. Her son Douglas Mahnkey was a historian, an attorney, and also an Ozarks author.[27]

At least three other Ozarks women certainly attracted Lucile's attention, and she met them during her first years as a Springfield reporter. Rose O'Neill, the larger-than-life illustrator, author, sculptor, and creator of the Kewpie dolls, had a home in the woods near Branson that she named Bonniebrook. Although O'Neill didn't live there permanently until the late 1930s, she was a well-known presence, especially in Branson, where people would spot her from time to time sweeping down the sidewalks in long rose-colored robes as she went about her shopping and other business.

Rose Wilder Lane, who hailed from Mansfield, was a very successful author and magazine writer in the US during the 1920s. Lucile met Lane when she lived on her parents' Rocky Ridge Farm off and on for several years in the late 1920s and early 1930s. During that time, Lane occasionally would invite Lucile and other area writers to join her for afternoon conversations. Lucile later spoke of meeting some of Lane's friends from New York, and also of seeing other regional writers she knew at those Mansfield gatherings. She invited Lane to contribute book reviews to her column. Lane turned her down.[28]

Lucile also made the acquaintance of, and wrote about, Lane's mother, Laura Ingalls Wilder. At that time, Wilder was a well-known regional writer and speaker in the farming community, and she wrote a popular column, "As a Farm Woman Thinks," for the *Missouri Ruralist* magazine. After Wilder's own mother died, she wrote a reminiscence of her childhood years in the big woods of Wisconsin and the prairies of Minnesota and South Dakota. Lane served as her mother's editor and agent, introducing her manuscript to New York publishers. After one publisher urged Wilder to target the autobiography to children around the ages of ten to twelve, it became a series of books about her growing up and early adult years. The first one, *Little House in the Big Woods*, about her very earliest years in Wisconsin, was published in 1932 to wide acclaim. That same year, Lane published a serial in the *Saturday Evening Post* called *Let the Hurricane Roar*, based on the story of Wilder's parents and covering some of the same family history. *Hurricane* was a success and was published as a book in 1933, but never had the acclaim of *Little House in the Big Woods* and the subsequent *Little House* books. Wilder died in 1957 at the age of ninety. The *Little House* books were turned into a successful television series in the 1970s and 1980s.[29]

Dale Freeman, later a colleague of Lucile's and executive editor of Springfield Newspapers, was a kid growing up in Mansfield during the years when she would visit there. His parents were friends of Lane's, and he remembered going to dinner at Rocky Ridge Farm. The Wilders, he said, "were lovely people. But they were 'Mr. Wilder' and 'Mrs. Wilder.' You know, in a small town everybody called everybody by their first name normally, but it was not 'Laura' and 'Almanzo.' " Freeman also sold magazines to Mrs. Wilder, and "one thing about Mrs. Wilder," he recalled, "unlike many during the Depression, she paid. Cash."[30]

BALD KNOBBERS

While Lucile was settling into her role as an Ozarks newspaperwoman, she was also pursuing her longtime interest in the Bald Knobbers. During her first days at the *Leader*, and then the *News*, she spent a good bit of her free time delving into newspaper clippings from forty years before, reading court transcripts, and cornering older Ozarkers who might have memories of those times to share. "Fortunately," she later told members of the Greene County Historical Society, "I wrote down my interviews and kept them carefully." Initially, some of the old-timers were reluctant to talk to her, on the basis that "thar's too much feelin' about it in these here hills.' " She persisted—and slowly uncovered a story that could rival almost anything in the movie theaters.[31]

Those times were well worth documenting. Taney County was isolated in the years after the Civil War and, as in other border states, when war ended, the bloodshed didn't: residents were terrorized by out-of-control groups of roaming ruffians who stole horses, burned barns, robbed homes, and occasionally killed someone. In the early 1880s, about a dozen of the county's leading citizens, most of them former Union officers and Republicans, organized the Bald Knobbers as a law-and-order group to deal with the chaos. Two former Union officers—Nat Kinney, a farmer, and Alonzo Prather, an attorney—were among those at the first organizational meeting when rules of conduct were decided.

The Taney County group was initially successful, but things got out of hand; before long, a far more radical band of Bald Knobbers appeared in Christian County that instigated its own reign of terror and murder. The Bald Knobber era ended when several of those involved were prosecuted in a long-lasting murder trial that went all the way to the Missouri Supreme Court. Three of the Christian County Bald Knobbers were executed by hanging in the Christian County Courthouse square on May 10, 1889. By that time, Kinney had been killed and Prather had been elected to the Missouri legislature, where he served off and on for nearly twenty years. "The whole thing was sensational, and made good copy for the eastern newspapers," said Lucile. "Governor Francis [David R. Francis, Missouri governor from 1889 to 1893] from what I've read, apparently felt all that publicity was giving Missouri a bad name. If he'd commuted the sentences, it would look as though the governor was in cahoots with people causing the trouble. It's sad he didn't."[32]

The end-time of the Bald Knobbers was many non-Ozarkers' introduction to the region: the story of the night riders attracted the national press, which covered the group's crimes and ultimate demise in sensational, if not always accurate, articles. By the 1920s, when Lucile was asking questions, most people had only vague memories of the group. To learn more, Lucile counted on her interviews, but she also needed documentation, which she found in old newspapers on file at the Springfield library. She became friends with the librarian, and would go after work and read through the old papers. She even lugged an old upright typewriter over and left it at the library so it would be handy when she found time for her research.[33]

As she learned more about the era of the Ozarks night riders, Lucile's fascination with the story only grew, and she made time to search out more files and meet more people who remembered. Later, she told an interviewer: "I talked to some wonderful people. The man who got me interested was an old native . . . I'm not sure he was ever involved with Bald Knobbers, just talked about them . . . Then I interviewed a preacher. He'd been a circuit rider. He was real old. When I went to talk with him, he said, 'I can't talk about that. I wouldn't tell you about that—there's too much feeling.' . . . And then I talked to a wonderful person who was among the well-intentioned men who helped organize the Bald Knobbers. He gave me a lot of very good information about why they felt they had to absolutely do something to bring law and order in the area. He didn't think the original group ever did anything of which they should be ashamed because they were well-intentioned and working for a peaceful atmosphere in the area."[34]

Her personal research, naturally enough, spilled over onto the pages of the newspaper from time to time. In 1930, one of her pieces received a special note in the editor's column: "Lucile Morris' story of the end of the Bald Knobbers . . . [was] one of the most interesting tales published [here] in a long while. People hereabouts commonly refer to the Bald Knobbers as a legend of the hills—but it is astonishing how few persons actually know anything about the history of that picturesque and sinister and fearsome band. Miss Morris, a native Ozarkian . . . did considerable research . . . and produced an authentic and dramatic record of the Bald Knobbers that will stand as sound history. Its value is great and its publication in line with the definitely established *Leader* policy of preserving the unusual history of the Ozarks."[35]

NATHAN BOONE

In 1931, her editors at the *Leader* showcased more of Lucile's historical work. This time, the subject was Nathan Boone (1781–1856), Daniel Boone's youngest son, whose home was deteriorating not far from the Morris farm. Stories about Nathan and his famous father were part of Lucile's childhood and, as with the Bald Knobbers, her return to the Ozarks piqued her interest in knowing more. And as she learned more, she became convinced that Nathan's service to the state made him far more important to Missourians than Daniel, but that few people realized this. As a history-focused newspaperwoman, she set out to change that.

She wrote several lengthy articles about Boone, which the *Leader* printed over the course of six days, with an overall title of "Neglected Hero NATHAN BOONE." On the Saturday before the first of her articles about "the Neglected Hero" was set to appear on Sunday, the newspaper ran a large promotional ad, a half column long, with "Thrilling!" "Strange!" "Forgotten!" across the top and then, in bold capital letters: *"A TRUE TALE OF PIONEER ADVENTURE AND THE BUILDING OF GREENE COUNTY, Now Told With Patriotic Enthusiasm After Nearly 100 Years By A* Leader *Writer Who Has Spent Many Weeks In Research Among Musty Records and on the Scene of the Incident to Write the Full Story For the First Time."*[36]

That "*Leader* writer" must have loved the ad. Her series described Boone's life as a surveyor, salt maker, and Dragoon Captain in the War of 1812. During that enlistment, he was an Indian fighter and negotiator, and, at least once, saved 150 members of the Miami tribe from being killed by his own Rangers. Boone was a member of the state's first legislature and served many years on the western frontier, patrolling from Minnesota to Indian territory and later serving primarily in what became Kansas and Oklahoma. After 1837, when he relocated his family and his enslaved people to property near the community of Ash Grove, he became a respected Greene County citizen.

He and his wife, Olive Vanbibber Boone, were the parents of fourteen children, and Lucile's articles included interviews with two of Boone's grandsons and photos of his great-great grandchildren, along with information about other Boone descendants in the area. One of the grandsons, Robert Hosman, told Lucile what his mother, Mary Boone Hosman, had said about Boone's military service. Boone was often away from home so long the family would give him up for dead, "then, one fine day he would come riding across the hills, hale and hearty, and gloriously glad to be home," Hosman relayed to Lucile. After he was settled in, Boone would take off his belt, which had two hidden canvas pockets. The pockets would be full of his gold soldier's pay. The family would gather around, and Mrs. Boone would hold her husband's upturned hat to catch the shining gold pieces as he counted them out. "Often," said Hosman, "by the time they finished, the hat would be well lined with gold." Lucile's six-part series concluded with her lament over the "historic grave of Lieutenant Colonel Nathan Boone . . . a level, unmarked, almost unknown spot, somewhere near the corner of a jumbled-up pile of stones that was once a burying ground and now is the unfenced border line between a clump of trees and a meadow."[37]

When Boone moved to the rolling prairie land of northwest Greene County, he built a large dogtrot cabin out of ash logs. Over time, his landhold expanded to 1,200 acres, the dogtrot was enclosed, and the "luxurious log cabin," which Lucile described, was 1,300 square feet on the first floor, with an upstairs, wallpaper, carpet, and walnut trim. Most of the time, Olive and their children lived there with a number of enslaved people who worked in the fields and maintained the farm. Boone retired as a lieutenant colonel and came home permanently in 1855, and, according to a 1932 column by Lucile, he was on hand to provide support and act as a trustee, along with several of Springfield's early civic leaders, for the first chartered school in Greene County, the Springfield Female College. Nathan Boone died in his home near Ash Grove in 1856.[38]

After Boone died, Olive continued to live on the property with their son Benjamin Howard and his family until her own death two years later.

The home of Daniel Boone's youngest son, Nathan, was neglected for many
years, despite Lucile's efforts to shine a spotlight on both the house and
Boone. Today the Nathan Boone homestead, which has been restored and
preserved, is celebrated as a state historic site. This photo was taken circa
1942. *Missouri Department of Transportation Photographs, P0453. Identifier
020911-2. State Historical Society of Missouri.*

Olive was buried next to Boone in the family graveyard on the property,
where some of their children and grandchildren already rested. Their son
remained on the property after Olive's death and passed the homestead
down to his son, Charles Boone, who later lost it to debt. After the property
passed out of the Boone family, the house sat, largely unoccupied, slowly
falling into disrepair.

When Lucile wrote her series of articles, the Ash Grove community
was full of Boone descendants and very much aware of the old pioneer,
but they had done little to nothing to commemorate him. Her articles
did seem to make a difference, although not a very big one: a few weeks
following publication of "Nathan Boone, Neglected Hero," the Ash Grove
American Legion Post passed a resolution urging the state to purchase

the Nathan Boone homestead and turn it into a state park. The resolution was a positive step, but in those Depression years, the state took little notice. Meanwhile, Lucile continued to push for someone—Greene County, Springfield, or the state of Missouri—to pay attention to the big log house and small family cemetery. Ultimately, the Nathan and Olive Boone homestead did become part of Missouri's state park system as the Nathan and Oliver Boone Homestead State Historic Site, but it took more than a half century and a lot of effort on the part of Lucile and some of her history-minded friends.[39]

| 5 |

THE HILLBILLY FEUD

Like the Lynch sisters at Marvel Cave, many Ozarks business owners were quick to see the financial benefits of promoting the natural attractions of the region and its hillbilly image. The idea of the backward Ozarks hillbilly had been building since the 1880s, when the East Coast press excited readers with sensational articles about the Bald Knobbers. Ironically, that image only grew as the Ozarks became less isolated and more visited by the outside world. When the Model T, paved roads, and the Ozarks Playground Association began to bring tourists to the Ozarks in droves, they came to see the countryside, to fish, to vacation and, as often than not, to see real hillbillies.

Many local Ozarkers were more than happy to help them do just that. One was Lizzie McDaniel, a banker's daughter from Springfield, who, in 1923, purchased property on a ridge above the White River that had belonged to J. K. and Anna Ross. McDaniel leased a part of the property to the state, including Inspiration Point, the blufftop where Harold Bell Wright had camped for several summers while he wrote the book. She then moved into the Ross home and turned part of it into a popular museum about the hillbilly novel. Around that same time, some Ozarkers even began to feel that being a hillbilly was chic. In Branson, a group of women organized a Hill Billies sorority that operated pretty much like a typical ladies' club, with luncheons, programs, and other get-togethers.[1]

Lucile did not consider herself a hillbilly. She was town-raised, bookish, and educated. Her family did not sing the old songs, although both of her brothers' wives did, and they did not take most Ozarks superstitions seriously. If it wasn't about something that had really happened, Lucile wasn't terribly interested. "Probably I am very literal minded," she conceded. "I hate fakes. Among other things, I don't like fabricated traditions—and there are more of them than you may realize that have been written about the Ozarks."[2]

She told of reading an entrancing story about a particular peak that had been a meeting ground for Bald Knobbers—one she hadn't found in her own research. A while later she met the writer of the story and asked about the peak. "Imagine my astonishment," she said, "when I was told that it was just a story concocted out of whole cloth for the newspaper article, and several other 'equally interesting traditions' were similarly invented. It makes me most resentful, for we have enough good old genuine history and tradition for writers who are not too lazy to dig it up." At the same time, she did get a chuckle about a truly made-up story in a local druggist's weekly humor column for the Dade County newspaper. That story, outrageous from beginning to end, discussed "strange doings" at an abandoned house near Dadeville and was so clever it lured a *Kansas City Star* reporter to the area to write about the place—including a few astounding elaborations that some of Lucile's old friends provided for the reporter's benefit. "That was the first time," she said, "I realized that we Ozarkers were good newspaper copy simply because we lived where we did."[3]

In the 1930s, a wave of back-to-the-landers arrived in the Ozarks. These people were leaving cities in search of a simpler—and less expensive—life in an out-of-the-way and untouched American arcadia. As far away as New York City, newspapers took note of eastern and midwestern "furriners" moving into the Ozarks, buying up land, and taking up (or trying to take up) farming. Mostly, though, the public's need for those untouched arcadias and the growing academic interest in isolated parts of America was satisfied in the pages of newspapers and in books.[4]

W. H. Johnson, the man who had developed the little English village of Hollister, made a tongue-in-cheek pitch for bringing hillbillies even more to the forefront in the Ozarks. "We Hollisterites are seriously considering the establishment of a nest of 'Genuine Hillbillies' if we can find them on some nearby mountains," he wrote in May Kennedy McCord's "Hillbilly Heartbeats" column. "I honestly believe that the promotion of hillbillyism would draw more tourists than any other natural curiosity we have. We have overlooked our big native resource, although I must confess that in sixty years of Ozarks residence I have never run into the habitat of the Hillbilly as described by Randolph and Rayburn, or by other feature writers who drop in from Kansas or God knows where, and make astounding discoveries in a jiffy. Perhaps because we natives never see the real article is due to the fact that being of the great unwashed we have no occasion to look in a looking glass."[5]

STUDENTS OF THE OZARKS

Despite some grumbling here and there, hillbillies were good for business, they were good newspaper copy, and they were also good publicity for the anthropologists and quasi anthropologists who were streaming into the region to study and write about the peculiar people of the deep hills. Folklorists of various stripes—from bona fide academics to serious students of the region like Vance Randolph to others simply enamored of the *idea*

Vance Randolph was probably the leading writer about Ozarks folkways and Ozarks music. He and Lucile had an on-again, off-again friendship for almost a half century. *Missouri Writers Portraits Collection number P1195, Identifier 015018. State Historical Society of Missouri.*

of the Ozarks' backwoods culture. Those studies were a sign of the times. Like Margaret Mead in Samoa, American anthropologists seemed to be everywhere, and the Ozarks certainly had a share. Among those studying the Ozarks was state teachers college sociologist Walter Cralle, himself a Springfield native, who wrote about how change was affecting the region. Another anthropologist and former Missourian was Carl Withers, who lived in and studied the Ozarks foothills community of Wheatland under the name James West. As West, he authored a book titled *Plainville, U.S.A.*, which discussed the life phases of a small rural community.[6]

Serious scholarly writing tended to be rather dry reading and had a limited audience. Randolph did publish his share of intellectual work on Ozarks dialects and folksongs, but it was a short step for him to produce more general, more readable, and far more profitable articles and books about old ballads, superstitions, folktales, magic, and, at the end of his life, bawdy jokes. Probably the fact that for years he supported himself by self-described "hack writing" had a bearing. Randolph's first published work on the Ozarks, for example, was a scholarly piece in *Dialect Notes*, a journal of the American Dialect Society, in 1926. It was a vocabulary list of words he heard used in the Ozarks backwaters—words like *cripple* (a verb, as in "I got so's I caint hardly *cripple 'round*") and *bait* (bit of food, as in, "Afore I lit out I et me a leetle *bait o'* vittles"). It was good for his scholarly reputation but not his pocketbook, as it didn't pay anything. In 1931, however, he published *The Ozarks: An American Survival of Primitive Society*, a very readable volume about backwoods Ozarkers. A year later, his book *Ozark Mountain Folks* cemented his reputation as an expert on all things Ozarks, and the two books provided grist for the hillbilly mill. As Ozarks scholar Lynn Morrow points out, "Randolph continued this successful journalist's formula for writing about the Ozarks, and like a comedian at a country music show who needed sales to support himself, told his audiences what they wanted to hear—stories about the most anomalous Ozarkers of the day." The books were grabbed up by the general reading public but ignored by the academic journals.[7]

Randolph and Otto Ernest Rayburn and, of course, McCord, were probably the best-known Ozarks folklorists, but there were many others who spent at least parts of their careers learning about and writing highly dramatic and/or romantically charged stuff about the Ozarks mountain people. Charles Joseph Finger, an English adventurer who settled in Fayetteville, reflected the rest of the country's interest in the Ozarks when his memoir, *Seven Horizons*, was touted on the front page of the *New York Times* book review section in 1930. Charles Morrow Wilson, a protégé of Finger's, penned several books about Ozarks folkways on the way to becoming a nationally known magazine writer, including *Acres of*

Sky (1931), which was described in the *Springfield Leader* as a "novel of the soil" with an Ozarks background. Charlie May Simon, a prolific writer of books for young people, is best remembered for her children's classic, *Robin on the Mountain*, about a pioneer Ozarks boyhood. Simon's second husband, John Gould Fletcher, was an Arkansas-born poet whose work won a Pulitzer Prize in 1938.[8]

Another Ozarks writer during that era was Simon's father, Charles Wayman Hogue, whose 1932 memoir, *Back Yonder*, told the story of his own hardscrabble Ozarks childhood. Lucile reviewed Hogue's book in the *Springfield Leader* and pointed out that, once more, the *New York Times Book Review* had considered an Ozarks book so significant that it was featured on the section's front page. She also wrote that "the Ozarks as a theme for writers seems to be gaining in popularity. And it also should be added that there is a large improvement in the type of things that are being written about our section. And students of Ozarks dialect should find Mr. Hogue's book decidedly interesting." She continued: "This is the first book I have read by a native Ozarker who actually knew from firsthand experience the pioneer customs and traditions." Then in the next paragraph, she made an offhand mention that "Vance Randolph recently published a splendid study of Ozarks folklore and customs, but he obtained his information from others."[9]

Lucile's music and book columns for the newspaper made her doubly attractive to Randolph. She was often the recipient of old folk songs from her readers, as well as a source for reviews of his books. When *Ozark Mountain Folks* came out in 1932, she gave it a glowing review in her book column, but even though she continued to write favorably about Randolph and his success, she was not happy with Randolph's promotion of backwoods Ozarkers. In his introduction to his 1931 book, *The Ozarks: An American Survival of Primitive Society*, Randolph wrote, "This book . . . is not concerned with the progressive element in the Ozarks towns, nor with the prosperous valley farmers . . . it deals rather with the 'hill-billy' or 'ridge-runner' of the more isolated sections." Despite this disclaimer, the public at large, taken with Randolph's portrait of the isolated hill people, immediately folded every person who lived in the Ozarks into that camp.[10]

HILLBILLY VS. TOWNIE

As Ozarks scholar Morrow points out, "Hillbillyism" can be seen as a symbol "of the age-old tensions between rurality and the city." In the case of Lucile and a good number of other Ozarkers, the idea of "city" also defined prosperous little towns like Dadeville. A couple of years after Randolph's books captured the American imagination, those hillbilly/non-hillbilly tensions boiled over, much to the delight of Ozarks-watching journalists.[11]

Ozarks hillbillies had gotten a boost in 1919, when *The Shepherd of the Hills* was turned into a movie. When a second movie was made in 1928, Lucile panned it in the *Daily News*. The movie was filmed high in the mountains in Utah, which she thought was a bad place to represent the Ozarks, but at least, she wrote, it was somewhat better than "the shoddy backgrounds used in the first film version." Elsewhere, she said of the 1928 movie that since *"The Shepherd of the Hills* could not be written today of the country in which Harold Bell Wright laid the story . . . it is perhaps better that the movie scenes were laid elsewhere. For the Ozarks—every part of them—have progressed. But it seems there are a few persons in the world too backward to grasp that fact."[12]

On the other hand, she appreciated people who truly appreciated the Ozarks. As an example, poet Carl Sandburg, who was a student of American folk music and had published his *American Songbag* collection in 1927, arrived in the Ozarks in 1931 to give a talk at the state teachers college in Springfield and was so enthused by the people he met that he spent the weekend. Lucile was among a handful of newspaper people who accompanied Sandburg and McCord to Galena, the little town on the James River that had become something of a writers' haven and where Randolph was living at the time. It was also home to the Short clan, which included former-and-future Congressman Dewey Short, and a starting place for many float-fishing trips on the James and White Rivers. That evening, the group gathered in one of Galena's lodging places, listened to McCord and a few local people play their guitars and sing a number of the old ballads, and were thrilled when Sandburg took his turn performing. He left Missouri with several "new" Ozarks ballads to add to his collection, and he even wrote a guest column for the newspaper.[13]

NATIONAL FOLK FESTIVAL

In those years, interest in old songs and old ways was so widespread that in 1933 a folklorist named Sarah Gertrude Knott founded the National Folk Festival Association. Almost immediately, based on the popularity of the annual Mountain Folk Song and Dance Festival in Asheville, North Carolina, she sold the idea of a National Folk Festival to the St. Louis Chamber of Commerce. Her plan was to hold local and regional musical and dance competitions around the country, with the winners performing in St. Louis in May 1934. The St. Louis chamber bought into the idea, as did the growing cadre of folklorists and folk enthusiasts in the Ozarks. McCord and Randolph were particularly involved in the planning and execution of the Ozarks fests.

The schedule was tight: the first preliminary festival competition in the Ozarks was scheduled for the old spa town of Eureka Springs, Arkansas, on March 13 and 14, 1934. Subsequent festivals were planned for several Missouri communities, building toward an Ozarks regional event in Springfield in mid-April. From there, the winners would go to the National Festival in St. Louis. There, the Ozarkers would have a chance to show off their folk traditions next to other groups as varied as north country lumberjacks, Kentucky mountain people, and natives of the American Southwest. McCord helped oversee the regional gatherings, and she also promoted them in her "Hillbilly Heartbeats" newspaper column.

Across the Ozarks it was full steam ahead toward the National Festival—until the Springfield Chamber of Commerce got stuffy. At a chamber meeting about a month before the big Springfield regional festival, the

May Kennedy McCord sang, played her guitar, told stories, and authored a long-running "Hillbilly Heartbeats" column for newspapers all over the Ozarks. She was known as the Queen of the Hillbillies. *Photo by Vance Randolph. Printed here courtesy of Lyons Memorial Library, College of the Ozarks.*

chamber board expressed unanimous disapproval of "advertising to the world that we're ignorant." They hit a nerve. McCord asserted that the chamber didn't understand the purpose of the festival. She pointed out that the "things we are after are bringing thousands into the region each year." In St. Louis, the editorial staff at the *Post-Dispatch* agreed with McCord: "We fear these business men mistake the spirit of the folk festival . . . The Ozarks have a rich heritage . . . and should be proud . . ." A few days later, an interview with Randolph showed up in the *Kansas City Star*. Randolph was succinct: "Thar's tourist gold in them hillfolk but resort operators are making a mistake trying to do away with the primitive and stressing the modern . . . They advertise that they have bathtubs and good hotels . . . when any place has good hotels and bathtubs and only the Ozarks has log cabins and hillbillies and picturesque folklore. . . . One novel by Harold Bell Wright has brought more people to the Ozarks than all the chambers of commerce in the state."[14]

News of the hillbilly/anti-hillbilly brouhaha traveled across state lines. The *Nashville Banner* wrote of the furor in Springfield and asked, "Is the 'hillbilly' with his superstitions, his weird remedies, and his hoe-down dances, an asset or a liability to the Ozarks Mountain region of Missouri and Arkansas?" The editor of the Memphis, Tennessee, newspaper suggested that the chamber be put on show instead of the hillbilly. Closer to home, a perhaps more thin-skinned editor of the *Tulsa Tribune* came out on the side of the chamber when he wrote, "Neither industries nor better home seekers want to settle among people who glory in their crudeness."[15]

Before the regional gathering in West Plains on April 5, McCord again defended "her" hillbillies: "We still sing songs of old England and Bonny Prince Charley and tell the tales of love and tragedy and pastoral peace as well, that our granddaddies and grandmammies told to us . . . Yes, we are an unworked mine for the folklorist and the student of tradition." McCord, Randolph, and a good number of others relished the opportunity to celebrate and showcase the old ways and provoke the chamber. However, chamber of commerce president John T. Woodruff was not amused. The night before the Ozark-wide festival, the Springfield chamber sponsored a dinner for the event's leaders and folklorists from the area, including McCord and Randolph. The dinner, which did not go exactly as planned, brought even more attention to the hillbilly controversy. According to an Associated Press account, "John T. Woodruff, president of the Chamber . . . told sponsors of the Ozarks folk festival across the table last night that writers on Ozarkian subjects are 'a lot of carpetbaggers' and that Harold Bell Wright who first 'touted' the Ozarks, hardly knew a thing about them . . . He said that Vance Randolph, Ozarks author who was present, 'had been consorting with some of the undercrust and took them as typical . . .

The real Ozarkian is high-minded, patriotic and God-fearing and he made . . . as nearly perfect a civilization as it is possible to make in a wilderness.' Randolph . . . refused to comment . . . Mrs. May Kennedy McCord, another Ozarks writer, said that Vance Randolph is 'the greatest authority on the Ozarks living today.' "[16]

The next day, the *Jefferson City Post-Tribune* emphatically agreed with Woodruff. Under the heading "Hillbilly Heartbeats," the *Post-Tribune* opined: "A bitter debate has arisen in the capital of the Ozarks between those who would encourage children of nature to do their best or worst and other progressive citizens who want to portray Southwestern Missouri as the land of the million smiles and life-giving health . . . John T. Woodruff of Springfield . . . has taken up the cudgels . . . and has brought them down with handsome whacks upon the bloody but unbowed head of Vance Randolph and other alien interpreters of things Ozarkian. . . . There has been a lot of guff written about the quaint folk of the hills . . . Vance Randolph and his fellow enthusiasts, brother and sister, may look upon their work and call it good, but there is no reason why others should not frankly condemn a movement which harms a forward-looking and progressive section of the state more than it helps." Interestingly, two months earlier, the *Sunday News and Tribune* had announced, "National Folk Festival to Glorify Hillbilly."[17]

Later, Woodruff retracted his words—sort of. He attended the Springfield regional festival, had a good time, and said he had only been worried about "rough stuff" like the works of Randolph and Thames Williamson's popular novel *The Woods Colt*. Besides Woodruff, several hundred self-described "hillbillies," including the mayor of Springfield, a couple of judges, and other local dignitaries, attended and reported they thoroughly enjoyed the Springfield competition.[18]

A few weeks after the Springfield brouhaha, the weeklong, and hugely successful National Folk Festival in St. Louis captured America's attention. Afterward, McCord wrote, "Well the papers are full of Folk Festival now, not only in our town but all over the Ozarks and in fact all over the nation. Even the *New York Times* is picking up our stuff. Everybody is writing about folk songs, and spinning . . . and weavin' and play parties and dancing . . .' " A few months later, the Asheville, North Carolina, *Citizen-Times*, perhaps envious of all the attention paid to the Ozarks, pronounced that since the Southern Appalachians are the "richest region of folk songs and folk dances in the English-speaking world," Asheville should be the permanent home of all future National Folk Festivals. In fact, the St. Louis festival was such a triumph for its organizers that it launched many years of similar celebrations in cities across the country and even on the National Mall in Washington, DC.[19]

Through most of the ups and downs of the hillbilly/anti-hillbilly debate, Lucile was busy doing other things. She wrote her articles about books and music, covered politics and murders, wrote her Ozarks feature stories, worked on her Bald Knobbers research, and generally held her tongue, except to denigrate those who veered too far from the truth. Then in 1937, after her world seemed to have accepted the "hillbilly" moniker as something between benign and valuable, she had her say. In a piece that was widely reprinted, she wrote, "If you've never been a hillbilly, then you can't imagine how rich and full life has become to us native Ozarkers. After going along all these years, struggling to conform to tiresome standards of civilization, we suddenly are pounced upon by an excited world begging us to be primitive."

She went on to say, "I am not one to take offense at the fact that Ozarkers are being portrayed in popular literature as ignorant. Some of our hill people are crude and unlettered. So are some New Yorkers . . . With all the wealth of folklore available in the Ozarks, we natives might as well make up our minds that the radio, movies, and fiction writers are going to exploit it. We shouldn't blame them." Then came her parting shot: "The public, however, is entitled to know the difference between the genuine and the synthetic."[20]

| 6 |

COVERING THE NEWS

Like everywhere else, the largely small-town and rural Ozarks suffered during the 1930s. The number of tourists dwindled, communities reeled from bank failures, Route 66 was the motorway of choice for bank robbers and bootleggers, thousands of individuals faced unemployment, homes and farms were foreclosed or sold for taxes, and the countryside was scorched by throat-parching heat and droughts.

Yet the Depression did not hit everywhere—or everyone—at the same time or in the same way. Lucile was caught up in her work as a reporter. Springfield, by then more than half-again as large as when she had matriculated at Drury College a decade earlier, laid claim to a population of 57,527, with more than enough things happening to keep three newspapers fully occupied, at least for a while. Springfield's downtown square was surrounded by busy shops, and the small city was headquarters for the Assembly of God, the nation's largest Pentecostal organization, plus the two major regional colleges, Drury and the state teachers college (now Missouri State University). Springfield was also becoming a cultural center. In 1923, the Shrine Mosque had opened with a stage second in size only to that at the New York Metropolitan Opera. The Landers, which opened in 1909 as a vaudeville theater, morphed into a movie theater, and in 1934, it became home to Springfield's Little Theatre troupe. The Gillioz opened as a movie theater in 1926. In 1928, members of an art club led by a state teachers college art instructor incorporated as the city's art museum. While the group was working toward building up a collection and a home for the museum, they held their first art show at Springfield City Hall. In 1935, community leaders established the Springfield Symphony Orchestra. The city was also a transportation hub. In 1926, the local state highway that went through Springfield was designated as national US Highway 66. The aviation world came to town in 1928 and 1929 with the Ford Air Tour, then in the fall of 1930, Transcontinental & Western Air, Inc., brought airmail to Springfield's small airport, along with regular passenger service in the form of ten-passenger Trimotor Ford planes. At the time, a person could fly to St. Louis for $14 to catch a plane to New York or to Los Angeles for $106.[1]

REPORTER ABOUT TOWN

Lucile was a noticeable person around town. She dressed smartly, like the professional she was; tall and good looking, she stood out in a crowd, and she made a point of getting to know nearly everyone she met. One of her fans wrote a letter to the editor praising her as "the color columnist of the *News*. She is so sincere, so exact, so interested in everything about the Ozarks . . ." She enjoyed the camaraderie of the newspaper family, lived in a local boardinghouse on her own, and she had a regular escort in the person of John Chapman, a fellow reporter. It didn't hurt at all that she obviously loved what she was doing and was dedicated to her job. By the 1930s, newspaperwomen were nothing new in Springfield, of course, and they were also regulars on the big screen. *Dance, Fools, Dance* in 1931 starred Joan Crawford as cub reporter Bonnie Jordan. In 1933's *Mystery of the Wax Museum*, actress Glenda Farrell played a spirited girl reporter, a role that may have led her, a few years later, to play newspaperwoman Torchy Blane in a series of Warner Brothers movies. Farrell's Torchy Blane, in turn, was the inspiration for Lois Lane, the hard-boiled *Daily Planet* reporter who was Superman's girlfriend. Lois Lane appeared in the very first *Action Comic* in June 1938.[2]

While Lucile may not have been quite as well-known as Torchy Blane or Lois Lane, she was spunky enough to make it through the tough times of the Depression. Her mother and brothers were also faring well. Veda was still in Everton, by now in a house of her own and surrounded by many of her Wilson relatives. She was also a grandmother three times over: Etna and Helen had two children, June and John Albert; and George and his wife, Verna, had a son, Allan George. Etna was cashier at the new People's Bank of Miller, which he helped found with his father-in-law and fellow Democrat, John E. Adamson, scion of an old Lawrence County family. In 1932, as part of FDR's Democratic landslide, Etna's neighbors elected him one of the only Democrats from Lawrence County to sit in the Missouri House of Representatives. George, who had been in Cushing, Oklahoma, working in the oil industry when the decade opened, returned from the Southwest to join the Missouri Fish and Game Department's fish hatchery in Chesapeake, just down the road from Miller. Since Fish and Game director Wilbur C. Buford had announced a "complete turnover of personnel" shortly before George was hired, and since nearly all Fish and Game appointments in those days were political, there is a high probability that state representative Etna Morris put in a good word to Buford to hire George for the Lawrence County–based hatchery. It was a good move. During George's years at Chesapeake he devised a system for raising catfish in captivity and also wrote both technical and popular articles about fish culture and fishing.[3]

THE COURTHOUSE RUN

Over the next few years, Lucile moved from being a general assignment and "downtown" reporter covering hotels and businesses to handling what she called "the courthouse run"—the first woman to hold that position in Springfield. She was familiar with the courthouse, and she had covered stories there over her time at the newspaper, but she earned her prized courthouse beat more or less by accident. When the newspaper's police and crime reporter, Frank Rhodes, was in a taxi accident the day after Christmas in 1930, assignments had to be realigned, and that meant a shifting of staff. John Chapman, the courthouse reporter, was moved to the police beat, and Lucile was assigned to the courthouse.[4]

According to Lucile, "I was sitting at my desk banging out the usual end-of-the-year-story about how prosperous the city had been during the twelve months just closing," when the city editor told her, "You go over to the courthouse. There won't be much going on over there, and you can watch it until I can get a man on the 'run.' " She headed over there that late December afternoon and she kept covering the courthouse until she married and left the newspaper several years later. "I already had enough experience writing feature stories on runs to the courthouse to have a secret desire to cover it all by myself," she said. "My boss of course didn't know that when he gave me the assignment, and he was utterly amazed when he discovered that a woman was seriously trying to handle what traditionally had been a man's work."[5]

Being on "the courthouse run" meant covering the various county divisions lodged in the massive four-story classical revival stone building about a mile north of the newspaper office. This included not only county government, the courts, the Springfield City Hall, and the mayor's office, which were located on the third floor, but also the sheriff's office and, like the Chicago sob sisters of a decade before, the county jail and its inmates in the building next door. It didn't take long for Lucile to know everyone in the courthouse complex. She delighted in the drama and being in on the action, and she had an unshakable belief in the importance of what she did. "I figure it is my duty to record the courthouse happenings completely and impartially," she explained. "The readers of the *Leader and Press* look to their newspaper for information. The paper in turn trusts me to give it to them. If an official of the city or county squanders the taxpayer's money or neglects the office to which he has been elected, the people ought to know it. On the other hand, if an official does his duty well the citizens also should be informed about that."[6]

She also thoroughly enjoyed being the first woman in a man's world. "I never will forget the expressions on the face of the sheriff and his deputies when I first walked in that office and asked for news," she told a group of

Docia Karell   Lucile Morris   Beth Campbell

Three Ozarks newspaperwomen: Lucile Morris, center, and colleagues
Docia Karell, at left, and Beth Campbell pose in front of the Springfield
Newspapers building, circa 1933. *Morris family photos.*

high school girls a few years later. "The sheriff's office long had been a
favorite loafing place for men and it took them considerable time to get
used to a woman popping into the office every little while."[7]

Eventually she was accepted as a professional, even by the sheriff's
office, and respected for her ability to do her job—but not immediately.
Very early in her time at the courthouse, she was standing in the prosecuting attorney's office and watching through the window as two deputies
marched a half-dozen prisoners from the jail to a dental clinic in the courthouse. "Just as they got to the front steps, one of the prisoners broke and
ran," she said, "and as he crossed the street, a deputy shot him." Lucile's
instincts were good, but her experience limited: she rushed to a telephone
and called the newsroom. When the editor answered, she yelled into the
phone, "I've just seen a man killed! Send a reporter!"[8]

The reporter duly arrived, the man was not killed, and Lucile never
managed to live down that memorable day—not even when she exonerated herself a week or so later: That day, as the jailer was bringing a
prisoner to the jail office to meet with his lawyer, the prisoner suddenly
pulled a gun, began firing at the feet of his attorneys, and headed toward
the door. Before the fellow could get away, a Frisco Railroad detective who

happened to be in the building shot the escapee in the shoulder, splattering blood all over the office.

"I heard the shots and ran down the courthouse steps to the jail," Lucile remembered. "I waded right into that gory office, talked to the prisoner as they examined his wound, then grabbed the telephone. 'We'll send a reporter over to cover it,' the boss said when I told him what had happened. 'But I have all the story,' I protested indignantly. He had just supposed I wouldn't want to cover it. When I got to thinking about it, I was surprised at myself, but the incident hadn't bothered me a bit."[9]

DOB ADAMS

"Mostly they are courteous to me because I am a woman," she conceded, adding, "Where they would curse a man reporter, they merely snarl at me or stubbornly refuse to talk." One of the prisoners, though, went out of his way to earn her respect and gratitude. Newell "Dob" Adams, under a death sentence for murdering his mother-in-law and a detective, was kept in a corner cell next to the jail door for more than a year. In those days before she was a regular at the courthouse, if Lucile had a need to talk with a prisoner, she would be taken into the jail past Adams's cell. "As the door would swing open and I stepped into the cell room, Dob would yell, 'Ladies in the hall,' " she recalled. "That meant, 'Shut up all dirty talk, keep your clothes on and behave yourselves.' If any prisoners had disobeyed the order there would have been trouble for he was big enough to enforce his edict."[10]

Adams, who was known to the authorities during those Prohibition years for hauling liquor into the Ozarks from Kansas City, was twenty-six years old. When his wife walked out on him and filed for divorce, he flew into a rage, and when his mother-in-law and sister-in-law wouldn't give away his wife's whereabouts, he shot and killed his mother-in-law and slashed his sister-in-law with a knife. Then he headed to the home of his wife's best friend, Zella Sinclair, who was a hairdresser, a strong Christian, and the sole support of her elderly and poverty-stricken mother. Adams lured Sinclair into a taxi and directed the driver to take them out of town. After the taxi stopped, Adams dragged Sinclair from the vehicle and began beating her, oblivious of the taxi driver, who took one look and went for help. When the police, including detective Francis DeArmond, showed up, Adams shot and killed DeArmond, and as Sinclair tried to run away, he shot her in the back.[11]

Adams's killing spree ended there; he was arrested and put in the Greene County jail. Sinclair's story had one more chapter, which Docia Karell described in great detail for the *News and Leader*'s front page: Emergency surgery on Sinclair to remove the bullet in her spine was

not successful: doctors told her she would never walk and probably
only live four to six more months. Bedridden at her mother's house, she
depended on prayer and on friends who collected money for her support. A few weeks after her surgery, when a Welsh evangelistic healer
named Stephen Jeffreys came to town to preach at Springfield's Gospel
Tabernacle, Sinclair's friends convinced a local funeral home owner to
use his ambulance to take "Poor Zella" to every night of the revival, where
the friends would wait with a stretcher to carry her inside. Reportedly,
hundreds of people were healed, although Sinclair—lying unresponsive
on her stretcher—was not one of them. On the final night, the tabernacle overflowed with worshipers, a two-hundred-voice choir sang "Jesus Is
Passing this Way," and the whole congregation stood and began to pray for
Sinclair. Preacher Jeffreys exhorted her to "arise and walk!" At his urging,
the young woman struggled almost to a sitting position, then fell back,
unconscious. Moments later, she regained her senses, turned her head
toward the congregation and shouted, "I have felt the power of Jesus!"
Unfortunately, that power did not enable Sinclair to walk, and she died
a few weeks later (August 11, 1928) at her mother's home. Hundreds of
people attended her funeral.[12]

Because of the notoriety of the case, Adams's trial was moved from
Springfield thirty miles north to Bolivar, but it didn't change the predicted
outcome: Polk County Judge C. H. Skinker declared Adams guilty and
sentenced him to be hanged. Adams then spent many months back in his
Springfield jail cell awaiting the scheduled hanging. But as the date closed
in, Adams foiled his executioners: he downed poison tablets someone
smuggled to him in the jail. The poison apparently didn't work instantly,
and he spent his last hours with Sheriff Marcell Hendrix—and also his
estranged wife. "I didn't deserve to hang," he told Sheriff Hendrix as the
poison took effect, "but I guess I do deserve to die." As he died, he thanked
the sheriff for how well he had been cared for at the jail.[13]

YOUNG BROTHERS

For Lucile, it was exciting to cover the courthouse and be in the know
about what was happening and what was going to happen in the county,
but one wintry afternoon, she got more than she bargained for. On
Saturday, January 2, 1932, as she headed back to the newspaper office
after making her courthouse rounds, she saw Sheriff Hendrix and Deputy
Wiley Mashburn leaving the courthouse complex in a big hurry, rifles in
hand. As they hustled out, Hendrix called over his shoulder, "We may
have a story for you after a while." She learned later that they had received
a tip that murder suspect Harry Young had been seen at his mother's

farm west of Springfield. The Youngs were not unknown to Springfield law enforcement. More than a dozen years earlier, Greene County's then-prosecuting attorney William Vandeventer had brought action against two other Young brothers, Jennings and Paul, for burglary and grand larceny. Sentenced to ten years at the Missouri State Penitentiary, they walked free after serving only three.[14]

A couple of hours later, after Lucile was back at her desk in the newspaper office, managing editor George Olds yelled across the newsroom to her, "Get over to the county jail as fast as you can—Marcell Hendrix may be shot!" She did, and he was. Lucile remembered: "As I reached the door of the old red brick jail, which adjoins the residence of the sheriff, and saw the face of jailer Frank Willey and heard heart-breaking screams from Mrs. Hendrix, I knew there was no doubt of the situation . . . Hours later, we learned that six police and county officers had been killed trying to serve a warrant to Harry and Jennings Young at their mother's farmhouse." The brothers were wanted for car theft and the murder of a deputy in nearby Republic. All told, Sheriff Hendrix took ten deputies and one layman with him to make the arrests. The two Young brothers were long gone when police reinforcements arrived at the farmhouse—they had managed to steal a car in Springfield and drove south—but the bodies of Sheriff Hendrix and five of his deputies were on the premises. Another brother, armed and inside the house, kept reinforcement officers at bay for several hours, preventing anyone from picking up the bodies. When Harry and Jennings's mother was eventually brought to the courthouse for questioning, she told the newspaper reporters, "I hope they kill themselves, because I know I'll never see them alive again. I'd rather they would do that than have the law kill them."[15]

Lucile was devastated. Almost immediately, she wrote a highly emotional column about the tragedy, her friendship with Sheriff Hendrix, the courage of the slain officers, and the horror of the event: "It's impossible to estimate the loss that has come to this section in the death of these six splendid officers," she wrote. "It will be a long time before the city or county recovers from the shock of their murder." What became known as the Young Brothers Massacre was the worst police disaster in the US until September 11, 2001. As details of the slaughter on the Young farm and new developments became available, the newspaper staff went to work. "Our newspaper staff worked all night," recalled Lucile with relish. "We published Extras every time additional information was obtained, then most of us went home after meeting at the Colonial Coffee Shop for early breakfast."[16]

News of the shootings—and the escape—spread across the country. The state of Missouri offered a reward for the capture of Harry and Jennings Young. Kansas City and Houston, Texas, put watches on the homes of

Young relatives in those towns. Newspapers all over the Midwest and Texas carried detailed stories about the massacre. Even the *New York Daily News* had a front-page headline that the "Killer of Six" was still on the loose. A series of mishaps on the Young brothers' part, including a wrecked car, enabled law enforcement officers to trace them to Houston, where they had holed up in a rented room. But word was out; the landlord figured out who they were and notified local police. Following a brief shootout on January 5, the brothers locked themselves in a bathroom and, true to their mother's wish, avoided arrest by turning their guns on themselves.[17]

Nearly a century after it occurred, the horror of the Young Brothers Massacre is recalled in a monument that stands in front of the Greene County Courthouse in Springfield. *Photo courtesy of Mike O'Brien.*

In Springfield, both newspapers followed the developing story closely, covering any angles of the goings-on they could think up. At the competing *Springfield Press*, Nancy Nance wrote about one of the Young children ("Youngest Member of the Young Clan Visits in Springfield") and about the crowds that descended on the jail and sheriff's office ("Excitement Prevails as News of Youngs' Deaths Is Spread"). *Press* reporter Lon Scott wrote a long and detailed story about helping one of the deputies drag a body out of firing range from where it had fallen many hours before. The newspapers stayed on the story of what happened to various other members of the Young family, covered the lawmen's funerals, and publicized memorial collections being taken up for the grieving families. Fifty years later, in January 1982, Lucile devoted nearly the whole of her column, "The Good Old Days," to a retelling of the grizzly tale.[18]

As soon as the dust cleared, Mrs. Hendrix—Maud—was appointed interim sheriff to serve until an election could be held. A few months later, the local Republicans nominated her for the job, but she lost the election by a small margin to Scott Curtis, a longtime city constable. Interestingly, Maud was the third woman appointed sheriff that year in the Missouri Ozarks. Just two weeks earlier in West Plains, Lulu Kelly had been named sheriff of Howell County following the death of her husband, Sheriff C. R. "Roy" Kelly, in a shootout with members of the Barker-Karpis gang. One of Lulu's first actions as sheriff was to join with the West Plains police chief in offering rewards for the arrest of members of the gang. Those rewards included one hundred dollars for "Old Lady Arrie Barker." That special offer was significant: it was the first official law enforcement mention of Ma Barker as the gang's leader. Lulu Kelly served as sheriff for about a month—until a special election when voters chose Els Seiberling to succeed her. The third woman sheriff was Bessie Kelly of Houston, Missouri, who was appointed to fill the remainder of her husband, Harry's, term as Texas County Sheriff after he died from blood poisoning as the result of an automobile accident. Bessie Kelly was appointed in mid-December to serve only until January 1, when her husband's already-elected successor, chosen in the November election, was slated to take office.[19]

WOMAN ON THE BEAT

While none of Lucile's other crime stories ever came close to the scope of the Young Brothers Massacre, she continued to savor the "courthouse run." She also believed that she often benefited from being a woman on the beat. "I frequently got stories from offices and meetings where a man reporter would have been pitched out on his head," she chuckled. "The officials couldn't make up their minds how to deal with a woman who barged in and started asking questions, refusing to take gentlemanly, though pointed, hints to get out. By the time they decided they would go ahead and swear at me even if I was a woman, I had the story."[20]

Lucile had always stood up for herself; her success in covering the courthouse was proof that she was a reporter who could cover anything. And while she had always been ready to defend her position as a news-paperwoman, the Young Brothers Massacre probably further bolstered her ego. Whatever the reason, just a couple of months after the killings, she took her turn on a staff-written column in the *Springfield Leader* to take issue with the comments of a well-known New York editor about the role of women journalists. *New York Herald-Tribune* editor Stanley Walker, whom she apparently admired, had given an interview about "skirted scribes" that got her dander up. She objected to his declaration that newswomen were "terribly unfunny" and that men were better at writing human interest stories. "When women write it [human interest stories]," she sniffed, "they call it 'sob stuff.' " She also used Walker as a starting place to revive her animosity against the *Kansas City Star* and *St. Louis Post-Dispatch*, "two large Missouri daily newspapers which will not employ women at all . . . They give as their excuse the fear that some-time they might want to send a woman out on a story not suitable for her to cover. That," she wrote, "is too absurd to discuss." She opined that "about as large a percent of women make good on newspapers as men" and that the work "brings a lot of satisfaction, variety, entertainment, and some-times excitement." The difficulties and hard knocks, she said, "keep one interested as much as do the many pleasant encounters along the way . . . Most newspaper workers, both men and women," she concluded, "have the vague notion that someday they'll get out of the game and do other types of writing. Yet if they are successful, they usually like their work too well to desert it." Lucile certainly felt that way. Throughout her life, she took pride in being and, later, having been a reporter. When she gave talks, she often found a way to sing the praises of newspaperwomen and raise her eyebrows at men-only newspapers and editors that didn't appreciate them.[21]

THE REST OF THE COURTHOUSE

During her years covering the courthouse, Lucile wrote not only about meetings and shootings but also about juvenile court, parole board hear-ings, and divorces. Some of what she reported broke her heart: "At the parole board meetings any injustices to the prisoners and all the heart-breaks of their families are revealed. I always feel wretchedly sorry for ignorant youths who have stumbled into some crime and are sorry too late. I always feel sorrier for the prisoner's family than I do for him. It's pitiful to see a woman with a lot of children begging for her husband's release from jail." As when she worked in Denver counseling the lovelorn, she couldn't divorce herself entirely from the human drama she was covering: "I used to take the run as hard as I did the lovelorn column. I saw so much that needed to be done for the sake of humanity and the taxpayers that I was in an eternal stew trying to set things right. The old Greene County jail used to haunt me at night. I couldn't understand how a humane and prosperous people could put other humans in such a place. For years I wrote stories trying to arouse interest so a new jail would be built . . . I still don't like to interview the prisoners in the cells of the old jail." She actually wrote one of those "replace the jail" stories in February 1932, only a couple of months after she became a regular at the courthouse.[22]

Later, while a new jail was under construction by the Works Progress Administration (WPA), she said of the old jail: "I worried as if I were personally responsible every time I saw some intelligent first offender locked up there. I raised Cain in one news story after another about that jail. I couldn't get the average citizen excited about it because most people have an unchangeable feeling that any kind of horrible quarters are good enough for people that get into jail. I did pester the county officials about it so much, however, that they called a bond election or two trying to remedy matters." That 1929 bond issue, proposing to raise $60,000 to refurbish the jail, seemingly had the support of the civic and business communities, but nonetheless failed to light a fire under the voters. One possible reason was simply the economics of the time. Lucile, however, believed that "those elections all failed, due to the sanctimonious attitude of good citizens who said, 'If they don't like our jail, let them stay out of it.' I'm glad to report, however, that there now is under construction as a WPA project a modern jail that will be sanitary and have ample room." After she retired from her long newspaper career, Lucile would run for Springfield City Council, push for a newer jail than the one built by the WPA, and take on some of the other challenges she saw at the courthouse.[23]

During her courthouse years, she made notes, probably for future speeches, about the conditions there: the building, dirty with full spittoons, had a shiny white space on the wall where a Western Union clock had once hung but had been discontinued as an economy move, and a circuit court room sported a broken-down chair where the sheriff sat. In her notes, she described a "fat attorney who looks like a bullfrog ready to jump," a "square dancing probation officer" with black hair "although old," and an unappreciated county health director who tried to save the county money. She also mentioned a "proud" widow who had begun making home brew to support her six children following the death of her husband. "I could get along and barely exist," the woman had told Lucile, "but my children are entitled to better than a bare existence. They are brilliant and talented. If I can't help them now, it'll be too late when they are old."

"All these things," Lucile wrote, "are none of my business. I'm at the court house to record the news. If some poor kid that never had a break in life gets thrown in jail then I should write the cold facts and not be stewing around about doing something to help him. If the county court wants to pay out thousands of dollars for disinfectants when soap, water, and elbow grease are what is needed then that's nothing for me to get excited about. But, just the same, I'm likely to take such things pretty hard."[24]

Other notes involved her pride in the power of the press. For a Rotary speech she mulled the thought that "the only thing that will put the fear of God in some political circles is the newspaper. Many politicians keep one idea on the impression their activity is going to make on the front page. 'I can't do that—it would get wrote up all over the newspaper.' " In the same set of notes, she also ruminated about a newspaper publisher "who frankly admits to the Rotary Club that a newspaper first of all is an enterprise for the making of profit," then "turns around and editorializes on the sacred institution of journalism that is above money or governmental control." If nothing else, reporters have a front-row seat to the contradictions of everyday life—Lucile watched, paid attention, and took notes.[25]

UP IN THE AIR—AGAIN

Her courthouse run kept Lucile busy, but not all the time. She was still one of the newspaper's two most visible and popular reporters, which kept her in line for the occasional special assignment, or airplane flight, as happened again in mid-1932 when Transcontinental & Western Air, Inc., began flying into the downtown airport. A TWA public relations man convinced the newspaper to send Lucile and Docia winging across the country to show people what it would be like to travel by air. Docia's trip was to San Francisco, where her family had moved; Lucile's adventure took her to New York City. Docia left first, and, as she wrote to readers, "For fourteen hours, from the bright morning sun of Tulsa," her plane skipped and hopped across the broad spaces and the small cities of the Southwest before arriving in Los Angeles. After a quick night in LA and an early bus back to the airport, she boarded a plane headed north to the landing field in the Bay Area, where, as they circled the field, she wrote, "I can see my mother" and "the tall brown-eyed brother with the old flashing smile that I have not seen for nearly ten years."[26]

For her trip to New York City, Lucile flew first to St. Louis, then picked up a transcontinental flight headed for New York. "As I left Springfield," she reported, "the TWA rep there gave me cotton and chewing gum for air pressure and noise." The air was smooth, the scenery "gorgeous," and "everybody was happy and agreeable." This was significant; three years earlier when had she covered the same route with Wiley Post as part of the Ford Tour, Lucile told readers, she "nearly bounced out of the seat."

She was flying "as space permitted" without advance reservations, so she felt lucky to leave St. Louis in the one extra seat on the next plane headed east. However, her luck didn't last: she got bumped first in Columbus, Ohio, for the night, then again in Pittsburgh, which, she reported to readers, was "Eastern and brusque." Her connecting plane out of Pittsburgh didn't take off until 10:30 p.m., which annoyed her, but her late-night flight to New York turned out to be a wonderful surprise: she was mesmerized by the lights she saw below. "Never have I seen such a show," she wrote. "As the plane rocketed eastward there was the flare of light from the exhaust of each powerful motor. Light on the wings outlined our ship . . . Lights at irregular levels in towns and farmhouses . . . revolving beacon lights . . . miles and acres and swarms of lights . . . I saw steamboats outlined in lights." At Newark, she wrote, "We circled this, the busiest airport in the world, and I gasped again to realize that I hadn't been dreaming or imagining things—that all this unreal, unbelievable scene which I had watched from the skies actually existed."[27]

Coincidentally, on the day Lucile was flying between Columbus and Pittsburgh, Amelia Earhart was flying across the US. That day, Earhart, who had already set the record for being the first woman to fly solo and nonstop across the Atlantic, set a new women's record for transcontinental flight, crossing the country in nineteen hours and landing at the Newark airport just about fifteen hours before Lucile. "Aviation is a woman's game as well as a man's," Earhart told a reporter. Since Lucile felt that way about newspaper reporting, she surely agreed about aviation.[28]

Once in New York, Lucile stayed with friends, was taken to Coney Island, toured the city, was awed by all the liveried doormen and waiters, gawked at the swell New Yorkers, went to a couple of speakeasies "just to look," and dined at the Biltmore Hotel, where Paul Whiteman and his orchestra were performing. She learned that Whiteman's manager had played in stock companies in Springfield. "He said a lot of nice things about the old home town—and I believe he meant them, too," she wrote.

Before she left New York, Lucile had another adventure. Someone, probably the TWA public relations people, had arranged for her to make a nationally broadcast radio talk. She wrote her speech and practiced ahead of time, but, as she reported to readers the next day, her brief time at the National Broadcasting Company (NBC) studio was nerve-wracking: "If you don't think it's something to scare a country gal to walk into the impressive offices of a great radio company and say a speech, you just try it yourself." When she was introduced on the air, she related, "I took a crack at the first sentence of my carefully typed speech . . . I sounded like a jaybird imitating a hoot owl." She stopped, momentarily, horrified, then, "I decided that I really wasn't scared—and I settled down to reading." The text of the fifteen-minute talk was a defense of her Ozarks, and of hillbillies. "We find it amusing that outside stories about our section usually feature it as a primitive place in which cavort uncouth natives with bare feet," she told her international audience of American and Canadian listeners. But "they fail to mention the prosperous towns and cities, the paved highways that wind along the backbones of our ridges or the modern newspapers . . ." She described the Ozarks hills as being "characterized by a blue haze which hangs over the distant ridges, ever changing in its tints, and lending glamor and beauty to every scene." She spoke about Osage people, Spanish treasure, shape-note singers, and pioneer Ozarkers with their old English roots. She discussed Ozarks fiddle music, the old ballads, square dancing, Daniel Boone and his son Captain Nathan Boone. She told listeners about Ozarks writers, too, from Rose O'Neill at Bonniebrook, to epic poet John G. Neihardt on Lake Taneycomo, to Rose Wilder Lane in Mansfield, Emily Newell Blair, who came from Carthage, and even Vance Randolph, whom she described as "another writer from our section who has recently published a book."

She also made a point to assure her listeners that in the Ozarks, "Women have much freedom of choice in occupations. The newspapers on which I work probably have the largest percent of women reporters of any dailies in the entire country. They are actual reporters, too, not merely feature writers. They cover the same type of news assignments that are given men reporters . . . Our stories are as varied as are the blue tints on the distant ridges." She told listeners about the Young Brothers Massacre and about a huge power dam that had just transformed the Osage River "into the largest artificial body of water in the country. The Lake of the Ozarks."

Once she finished speaking and was off the air, a woman called the studio: her brother lived in Springfield she said, and she wanted Lucile to know she appreciated the speech. Then came a telegram from Docia's sister Joanna in California, who had also been listening. "I was thrilled to pieces," Lucile acknowledged. "For the first time I realized what I actually had done—talked to people clear across the continent." Unfortunately, the people at home were unable to hear Lucile. NBC broadcast her speech to big cities like Toronto, Chicago, San Francisco, Washington, DC, and Kansas City. The *Leader* announced it, but told readers the closest place to hear Lucile would be in Lawrence, Kansas. Later, after she was back home, they reprinted the script of her talk for her fans.[29]

Almost a half century later, *News-Leader* columnist Hank Billings also wrote about Lucile's trip to New York, letting readers know about the two things that impressed her most about the trip: her night flight from Pittsburgh to New York, and on her way home, a storm between St. Louis and Springfield. "Of the latter," Billings wrote, "she recalls that she was nervous, but determined to act brave; that two men passengers were airsick and scared. 'The pilot started writing notes to us trying to calm us down, though plainly he wasn't too happy about the situation either.' "[30]

Despite the newspaper's, and Lucile's and Docia's efforts to encourage passenger business, Transcontinental & Western Air, Inc., couldn't outlast the effects of the Depression in the Ozarks. Plus, because of power lines and telephone poles at the end of the runway, the TWA planes were making only about half their landings. Airmail officials cited those hazards and announced that if they were not removed, not only airmail but also passenger service would cease in Springfield. The small downtown airport with its too-short and unpaved landing strip was outdated, and the city had no extra funds to deal with it. In February of 1934, TWA left Springfield.

A few months later, American Airlines moved in to provide airmail and passenger service, but that, too, did not last. In 1935, Springfield's acting postmaster, C. W. Greenwade, complained that "American Airlines is attempting to force the Springfield Park Board [the group that managed the airport] to pave the runways." When a Department of Commerce engineer came to town and officially made the same recommendations, the city was unable to comply. Mayor Harry Durst met with chamber of commerce president Lester Cox and members of the park board. They knew what to do, but their conclusion was that there simply was no money to make the needed improvements. Park board member J. H. Karchmer probably did not help the situation when he observed, "Those people are asking us to build a port to suit their ships. Wouldn't it be just as reasonable for us to ask them to buy some ships to fit our park?" By September 1936, American was no longer flying to Springfield and the US Postal Service announced that Joplin would become an airmail stop on American Airlines' St. Louis-Fort Worth route.[31]

| 7 |

DEPRESSION, BOOKS, AND BALD KNOBBERS

As the Depression deepened, many businesses couldn't hang on—or if they did, business owners couldn't afford to advertise, which made life very difficult for newspapers. In Springfield, the newspapers survived, but just barely. For almost four years, the town had supported three newspapers —the Bixbys' *Springfield Daily News* and *Springfield Leader*, plus Harry Jewell's *Springfield Press*—but finally, in May 1933, the economy forced a change. Jewell and the Bixbys merged their publications into what became Springfield Newspapers, Inc.: the morning *Daily News*, the after-noon *Leader and Press*, and the *Sunday News and Leader*. Under the new arrangement, Lucile continued on her courthouse run, edited her Sunday book column, and occasionally worked on other assignments from the city desk. She also gave up her pseudonym. Docia, on the other hand, tried to give up hers, but couldn't. Readers refused to believe that the "Helen Laverty" whose name suddenly showed up on the newspaper pages could write half as well as the better-known "Docia Karell." Docia liked the name, so under the circumstances, she decided just to keep it.[1]

All over the Ozarks, local newspapers were holding their breath. Some, like the Springfield papers, merged; others were forced to shut down their presses. In Marshall, Arkansas, *Republican* publisher James H. Tudor announced he was accepting hay, chickens, corn, or potatoes— or cash—as payment for ads or subscriptions. He had a mortgage on the newspaper office, but he also had one on his home. In the end, unable to make both payments, he saved the newspaper and lost his house.[2]

COUNTRY CORRESPONDENTS

One thing that helped keep the small newspapers going was their country correspondents, those unpaid contributors who provided them with chatty neighborhood news and enough words to fill their pages when hired help, real news, and advertising were scarce. Among them, poet Mary Elizabeth

Mahnkey was beloved of both readers and editors, not only because of her long-running column in the *Taney County Republican* but also because of a series of articles she wrote in 1933 and 1934 about pioneer times that not-so-subtly covered many issues of the day. These articles, titled "When Roseville Was Young," ran in both the Taney County newspaper and the *Springfield Press*. When the *Press* introduced her column in February 1933, the editor, clearly an Ozarker of the Woodruff school, wrote that "Mrs. C.P. Mahnkey, (a 'self-styled "hill billy" and writer') resenting the work of 'these poisonous feature writers' who have emphasized the crudities of the Ozarks region, has sent the *Press* . . . chapters out of the life she has lived. . . . Mrs. Mahnkey has presented an Ozarks which . . . is more fascinating than that presented by most writers."[3]

One of her first pieces in the *Press* began this way:

> When Roseville was young, there was no poverty; to be sure, there were some not "well fixed," but they never felt any difference in their position in the community, for here was no difference made. We would have been amazed, bewildered, at hearing them termed 'underprivileged' or to have them the objects of community chest drives, or a study for welfare bureaus and so on . . ."[4]

Mahnkey's attitude reflected the feelings of many Ozarkers who had grown up and "made do" for generations in that rocky region. But her words echoed beyond the deep valleys and river bluffs of the Ozarks: in 1935, she was selected as the best from among 1,500 country correspondents in a contest sponsored by national farm magazine the *Country Home* and Crowell Publishing Company. She won a trip to New York and Washington, DC, to see the sights, talk on the radio, and meet dignitaries like New York mayor Fiorello LaGuardia and former mayor Al Smith, her favorite politician despite his being a Democrat. In Washington, which she told friends she preferred to New York, she visited the Library of Congress and lunched with Congressman Short, but she turned down an opportunity to meet President Franklin Roosevelt. On the trip she also endured interviews by a large number of big-city reporters. "At one time," she later told some of the home folks, "I was interviewed by sixteen reporters, and of them only three had journalism training." Like Lucile, she must have been sensitive about her lack of formal training—but certainly not because she lacked knowledge. One male reporter it turned out, was surprised that Mahnkey knew far more about literature than he did.

As for all those reporters, "They asked me what the Ozarks thought of the New Deal and I told them the only ones for it are those on relief," she related. "All I've got to say is that the Constitution, Carter Glass [US senator from Virginia and former secretary of the treasury] and Dewey Short will

Poet and local columnist Mary Elizabeth Mahnkey beat out 1,500 other
country correspondents to win a national contest and a trip to New York and
Washington, DC. *Photo by Townsend Godsey courtesy of Lyons Memorial
Library, College of the Ozarks.*

save the country." When a *New York Sun* reporter interviewed her, she
said, "I promised not to talk about the President or politics. I'm a staunch
Republican," adding, "The people in my section of the country look to God,
and not the administration, for prosperity. Out our way, prosperity means
do we have rain or don't we have rain. If we have rain we are prosperous."[5]

DROUGHT AND HEAT

As the 1930s progressed, the Ozarks did not prosper. Nor did many opinions change regarding the New Deal. In Mansfield, Laura and Almanzo
Wilder's attitude toward FDR and the federal government's "handouts"
matched that of Mahnkey, Congressman Short, and a good part of southwest Missouri. Historian Carolyn Fraser, whose Pulitzer Prize–winning

Prairie Fires looks deeply into the lives of the Wilder women, suggests that their anti-FDR attitude was at least in part related to Laura's impoverished childhood and the Wilders' hardscrabble existence during Rose's childhood as well. In other words, if they could survive, others should be able to. One day, when a federal farm agent came to Rocky Ridge Farm to talk about Congress's newest programs, Almanzo, eighty-one at the time, told the agent to "get the hell" off the farm and warned, "If you're on it when I get to my gun, by God I'll fill you with buckshot."[6]

During those years, there was almost no rain, summer temperatures hovered over one hundred, and there was not much FDR or the New Deal could do about it. Dade County native John Hulston, whose father had purchased the Morris Hardware store from Veda, remembered those years vividly: "Looking back, it seems to me that the Great Depression meant droughts, interspersed with tornadoes . . . My father hired a sawyer to cut trees in early July, 1934, so his cattle could eat the leaves and beat starvation . . . There was no reserve water in the sub-soil . . . many wells and springs that were never known to go dry before did so now . . . the dust was like a fog . . . people went to bed with wet towels over their faces . . ." July 1934 was the state's hottest month on record, and 1936 was the driest summer.[7]

Despite the drought, the economy, and the plight of many Ozarkers, Lucile's job kept her busy, and her family continued to be okay. Veda rented out half her house in Everton and took a job as a seamstress and postmaster at the Missouri State Sanitorium in nearby Mount Vernon. George's hatchery at Chesapeake, which raised bass, crappie, and bluegill, was producing more fish in 1934 than any of the state's other hatcheries, and it was expanding: the young men from a nearby Civilian Conservation Corps (CCC) camp were in the process of building twenty new lakes there, allowing George and his crew to raise even more fish for the state's anglers. George was also beginning to talk about raising channel catfish, which would make Chesapeake only the second hatchery in the US to raise the popular fish.[8]

Because Chesapeake was in Lawrence County and just fifteen miles from Etna's family in Miller (by way of Veda in Mount Vernon), George and his wife, Verna, could vote for Etna, who was running for his second legislative term in that blistering summer of 1934. As an elected member of the state legislature, Etna was doing what politicians do: he met regularly with a group of area bankers to discuss issues and hear talks by local leaders, and he could often be found volunteering as a sometime auctioneer, funeral orator, or emcee at local events. At more than a few funerals, his deep, sonorous voice comforted the bereaved with a recitation of William Cullen Bryant's poem "Thanatopsis."[9]

POLITICS

In 1934, there was no guarantee Etna would be reelected. Although a large majority of Missourians—63.69 percent—voted for Democrat Franklin Roosevelt in 1932, many Ozarkers, like the Mahnkeys and Wilders, were long-standing conservative Republicans, and Democrats had to fight for their attention—and their votes. In the area that included Lawrence, Dade, and rural Greene Counties, however, there was one place where local politicians—even Democrats—could count on being able to press the flesh and visit with a lot of voters, and that was at Everton's annual midsummer "picnic." The Everton picnic generally attracted thousands of people over the course of three or four days. It was always a time for family reunions, a shooting gallery, horse show, midway, fair food—and political speeches. It was such an important part of local life that even back in 1931, when the Everton Bank closed "for reorganization," the local newspaper assured readers that the picnic would "not be interfered with by the closing of the bank." The next year, the *Greenfield Vedette* enthusiastically estimated that a staggering fifty thousand people had attended the four-day event.[10]

If they didn't visit Everton any other time of the year, Lucile, George, and Etna made a point of being on hand at the picnic to renew acquaintances with old friends, visit with family members in from out of town, and for Etna to do some politicking. So even in that summer of 1934, with temperatures hovering around one hundred degrees, wells running dry, and money scarce, Everton had its picnic. The *Vedette* announced: ". . . once more the big Everton picnic is in progress, four whole days of fun and forgetting how hot the weather is—maybe. Ferris wheels, merry-go-round, popcorn and peanut stands, hamburger joints, shooting gallery, ice cream cones, lemonade, and all the other stuff with which one may stuff himself. Then as an added attraction this year there is the saddle horse show. Come and enjoy the picnic." Friday was the horse show and Saturday was "State Candidates Day with addresses by Many Candidates."[11]

That year there was an added attraction: word had come down that Kansas City political boss Tom Pendergast was backing a new candidate for US Senate and was sending him to meet Ozarks voters. In that sweltering summer, Pendergast's people called local Democratic committeeman Fred Hulston to take charge of the candidate and introduce him around. "I think that's the first time my father had heard of Harry Truman," remembered Hulston's son, John, "and . . . I think he used the words, 'Who the Hell is he?' [and] was told that Harry was a very fine county judge in Jackson County and that he had Tom's support, and that he was going to be the next senator of the United States and that he'd like to meet some of the people in town." Ash Grove, where the Hulstons lived, was like most of the area in that Democrats were sparse, but as a good party man the elder Hulston agreed to meet Truman. "There's not any Democrats here," he told Pendergast's man, "but bring him down and we'll take him to the Everton picnic."[12]

Hulston first took Truman to Ash Grove to shake hands with the mayor, who was a Democrat, and to meet the banker, who was the other leading Democrat in town. Then he drove the candidate over to Everton. At the picnic, it's a sure bet that Hulston introduced the unknown US Senate candidate to Dade County native and Democratic legislator Mount Etna Morris, and he probably introduced Truman to Morris's family—especially his newspaper-reporter sister.

Over the course of the very hot day, Hulston learned Truman had been born on a farm in nearby Lamar, so when it came time to introduce the candidate, Hulston presented him to the crowd not as a Kansas City politician, but as a neighbor: "Now, you folks will want to be for this man because he's a farmer just like we are. You know, his hands fit a plow handle just like an owl's claws fit a limb." Truman, dapper in a light-colored suit and tie despite the ninety-plus degree temperature, and, by 1934, a long way from being a Lamar farmer, made a folksy, down-home talk and totally captivated his audience.[13]

Despite Truman's rousing success at the Everton picnic on that sweltering day, however, it turned out not to be enough to win Dade County's vote in the August primary election a few weeks later. To be sure, Truman won the primary statewide, and then went on to win the US Senate seat in November, but he came in second in Dade County in the primary, getting 240 votes to fellow Democrat John Cochran's 268, and to Republican incumbent Senator and Springfield native Roscoe Patterson's 2,380. Democrat Etna Morris, on the other hand, was returned to the Missouri legislature by the overwhelmingly Republican Lawrence County electorate: he won by thirty-four votes.[14]

NEW DEAL IN THE OZARKS

Etna's return to the statehouse was good news, but it couldn't change the weather. Heavy rains and flooding in 1935 threatened the Chesapeake Hatchery. Then, in 1936, it was so hot and dry that George was part of a Fish and Game crew that went out across the southern part of the state to rescue dying fish from almost waterless streams.

As the 1930s shuffled toward the 1940s, the heat and economic disasters continued, yet people muddled through. Voters instituted a new Department of Conservation in 1936, and in 1937, George was promoted to section superintendent for the state's hatcheries. Congress passed Flood

Control Acts in 1936 and 1937 that included future plans for dams that would impound Bull Shoals and Table Rock Lakes, eventually meaning more Ozarks construction jobs—and a promise of more tourist money in the economy. Etna, who had not run for the legislature after his second term, was hired to be cashier of the National Bank of Trenton and moved to far northern Missouri in 1939. Dale Freeman, a schoolboy in Mansfield during those years, remembered, "We had the Depression, and we had the damnedest drought. You saw people lined up to get basic commodities. You saw the CCC camps; the boys would come in and hit the local beer joints. You were aware of that, but somehow the Ozarks was a good place to grow up."[15]

The weather didn't improve right away, but slowly, the economy did. In the face of opposition from many locals, including outspoken Congressman Short, the New Deal began to make a difference in the Ozarks. (Short had been voted out of office in the 1932 Democratic landslide, but was reinstated in 1934 to represent southwest Missouri in the US Congress for the next twenty-two years.) The Civilian Conservation Corps camp near Chesapeake that put young men to work at George's hatchery was one of about seventy CCC camps in the Missouri and Arkansas Ozarks, each with about two hundred occupants. The CCC Boys, as they were called, planted trees, built hiking trails and roads in state parks and national forests, and erected structures in fifteen of Missouri's state parks, including Big Springs near Van Buren, Roaring River near Cassville, and Bennett Springs near Lebanon.[16]

In 1935, when the Works Progress Administration (WPA) was authorized, impoverished men joined work crews to build—besides a new Greene County jail—highways, streets, schools, gyms, hospitals, courthouses, parks, post offices, swimming pools, sewage plants, airports, and water systems across the state. It has been estimated that the WPA was responsible for as many as ten buildings in every county in the country's then-forty-eight states. The WPA even put hired writers and artists to work documenting the state's history and geography, and the US Treasury Department's own Section of Fine Arts spearheaded another project that resulted in murals in the US post offices in several Ozarks communities, including Clinton, Eldon, Cassville, Monett, and Mount Vernon.[17]

OF BOOKS AND WRITING

During those Depression years, the *Springfield Leader*, with an eye to supporting the faltering tourist economy, kept the staff writing Ozarks features and book reviews, which Lucile was happy to oblige, and the newspaper—whether it was pro-hillbilly or not—also began reaching out to some of the more well-known folklorists and "professional hillbillies" to spice up the day-to-day news. May Kennedy McCord had become part of the Springfield Newspapers crowd in October 1932, when she brought her "Hillbilly Heartbeats" column and her pro-hillbilly point of view to the *Daily News*. In her first column she urged: ". . . come on, hillbillies, let's get together . . . Write some poetry and some essays and some love letters to the hills! Let's don't talk about our hotels and garages and banks and politics and the cosmic situation . . . This old world is progressing fast enough scientifically; it doesn't need us hillbillies to help along that line."[18]

Vance Randolph was a regular subject for the newspaper's pages, a reliably good interview, and he was still busy churning out books. *The Ozarks: American Survival of a Primitive Society* (1931) and *Ozark Mountain Folks* (1932) were followed by *From an Ozark Holler* in 1933. Randolph got in touch with Lucile about *From an Ozark Holler*; he had taken issue with her review of *Ozark Mountain Folks* and wanted to make a special point when he sent her the new book to review. Overall, Lucile's review of *Ozark Mountain Folks* had been very positive. She wrote that Randolph's Ozarks "is more primitive than any with which I ever have come in contact," but added, "I wish we had more of the pioneer peoples and customs left . . . I like the old-fashioned hill billy with his droll humor, shrewdness, honesty and good fellowship. Therefore, I have enjoyed reading *Ozark Mountain Folks*."

She enjoyed the book, but she also commented that Randolph wrote "in the raw." That is, if the teller used words not fit for polite society, Randolph put those words in his books anyway. Therefore, despite liking *Ozark Mountain Folks*—and despite the conversations she was party to in the sheriff's office and county jail—Lucile wrote in the review that "a few of Mr. Randolph's paragraphs made me feel as though I'd suddenly 'busted into' the livery stable and heard the loafers say some things not intended for my ears."[19]

Nearly a year later, when Randolph wrote her about his next book, he was still smarting from her comment: "That crack you made last year about my stuff being 'raw' disturbed me. I wouldn't in the least mind writing a dirty book—I think that smut has a legitimate place in literature—but I would want to do it intentionally and deliberately. If there was anything 'raw' in *Ozark Mountain Folks* it was unintentional— just clumsy and ambitious carpentry. In this new book, however, I think I have cut out everything (except perhaps one single sentence) that could possibly make you feel as if you had 'busted into the livery stable, and overheard something not intended for your ears.' " He ended his letter with a question: "How goes your book on the Bald Knobbers?"[20]

BALD KNOBBERS

Lucile's book was going very well. As Randolph—and nearly all of her friends, relatives, and readers—well knew, Lucile had become fixated on the Bald Knobbers as a teenager visiting her uncle George Wilson on Presbyterian Hill. She began researching the story almost as soon as she returned to the Ozarks from El Paso. At first, she was enraptured by tales told to her by old men who had been involved in the early days of the Taney County night riders. Then, as her curiosity shifted into serious thoughts about writing a book, she buttressed her interviews with newspaper accounts and court records.

While she was working on the book, Lucile got in touch with William H. Johnson, the elderly Springfield real estate developer who had founded Hollister. During the Bald Knobber trials at Ozark, Johnson had written newspaper stories about the men and made sketches for the *St. Louis Post-Dispatch*. "He gave me some of his stories with the sketches," recalled Lucile. With Johnson's permission, and that of the *Post-Dispatch*, several of the sketches were reproduced in her book.[21]

After a decade of research, many feature articles, and a good number of speeches on the subject, Lucile completed her "Bald Knobbers" manuscript in 1934. Then, as writers do, she spent the next year rewriting it. When it was finished, she sent the manuscript to the Caxton Press in Caldwell, Idaho. As she put it in an interview with the Christian County Library, "They were a fine small publishing company interested in western books, and apparently the Ozarks fitted into their western theme." Caxton had made a name for itself when it began welcoming writers who, like Lucile, had trouble getting the attention of East Coast publishers because of where they were located. One of Caxton's early authors was Russian American writer Ayn Rand, best known today for her two novels *The Fountainhead* and *Atlas Shrugged*.[22]

On May 23, 1935, Lucile received word that Caxton would take a serious look at her manuscript, and on October 19, Lucile's manuscript was accepted for publication. For the next several months, she worked with editors on rewrites and fixes, and by early March 1937, *Bald Knobbers* was typeset, the cover designed, and engravings made. Publication was scheduled for August 1 of that year. As a final step, when the editors at Caxton sent Lucile the page proofs of the book, they—almost miraculously—sent along all of Johnson's original illustrations because they wanted her to rewrite and shorten the captions. She gave the proofs a final read, rewrote the captions, and on March 17, 1937, she took her book package to an express office to mail.

Coincidentally, at the very same time she was mailing her package to Idaho, the Caxton Press was burning down.

The conflagration started in a paper stockroom, and by evening everything was gone: books were cinders, company records ashes—and Lucile's book, typeset and almost ready to go, had "flowed off in a river of lead." The editor sent her a frantic letter, telling her about the fire, and hoping against hope that she had received the proofs. She had, and despite crushing disappointment, she understood that her book and the original artwork were saved. *Bald Knobbers* would still be published. "That was wonderful, fortunate for me," she said when she told the story later. "How could I ever be so lucky when everyone else lost everything!" Once the fire burned itself out, Caxton lost no time in getting back to work. The company rented local buildings and presses in order to continue publishing what they could. Within two months, they had erected a new building. Before long, they gave Lucile another publication date, this time in 1939.[23]

A NEW CHAPTER

For Lucile, 1936 was a milestone year. Selling a first book manuscript would be an event of momentous importance for most people, and for Lucile it certainly was. But six months after she sold her "Bald Knobbers" manuscript, Lucile Morris, the straight-shooting, independent career woman who had lived through a vendetta against the KKK, worked on the Mexican border, covered the Young Brothers Massacre, and was comfortable talking with everyone from presidents to criminals, was married. Her new husband was Greene County Circuit Court reporter Eugene V. Upton, eleven years older, scion of a prominent Bolivar family, a widower of one year and father of three children: nine-year-old Rosemary, sixteen-year-old Eugene, and nineteen-year-old Joseph (JB). He was also a Republican. The Upton family was well-known in Gene's hometown of Bolivar; his late father had been a highly successful attorney, state legislator, Bolivar postmaster, managing editor of the *Bolivar Free Press*, and a delegate to the Republican National Convention several times. Gene's mother, Nanny (Nancy) Gravely, had been the daughter of Missouri's lieutenant governor.

Gene was one of seven siblings. A sister, Mattie Weaver, was married and living in the eastern part of the state. His brother Mark owned the Bolivar drugstore and was a leader in promoting better roads in Polk County, and his brother Ernest, a former Polk County prosecutor, was living in Los Angeles. Three other brothers had died. Gene himself had gone west as a young man, spent time in Canada, worked for a contracting firm in Oregon, married, then returned to Missouri in 1917 and became a court reporter for Judge C. J. Skinker of the 18th Judicial Circuit in Bolivar before moving to Springfield.[24]

Lucile, second from left, and Eugene V. Upton, in white suit, were married in the
Springfield Presbyterian Church parlor on her thirty-eighth birthday. Back row
from left: Lucile's brother George; Upton's son JB; Lucile's brother Etna; and Docia
Karell. Front row from left: George's wife, Verna; Lucile; Gene; and Etna's wife,
Helen. © *Springfield News-Leader—USA TODAY NETWORK.*

Lucile had known Gene since she started on the courthouse run in 1930,
and she quite liked the serious, quiet gentleman. However, it took a push
from another courthouse denizen to bring them together romantically. One
of the people she interacted with on a regular basis at the courthouse was
Deputy Circuit Clerk Irene Wilson, who kept her apprised of courthouse
gossip, upcoming trials, and other court news. Wilson, in turn, worked
closely with Gene, and his boss, Circuit Judge Guy Kirby. After Gene's
wife died in the spring of 1935, "several women were showing a good bit
of interest in him," Wilson recalled. When he confided that he wasn't sure
what to do about all the unsolicited attention, she gave him some advice:
"One day I said to him, 'Why don't you pick out your own? You did a good
job the first time.'" Gene asked for a recommendation, and she told him,
"If I were a man in your place, I wouldn't pass up Lucile Morris. She's a
lady." Gene demurred, with the excuse that a date "would just break up
a beautiful friendship, especially if she turned me down." Knowing how
direct Lucile generally was, Wilson told Gene that if Lucile didn't want to
go out, she would say so.[25]

On Wilson's advice, Gene asked Lucile to go out, and she agreed to a movie that very evening. The two dated, they were seen around town, and a few months later, they announced their engagement. A week after that announcement, Winnie Lucile Morris and Eugene V. Upton were united in holy matrimony in the parlor of Springfield's First and Calvary Presbyterian Church, in the presence of Lucile's brothers and their wives, her dear friend Docia, and Gene's son JB. Following a wedding breakfast, the new Mr. and Mrs. Upton took a three-week tour of the West, including a sojourn on Galveston Bay in Texas. The grand Galvez Hotel, where they stayed, became a favorite vacation spot for the two. When they returned to Springfield, the couple settled into their new life in a large home about a mile north of downtown.

FORMER NEWSPAPERWOMAN

Lucile quit her job, as was the custom for married women in those days, as well as a requirement at the newspaper. According to historian Megan McDonald Way, prior to the 1930s, nine states actually barred married women from being employed. Missouri didn't, but married women were encouraged to focus on home and family, especially during the Depression, when so many men were out of work. Back in the days when Lucile had been the advice columnist for the *Denver Express*, she often was asked to address the question of whether women should continue to work after they married. Now, given that her new husband had two teenage sons and a nine-year-old daughter, Lucile didn't feel that she could do anything else but leave the newspaper.

Lucile's place on the staff was filled by a young woman named Ann Fair. Unlike Lucile, Fair had gone to the University of Missouri's journalism school. She graduated in 1933, but when she began looking for a newspaper job, she found, as Lucile had eight years before, that St. Louis and Kansas City were hiring women only for the society pages. "I didn't want to do that," Fair remembered. "So I worked at weekly newspapers in Eldon and Marshfield. Then, when Lucile married and quit the Springfield newspapers, I got her job."[26]

Before Fair was hired, Docia and Lucile had been the only women in the newsroom. By this time, Docia was more of a columnist and Lucile, of course, covered the courthouse and city hall. A few days after Fair joined the staff, Lucile invited Docia to bring her for tea at the grand residence in north Springfield that Gene had purchased when they married. When they rang the bell, Fair remembered, "Lucile came down the big staircase to open the front door—I was so impressed!" A slender woman who shared Lucile's dedication to journalism but not her glamorous presence, Fair stayed at the newspaper until her own marriage to golf pro Ray Dodson in 1949, then returned following his death in the mid-1950s. Fair and Lucile became good friends.

In the meantime, Lucile took on her new assignment with gusto. She did her best to learn the ropes of being a wife and stepmother, even nursing Rosemary through a serious childhood illness. She also became a sought-after speaker by club groups and schools, sharing her experiences from the newspaper world, lamenting the neglect of Nathan Boone's home, and offering encouraging advice to young women about careers and their lives in a changing society. She even, very occasionally, wrote an article for the newspaper, under the name Lucile Morris.

When she gave talks about her newspaper years, she always included names of other newspaperwomen, past and present. In a talk to the Saturday Club, she told her audience about colleagues at Springfield Newspapers, from McCord to Mahnkey to Docia and Fair, describing the latter two as "Docia Karell, whose brilliant writing has become an important institution in the community, and Ann Fair, a competent reporter . . ." Others she mentioned were the women publishers, from the Williams sisters in West Plains to women publishing papers in Monett, Mount Vernon, Greenfield, and Clinton, plus "no doubt others I have overlooked." She observed that Frances Willard, founder of the Women's Christian Temperance Union (WCTU), had been a newspaperwoman-turned-temperance-crusader, and ". . . as I read histories of women in early journalism . . . most of those who made newspaper reporting their business were crusaders. It seems to me that is all right. It is very difficult for us women to see a wrong without wanting to do something about it."[27]

PUBLISHED!

Bald Knobbers ultimately was reset and published in 1939, and received with great fanfare in Springfield and beyond. The *St. Louis Post-Dispatch* proclaimed Lucile's book "far and away, the best that has been written on the Knobbers!" The *Kansas City Star* ran a two-column story on the editorial page with an illustration from the book, noting that it had been written by a Springfield newspaperwoman and commenting that "Miss Morris's account of the Bald Knobber terror is valuable social history. Never before have the many diverse elements been gathered together." In Springfield, the Sunday newspaper devoted a half page to the new book, and one of the bookstores launched *Bald Knobbers* with a tea. The public library was "elated" when she brought them an autographed copy; no local author had ever done such a thing before. The local writers guild named Lucile "First Citizen" at their annual spring banquet and gave her a basket of roses. Banquet speaker Dr. Virginia Craig of the state teachers college English department said the book was a "fascinating, entrancing, and convincing account of a very human incident" and predicted that as years passed it would become an "authoritative source for its period." Walter Cralle, the state teachers college sociology professor, praised *Bald Knobbers* as helping to preserve the "history, traditions and dialect of a vanishing pioneer society with a convincing authenticity."[28]

Lucile saved excerpts from some of the reviews that appeared in the rest of the country, which by and large questioned the value of a book about a group of vigilantes. The San Jose, California, *Mercury-Herald* review pointed out that the Bald Knobbers "brought law, or at least retribution, in Taney County, and then, again in the process inherent in vigilantism, they reaped the whirlwind of their violence by becoming themselves a terroristic group . . ." The Lowell, Massachusetts, *Courier* review opined, ". . . it contains a lesson worth heeding regarding the danger of going outside the law for the preservation of order and the punishment of crime."[29]

Despite the national distribution of the book for reviews, *Bald Knobbers* was a very regional book and never sold a lot of copies. One of those copies, however, somehow found its way to Hollywood and garnered a good bit of attention. When the Caxton people told Lucile that her tale of night riders in the Ozarks hills had piqued the interest of the movie people, she hired an agent and crossed her fingers. A few months after *Bald Knobbers* was published, she and Gene were on vacation in Galveston following a conference in New Orleans for court reporters, when Lucile received a telegram: MGM might be interested in the book. That was certainly heady stuff and confirmed the speculation among her family that John Wayne should be cast in the role of Nat Kinney. However, as she and Gene began their drive back to the Ozarks, word came that Europe had gone to war. "On the way home," Lucile later told friends, "I said to my husband, 'I'll bet that will never be made into a movie if this war keeps up.'" It never was. "I still think that was the reason. People didn't want to hear about turmoil."[30]

| 8 |

WAR AND WAITING

Once the war in Europe began officially, the US initiated a nationwide "precautionary mobilization" drive that brought several massive construction projects to the Missouri Ozarks. The three largest were the US Army's Camp Crowder, near Neosho; O'Reilly General Hospital, built on land that had been the Springfield municipal golf course until the US Army took it over; and Fort Leonard Wood, about ninety miles northeast of Springfield.

The army announced plans for Fort Leonard Wood, an infantry training center, in January 1941. Originally intended to be the home of the 6th Infantry, Fort Wood was soon filled with infantrymen from multiple divisions, and very soon it became an engineer replacement training post as well. Before the war ended, more than three hundred thousand soldiers passed through Fort Wood on their way to active duty.[1]

Also in 1941, the army announced it would build an infantry and Signal Corps replacement training center near Neosho, with the expectation that Camp Crowder would house seventeen thousand draftees for their thirteen-week training camps. It did that, but along with draftees and contingents of the Women's Army Corps, the Signal Corps maintained the Signal Pigeon Corps. During the war, that special unit housed and raised as many as thirteen thousand carrier pigeons, later reported to carry ninety percent of their messages successfully.[2]

That same year, the US Army selected the grounds of Springfield's 160-acre municipal golf course as the site for a one-thousand-bed temporary military hospital—one of nine to be built across the country. O'Reilly General Hospital eventually took care of more than fifty thousand patients and was enlarged six times before its doors closed as a hospital in 1946.[3]

By mid-1941, signs of the war were everywhere in the Ozarks. Docia summed it up in a story for the *Daily News* that ostensibly announced the September 7 opening of the Ozark Empire Fair. Titled "Looking Back on One Year in the Ozarks," she wrote that since the prior year's fair:

- More than 2,000 men from the Springfield area were employed at soon-to-be Fort Leonard Wood.

- Camp Crowder was under construction in Neosho.
- O'Reilly General Hospital opened its doors to its first patients.
- The Frisco Railroad added a third more workers in the Springfield shops, increased the number of trains from St. Louis to Fort Wood, and began Pullman service from Kansas City.
- Springfield's population had grown by about 2,800.
- Hog prices doubled over the year before.
- More than 400 new homes were built in Springfield alone, along with St. Agnes High School, a new elevator at MFA Milling, a phone company expansion, and upgrades to downtown's Woodruff building.
- Seventy-five to one-hundred boxcars a month were pulling out of Springfield with eggs, milk, and millions of pounds of cheese bound for Britain.
- Springfield's National Guard Unit in the 203rd Coast Artillery had departed for Camp Hulen in Texas.
- 442 young men from Greene County had been drafted since the Selective Service Act was passed in September 1940.
- More than 1,500 Ozarkers volunteered for the Army, Navy, Marines, or Coast Guard.[4]

Among the young men who left town were Gene's sons and, later, Lucile's brother George. Eugene Jr., who had grown up planning to spend his career at sea, had enlisted in the US Navy in 1939. JB finished Drury College, and then enlisted in the Army Medical Corps in September 1941 at the age of twenty-four. Both young men served in the Pacific. George was drafted in 1943. The Selective Service was drafting men up to age thirty-eight, and George was sworn in at Jefferson Barracks in St. Louis on the day before his thirty-eighth birthday, making him, according to the *Springfield Daily News*, "perhaps the oldest draftee of the year." He also was sent to the Pacific. There was some speculation in the family that George was drafted in retribution for some of Etna's political activities. Subsequently, because of his age, the politically connected family set about getting George discharged but finally decided it would only cause problems for him. At one point, Lucile wrote to George that she had received a letter sent by Congressman Short in which he said he thought he should do nothing further at this time—that it might hurt, rather than help.[5]

O'REILLY HOSPITAL

Beyond the general worry about the war, the next few years hung heavy on Lucile and Gene as they waited for news of their loved ones. They filled their time with work—Gene at the courthouse and Lucile with various writing and speaking projects—and by volunteering at O'Reilly Hospital. When O'Reilly opened in mid-1941, post commander Colonel George B. Foster vowed to make it "the hospital with a soul." Two years later, Army Surgeon General James Magee told Colonel Foster that O'Reilly was the best of the US Army's hospitals. After that, it became a model for others across the country. Part of O'Reilly's success was the result of widespread support from the Springfield community: more than a thousand civilians were on the O'Reilly staff as cooks, guards, postal clerks, telephone operators, and the like; and probably a thousand more spent time there as volunteers. The volunteers took recuperating soldiers on day trips around the Ozarks, saw to it that each patient received Christmas gifts, and generally made them feel welcome. Lucile and Gene were regulars among the volunteer corps. She worked with her writers group to teach a class as part of the hospital's rehabilitation program, and Gene went along on class nights to play chess with the soldiers. Lucile wrote to Gene's sister and brother Ernest about one of his regular opponents, a young soldier who had been paralyzed from the waist down with no hope of regaining the use of his legs.[6]

In that same letter, Lucile also told Gene's siblings about her writing class: "There are about six or eight of us—all women—in the writers group working at O'Reilly but we have managed to do quite a bit. We brought three speakers . . . big shot writers that we just tell to come . . . Lester Dent who writes the Doc Savage stories, flew down in his own plane from La Plata, Missouri, in January. Marge Lyon . . . was here in February . . . the boys just loved them . . . In March, we had [creative writing] Professor Edwin L. Peterson of Pittsburgh (Pennsylvania) University who was here to talk at state teachers college. He was VERY good." The class was a success, and the O'Reilly commander asked Lucile to lead a second writing class in the afternoons, which she agreed to do, leaving the evening class under the charge of a friend and short story writer Donna Ashworth (later Thompson).[7]

On several occasions Lucile and Gene brought O'Reilly patients home with them to dinner. Lucile wrote about a twenty-three-year-old who had been wounded in Italy almost a year before, and who was walking on crutches and possibly facing a bone-grafting operation. His visit to the Upton home was his first day away from O'Reilly since he'd arrived. "If I never do anything else," she noted in that letter to Gene's siblings, "I can know I've done some good there."[8]

She also gave talks at the hospital from time to time, often to tell people there about the region. Once, she spoke about how hillbillies had become fashionable again in the Ozarks: "Now that it is good box office, our attitude has changed." She told her audience about a time when she and Gene were entertaining a couple of young soldiers from Boston, and "they were so interested in learning about the Ozarks, I tried to tell them all the tall tales I could remember." When one of them said he had expected the Ozarks to look like the *Li'l Abner* characters that were popular in the newspaper comics sections, she began trying to think of "some evidence of hillbillyism" and remembered the picture she had taken years before for a Kansas City newspaper "of an aged, bearded man, dressed in overalls and leaning on a gnarled cedar cane . . . posed with my little niece . . . [that was] framed to hang over my desk." The old man, of course, was Uncle Ike of *The Shepherd of the Hills* fame. "The two soldiers were intensely interested . . . They started asking questions. Then I was struck by a shattering thought. 'That man,' I gasped, 'Is no hillbilly—he's from New England—where you're from.' And that was the truth." She went on to tell her audience that most of the region's best-known writers were " 'furriers' who have come into our region and liked it well enough to make it their home. In many cases they had a perspective on the Ozarks that we natives could not get on ourselves, and have presented a clearer picture of it than we could have done. In fact, there was a time when some of us were saying that if things kept up the way they were, we would have more writers about our hillbillies than we'd have hillbillies to be written about."[9]

"THE GOOD OLD DAYS"

Another place in Springfield where help was needed during the war was in the big building on Boonville Avenue that housed the newspaper offices. Lucile was well aware that many of her former colleagues at the newspaper were gone—volunteered or drafted. That meant that the newspaper management went looking for people to fill the empty jobs. One of the people they called, of course, was Lucile. "I was a housewife with two college-age stepsons in the service. It never occurred to me that I'd ever be a reporter again. No married woman could hold such a job on Springfield Newspapers even if she wanted to do so, which I didn't at the time," she said. "Any urge I had to write was appeased with occasional short stories or articles for magazines, or an Ozarks feature for some out-of-town papers."[10]

In those days it was not uncommon for businesses to have rules, like Springfield Newspapers did, against employing married women. However, during the war years, a lot of women, including newspaperwomen, were filling jobs that wouldn't have been dreamed of a decade before. Virginia Irwin, a *St. Louis Post-Dispatch* reporter who made a name for herself with an eleven-part series of articles on women in the American war industries, became a war correspondent in a way not dissimilar to Peggy Hull a generation before. Her editors at the *Post* refused her request to go overseas but finally agreed to give her a year's leave. On her own, she made her way to England and hired on in the public relations department of the American Red Cross. Eventually she convinced *Post* publisher Joseph Pulitzer II and *Post* Washington bureau chief Raymond Brandt to support her application, which was accepted. As an accredited war correspondent, she was one of the first three Americans to enter Berlin. Her dispatches back to the US were picked up by the Associated Press and landed on the front pages of newspapers across the country. Pulitzer was so pleased he gave her a bonus of a year's pay. On her return to the US, she joined the *Post*'s New York bureau for several years, then moved back to St. Louis, and then, after her retirement, moved to Webb City in the northwestern Missouri Ozarks.[11]

While their work was perhaps not so exciting as Irwin's, a number of Ozarks women were covering the war on the home front. In Waynesville, *Pulaski County Democrat* owner and publisher Ruth Long wrote a regular "Dear Readers" column that kept the community apprised of details about the growth of nearby Fort Leonard Wood and the boom years of World War II. While many of her columns were not unlike those of the weekly correspondents like Mary Elizabeth Mahnkey, they were less about gardening than town life, as when she discussed the "rivers of rich brown tobacco juice all about the front door of the courthouse." Others often contained serious "real news" about the war industry.[12]

On the national scene, First Lady Eleanor Roosevelt made it a point to showcase female news professionals. She held women-only press conferences, 348 of them in all. Initiated in 1933, these sessions began by being all about Mrs. Roosevelt's daily schedule, White House décor, and scoops like the fact that the White House would serve beer as soon as Prohibition ended. It didn't take long, however, before she was discussing important national issues such as low-cost housing, equal pay, and the minimum wage. United Press reporter Ruby Black dubbed Mrs. Roosevelt's press conferences a "New Deal for newswomen." Lucile's friend and former colleague Beth Campbell, who had married and moved to Washington, DC, was one of those newswomen; she covered the conferences for the Associated Press.[13]

Although Lucile said she didn't want to go back to reporting, she did remain in close touch with her old newspaper cronies. One day only a few weeks after Pearl Harbor, she was having coffee with a group of newspeople, and managing editor George Olds again solicited her help. She remembered him asking, " 'Isn't there something you can do?' I said 'I might write a column, but it has to be something that is an antidote to war.' So I went home and tried to get an idea . . . The next morning, I went to the public library. I told Miss Harriet Horine, a longtime librarian, of my problem and she gave me permission to go to the basement and wander through the newspaper files . . . The newspaper had given precious old files to the library and Miss Horine was a great protector of anything related to Springfield history." Looking through the old newspapers gave Lucile an idea, and the next morning, when Gene left to go to the courthouse, she asked him to make a detour by way of the newspaper office and drop off a draft column. The column she'd written was in the form of a letter from "Celia" to her "Auntie" about the goings-on in Springfield a half century before: "I enclosed a note to Editor Olds that said 'This probably isn't what you want, but maybe it will help you suggest something more to your liking." She didn't get a response to her note, but the following Sunday— January 25, 1942—"the letter appeared just I had written it."[14]

Olds liked the column so much that he touted it in a front-page box, and again on the editorial page, calling it a "fascinating new weekly feature" with "rich and diverting information on life as it was lived in Springfield fifty years ago." He added that "Miss Morris is peculiarly qualified . . . as she has been a student of Ozarks history for many years . . ." The column did not disappoint. "Dearest Auntie:" it began, "When I promised to write you all the news while you are visiting Grandfather in St. Louis, I didn't count on the perfectly grand snow we've had this past week." What followed was a mention of the Springfield news of January 1892: people were busy storing ice for the year, and twenty-nine rail carloads of it had been brought in for local use; a successful rabbit hunt had taken place in nearby Ozark; there was also mention of an upcoming suffrage meeting, comment on former Governor McClurg's expert handling of the US land office, news of a train robbery and murder near Lamar, and discussion of a diplomatic crisis and possibility of war between Chile and the US. Of the latter, local Judge A. B. Appleby was quoted that "at this stage of the world's civilization, war is unnecessary."[15]

Olds's judgment about Lucile's column was sound. "The Good Old Days" ran as a part of the Sunday newspaper for more than forty years and became a must-read for anyone who cared about Springfield or Ozarks history. For the first five years, the column byline was "Lucile Morris." However, on February 2, 1947, with no explanation from Lucile or from managing editor Olds, the byline changed to "Lucile Morris Upton" and remained Lucile Morris Upton until she stopped writing "The Good Old Days" in March 1982.

When Lucile began the column, she was sharing history from the pages of old newspapers. By the time she retired the column, she was writing about things she remembered and had lived through. One of the most poignant (for her) was probably an item in her August 5, 1973, column about President Warren Harding's final trip to the West Coast fifty years earlier, which she had covered as a young reporter in Denver.

BETTY LOVE ON BOARD

A few months before Lucile embarked on "The Good Old Days," another woman joined the short-staffed newspaper. Betty Love was an artist and Drury College graduate who was teaching art at a local junior high until a combination of school politics and the pending world war managed to change her life. Upset over what was happening in the school's art department, she applied for a position at the *Leader and Press*. The newspaper's staff artist, Jon Kennedy, had recently left for the *Arkansas Democrat*, and Love was hired for the summer. Of the editor who hired her, she remembered, "He never told me I was fulltime. I just stayed." Love was not a total unknown. She had entered a number of paintings

Betty Love in 1945, about the time she gave up her paintbrushes for a camera. © *Springfield News-Leader—USA TODAY NETWORK.*

in regional art competitions, and in 1939, one of her paintings was hung in the state capitol building with the work of several other Ozarks artists. While she was teaching, she befriended a Kansas City artist who had come to the Ozarks on sketching trips. That artist was Thomas Hart Benton. They remained friends, and there are numerous stories about parties they both attended at the Riverside Inn, a popular restaurant and bar just south of Springfield.[16]

A year or so after she joined the newspaper staff as an artist and cartoonist, Love turned in her pens and pencils for the camera that would define her career. Within a few weeks of Love becoming a photographer, Olds wrote what, for the time, was a highly complimentary column about her. Love, he wrote, ". . . came to us a couple of years ago when we needed an artist. She thought she could hold a newspaper job. Even in filling an art job, we had that mysterious trepidation about hiring a girl. It was her idea—not ours. And it was a considerably harder job than teaching school. Faster, more exacting, longer hours, new tricks to learn. But after her hand stopped trembling, Betty settled down and learned to draw newspaper stuff, learned retouching and sketching and cartooning and all the variety of chores that go with a newspaper artist's job."

Not long before Olds wrote the column, nightside police reporter Scott Shadburne moved over to join Love as an illustrator/cartoonist. Among other aspects of his job, Shadburne illustrated Lucile's "The Good Old Days" and drew a regular sports sketch. Then Love let it be known that she wanted to become a photographer. "We smiled tolerantly," Olds wrote, "and said maybe we'd let her try some time . . . she persisted and finally we told Johnny McGuire [a staff photographer] to see what he could do with her . . . in less than a week Betty was turning out darned good prints, all by herself, and in another week she had learned enough of the fundamentals of the intricate camera to turn in some pretty fair shots . . . by golly she was getting to be a news photographer."

Olds's column was a rather backhanded tribute to Love, but its overall purpose was to compliment not only her but also the "extraordinary journalistic team" of Betty Love and Ann Fair that debuted in that day's newspaper. He cited "Miss Fair's excellent reporting" and noted that "girl reporters are not new in our experience—everyone knows we have boasted some wonderful ones—but a girl cameraman is a bit more unusual and a team such as we now present is unique in Missouri and probably in a much wider territory." The two women's "quite important . . . assignment"? A trip to Lebanon, Missouri, fifty miles northeast, for a three-part series on the year's gubernatorial candidates, Republican Jean Paul Bradshaw and Democrat Phil M. Donnelly, who both hailed from Lebanon. Olds did somewhat redeem himself when he pointed out that "we've always had girl reporters . . . because we've always tried to hire the best possible people—hired them as persons, as individuals, not as men or women . . . providing they had the ability, the personality and the loyalty. The only reason we haven't had more girls on the staffs is that good girl reporters are relatively much scarcer than good men reporters. But somehow it never occurred to us to have a girl photographer . . ."[17]

Love worked for Springfield Newspapers for thirty-five years. By the end of that time, she had a national reputation as a photojournalist, was celebrated in the National Photojournalism Hall of Fame, and was recognized as a pioneer in color newspaper photography. She was also known across the Ozarks as a talented but eccentric part of the newspaper staff. As one fan wrote in a *News-Leader* editorial on the occasion of her death in 1984, "When a reporter went on an assignment with Betty, it wasn't just a job. It was an adventure." There were tales of Love stopping her car in the middle of a busy bridge, heedless of other traffic, to get a picture and of her dropping a camera lens out of a plane that was flying low over a Springfield residential neighborhood so she could do some aerial photography. In the 1950s and 1960s, after Lucile was widowed and had returned to the newspaper, she and Love often worked together—sometimes on fairly dicey stories. According to Lucile, "Betty always said they sent us out on some of those difficult assignments because the men on the staff all were married and we weren't." The twosome became well-known across the Ozarks.[18]

LUCILE'S FICTION

In the meantime, during those long years of war, worry, and waiting, Lucile continued to volunteer at O'Reilly Hospital, but stayed busy in other ways as well.

Besides her public speaking during those years, Lucile tried her hand at writing fiction. She had sold a short story years before to *Capper's Farmer* magazine ("Woodsaw Charlie's Wife," October 1926), and during the war years she wrote dozens more, plus two novels. Neither of her novels was published, but both of them revealed her reporter's knack for seeing details. One was a traditional romance about a backcountry mountain girl who falls in love with a good-looking visitor from the city. She sent that one to her friend, the poet John G. Neihardt, who pronounced it "a sweet story, well written and essentially true," with "characters drawn with genuine understanding and sympathy," but "if the tale were more obviously dramatic, its chances might be increased." He recommended that she send it to Mathilde Weil, a New York literary agent of his acquaintance. The other novel, which Lucile originally called *On Wheels*, described changes brought to the Ozarks by the arrival of automobiles, as seen through the life of her independent businesswoman heroine.[19]

Over the next thirty years, Lucile kept at it. She attended writing conferences, even the venerable Bread Loaf conference in Vermont, where she hobnobbed with writers from across the country, including nationally known poet John Ciardi, and became friends with Goldie Smith, a children's book author from Tulsa. She took a correspondence course on fiction writing from the University of Oklahoma and turned out dozens more short stories, but none sold. She kept scrapbooks of her formal rejection slips and many letters from kind editors, all with the same message. Lucile's manuscripts would be praised for her characters and their surroundings—i.e., her reporting—but editor after editor wrote that her stories had no suspense or drama. She even got an agent. Lurton Blassingame was a well-known New York literary agent, and he accepted her on the basis of *On Wheels*. It was a bonus that he had been born in Fort Smith and had an affinity for the Ozarks, but it didn't help him sell her work. On his first reading of her manuscript in 1942, he wrote to her, "You have all the makings here for a really first-rate book, but I don't think you have taken your ingredients and worked them together nearly as well as you might. What you have here seems too much the work of a social historian, too little the work of a novelist." The problem, he said, was suspense: "You have almost none."[20]

She took his words to heart, rewrote the manuscript, and sent it back. This time, Blassingame wrote, "You have improved the novel (needs a better title) but I'm not sure if you've done enough. It's still written more from the head than the heart." He added, "It's still too early to say whether this means you should abandon fiction for non-fiction. However, if that does turn out to be the case there will be nothing to worry about . . . *On Wheels* is a competent job and an improvement. I'm going to try it out; as a matter of fact, it's with Doubleday now." Unfortunately, Doubleday editor James Zarbock agreed with Blassingame. He wrote, "The first part of the book I thought was especially well handled, but when the plot carried on to the girl's marital relations, I am afraid something went wrong. Sorry." In 1945, Robert M. McBride and Company, which had published books by Ozarker Charlie May Simon, agreed to read Lucile's book manuscript, now renamed *Joy Ride*. Again it was rejected, but this time with a slightly different message: "The characters are excellent but the plot is not sufficiently original."[21]

It was the romance of real things that captivated Lucile, not the romance and drama of things that were made up. For example, the "Bald Knobbers" manuscript wasn't fiction, but it was full of drama. Years before, when she had sent Rose Wilder Lane parts of her working manuscript to read, Lane saw the fictional possibilities right away. She wrote Lucile that "only the other day I was thinking about the wagon trip . . . You know, where the girl went to meet the fugitive sweetheart whom her brother hated. And was accused of betraying him. And he was later hanged. I am mad to know all about it. What drama. What really *did* happen? Or may or might not have." Lane had been eager for a novel from Lucile's book. Vance Randolph also saw the fiction possibilities. When he wrote to Lucile in 1935 about some work he was doing for the Kansas Teachers Association, he observed, "It seems to me that there is room for two books . . . First, a carefully documented historical treatment; second, a somewhat lurid and sensational novel, with a strong light on the sordid, sadistic side of the thing." It never happened. Lucile could write *about* drama and suspenseful events, yet she never learned to create that same drama and suspense in her own writing.[22]

Nor was she very good at humor. In 1945 she wrote a chatty letter to one of the former patients from her O'Reilly writing class. "Our preacher at the First Congregational Church is leaving," she wrote, "and we had a dinner—I had to make a speech presenting him a wool blanket. I tried to get funny and it fell FLAT. From now on I am going to be matter of fact. Apparently, I'm not the funny type. Everyone looked at me blankly as if they just didn't know what I was trying to say and didn't think I knew myself. I do better at writing than I do at speechmaking anyway. Even then, I don't get very far when I try to be funny." Truth and facts were Lucile's forte. Always.[23]

During her years away from the newspaper, Lucile joined a couple of writers groups. She had been a member of the Ozarkians, an Ozarks-wide group, since the 1920s, but during the war years she joined the Writers Round Table in Springfield and the Fiction Faction, Springfield women friends who met regularly to talk about their progress in writing and selling stories and books. She also joined the Missouri Writers Guild. This statewide organization, which had been founded in 1915, already had a good number of Ozarks writers among its membership when Lucile joined. Lucile's friend Donna Ashworth Thompson had been a member since 1929. O. K. Armstrong, a former congressman, founder of the University of Florida's journalism department, and a contributing editor to the *Readers Digest*, had been a member since 1932. Quite a number of others joined about the same time as Lucile, including the Reverend Guy Howard of Branson, known for his book *Walkin' Preacher of the Ozarks*, and Marge Lyon, the Chicagoan-turned-Missouri-sheep-farmer-turned-Eureka-Springs-resident who wrote books and columns about her Ozarks experiences. Other Ozarks members of the writers guild in the early 1940s included Eula Mae Stratton, author of several Ozarks cookbooks; Fred

DeArmond, a former associate editor of *Nation's Business*; and Lucile's friends Adelaide Jones (a former advertising woman in charge of Drury's night classes) and Docia. The guild membership elected Lucile president in 1945.[24]

REWRITING THE MISSOURI CONSTITUTION

Aside from her volunteering and her writing, Lucile was present when the Missouri State Constitution was rewritten. Since the last constitution had been put together just after the Civil War, it was past time to bring it up to date. Her old Drury professor and friend L. E. Meador was one of fifteen at-large delegates to the constitutional convention ("Con-Con"), and he asked Lucile to accompany him as his secretary. She readily agreed, although the position took her away from home many weeks during the last months of 1943 and nearly all of 1944. She handled Meador's correspondence, edited his speeches, and, because of his deteriorating eyesight, often acted as his chauffeur between Springfield and Jefferson City. She also paid close attention to the convention debates and decisions, two of which would turn out to affect her brothers.

As the delegates from all over the state considered every part of the old constitution and debated what should be done to update sections or do away with them altogether, Meador was particularly focused on the state's tax system. He urged delegates to revise the tax structure to divide the existing single general property tax into separate units, such as real estate, intangibles, and personal property, each taxed at a different rate. This change would benefit taxpayers, and it would save money for the state, as well, since Meador's efforts extended beyond defining new tax categories to transform the way taxes were collected. He urged that the new constitution create a revenue department to collect all of the state's taxes. "It was never intended that all these state officials should be tax collectors," Meador pointed out in a talk before the Springfield Chamber of Commerce. "It is not the function of the secretary of state; it is not the function of the attorney general; it is not the function of the state treasurer, to be a tax collector. Furthermore," he added, "consolidating the collections in the revenue department will save the state one million dollars a year." When it came time to vote, the delegates readily accepted Meador's suggestion and created a department of revenue to collect the state's new taxes.[25]

The purpose of the constitutional convention, of course, was to modernize many aspects of the state's governmental system, but the delegates didn't change everything, and they didn't touch the popular and successful Conservation Commission and its subsidiary Department of Conservation. The Conservation Commission was relatively new, having been approved by voters only eight years before to replace the old Fish and Game Department. During the convention Lucile was able to listen along with convention delegates when Conservation Department director I. T. Bode described the department's work. Bode spoke particularly glowingly of the Fisheries Division where George was employed. Bode told delegates that in the past eight years, that division had enlarged or rebuilt four hatcheries and distributed thirty-two million fish, fingerlings or larger, into state waters. The delegates voted to leave the Conservation Commission as it was.[26]

Over the course of those several months, the convention delegates adopted Meador's suggestions for reforming taxes, consolidated and streamlined executive branch agencies, endorsed continuation of Missouri's Nonpartisan Court Plan, made some judicial reforms and, among other changes, determined that larger cities and counties could adopt home-rule charters. In general, they revised the state's constitution to match the needs and changing technology of the twentieth century.[27]

Next, of course, they had to sell the result of their work to the voters. Over the course of several months, Lucile joined the delegates and others in giving speeches to civic and social groups to explain what the convention had done and to urge voter acceptance. As she wrote to an acquaintance, "between the adjournment of the constitutional convention in September 1944 and the adoption of the constitution February 27, 1945 I spent most of my available time making speeches for the document."[28]

FAMILY NEWS

The following months Lucile had family news to share: Etna was named state commissioner of finance. He would be leaving his job as cashier of Trenton National Bank in far north Missouri and moving to Jefferson City. In April of 1945, Lucile wrote to George, who was still in the Pacific, that she and Gene had driven up to Trenton to attend a "big dinner" for Etna given by the bank staff and that the Missouri Bankers Association was holding a luncheon in his honor the following week. "He is quite the stuff," she finished.

Etna's new job was good news. Word from the Pacific was not. JB had been with General Douglas MacArthur at Corregidor in the Philippines in May 1942 when the island fell to the Japanese, and it was 1943 before Lucile and Gene even knew he was alive: they received a card from him from a Japanese prison camp. In February of 1945 they heard again, this time that he was in a camp on the Philippine island of Luzon. The American and Filipino forces took Luzon the following month, but battles continued across that island and, as before, they had no word for some time. Later they did learn that JB was moved from the Philippines to a prison camp in Japan.[29]

Eugene, who was an Aviation Ordnanceman 1st Class, served on the aircraft carrier *Hornet* and survived the Battle of the Santa Cruz Islands, during which the *Hornet* was sunk by the Japanese. He came home for a visit in August 1944, and, when he returned to the navy, he was again assigned to the Pacific. According to Lucile, "When the war was about over, he was in Hawaii and thought he would take an assignment that would get him to Japan to perhaps see his brother. He went out on the [aircraft carrier] *Franklin*." Near the end of March, she wrote to Gene's brother and sister, "We have no word about JB. We think Eugene probably is in the current carrier attacks on Tokyo though that is just a big guess. We haven't heard from him since he left Hawaii, and he didn't know then where he was going . . ." Lucile had guessed correctly. Eugene was indeed on the carrier *Franklin* and about the time she was writing that letter, the *Franklin* was bombarded and almost sank. A terse telegram came to Gene and Lucile from the War Department to notify them Eugene had been killed. There were no details. His body was never recovered.[30]

An obituary in the *Springfield Leader and Press* on April 20 of that year noted that Eugene had been "crazy about the Navy, and from a schoolboy had planned to make a career." He had battle stars from his involvement in the battles of Midway, the Coral Sea, and Santa Cruz. A subsequent article on May 18 discussed the fact that Lucile and Gene were "quite confident" that Eugene had been killed—along with eight hundred others—in the USS *Franklin* disaster. They had no official news but said that all of his mail after March 19—the date of the battle—had been returned.[31]

A few months later, Lucile wrote to Gene's brother Ernest in Los Angeles: "We never have heard a thing about the circumstances of Eugene's death. I have written the Navy department to try to get some information, but they haven't even answered that letter. Gene is going to take it up with the congressman and try to find out something if we soon don't get word. The Navy never has sent us any word of any kind except the original telegram. The Japanese war drags on . . ."[32]

The stress on Lucile and Gene was enormous. Even as they mourned Eugene's death, they had no idea whether JB was alive or dead. More than once, they met with soldiers who might have had word of JB, including one in Springfield and another in northern Missouri who had been in the same prison in Corregidor and played chess with JB. After that trip, Lucile wrote to George that "Gene really enjoyed his visit with the boy. He is in MUCH better spirits about JB."[33]

GEORGE

George, on the other hand, was very much alive, and in touch. Originally sent to the South Pacific with an amphibious landing craft battalion, he contracted health problems after several months, spent time in an army hospital, and finished the war in a noncombat job in New Caledonia, a French island 750 miles east of Australia. Lucile, Etna, and Veda all wrote to him regularly, and they sometimes included clippings from Springfield newspapers in their envelopes. Mostly the news George received from home was good, or at least innocuous, but one clipping he received in mid-1945 worried him.

The article had to do with dams planned for the White River, a favorite float stream for recreational fishermen. Since the 1920s, there had been talk in the Ozarks and in Washington about building more dams for flood control and/or hydropower, and by 1945, when Congress finally did authorize funds for what would be Bull Shoals and Table Rock Dams after years of on-again, off-again votes, Ozarkers had developed strong opinions on the subject. Despite the fact that government dams had already created three other lakes in the region—Norfork Lake on the North Fork River, Greers Ferry on the Little Red River, and Clearwater Lake on the Black River, there was strong opposition to "ruining" any more Ozarks rivers. A bright line existed between the pro-dam business community, who saw the need for jobs and new industry in the impoverished region, and the pro-river wildlife, fish, and conservation people.

On May 9, Springfield newspapers were full of dam news: city leaders John T. Woodruff, L. E. Meador, and Democratic politician Rex Allaman were headed to Harrison, Arkansas, for a rally on behalf of Table Rock Dam and the jobs and tourists it would bring. In the same edition, the newspaper's sports editor, Perry Smith, worried that the dams would kill the goose that laid the Ozarks' golden tourist egg. "As we see it," Smith wrote, "Southwest Missouri is risking the things that made it famous as a resort country in order to enter competition for industries and factories ... Minnesota and Canadian lakes even now offer far more sport than our Lake of the Ozarks—yet they have nothing to compare with Missouri's widely-hullabalooed float streams."[34]

After George read Smith's article, he wrote a letter to the editor, which Smith printed a few weeks later: "I am in the habit of getting a bunch of clippings from my mother every so often," George wrote, "—on subjects from strawberry shortcake to the obituary column—and as I tell her, I not only read the right side but the other side as well. Anyway, today's supply included a clipping ... by you [Smith] on the dam proposition. I appreciated it, and not being a member of the [Conservation] Commission right

at the present time [he was on a military furlough] I can express myself
... I can't seem to picture the fact that someone would want to fill White and
James full of dams—and if some of the 'pork barrel' boys would take a
deluxe trip down them with [float fishing impresario] Jim Owen, I think
even that would convince them they should move on and let nature alone."
Continuing, George probably spoke for many of his fellow Ozarkers:
"Every night for the past year—and in a couple of days I will be over here
a year—whether I was sleeping with 155s [artillery shells] going over my
head, or whatnot, I've thought of two things . . . my family back home and
the nice holes of water and big gravel bars on the James River. You're forced
to think of something besides coconuts. Anyway, they are the things that I
want to get back to Missouri to do (and I have five months and a few days
to go before I am forty)." He ended his letter with a sigh: "Course that won't
keep the dams from being built—my wishes—but I wanted you to know you
had a well-wisher who is a few miles away from Greene County."[35]

A couple of months after the letter appeared, Japan surrendered.
George came home to resume his work with the state's fish, and he
watched as not just one but three dams were built on the White River. The
new dams, constructed between 1947 and 1966, created Bull Shoals, Table
Rock, and Beaver Lakes in southwest Missouri and northwest Arkansas.

JB

Besides George, the other member of the family still in the military was
JB. Very much alive when the war in the Pacific ended on August 15, he
was released from a prison camp in Kyushu, Japan, and sent to an army
hospital in Clinton, Iowa, to recover from his ordeal. In November, JB
got an eight-day furlough and came to Springfield. While he was there,
Docia interviewed him and wrote an upbeat story about the not-to-be-
forgotten day when the Kyushu prisoners—one hundred Englishmen,
175 Australians, more than three hundred Dutch, and only two other
Americans besides JB—realized the war was over. After his visit to
Springfield, JB went back to Iowa, but received a final discharge in time
to celebrate Christmas at home. Not many months later, he married a
Springfield girl and embarked on a long career with the Missouri Highway
Patrol plus an almost equally long commitment to the organization of
American Ex-POWs. He died in February 1989.[36]

MORE BAD NEWS

The war's effect on the Uptons—especially on Gene—had been terrible.
His blood pressure rose to unacceptable levels and, as Lucile described it,

"He had some attacks of what he thought were stomach upsets, but which alarmed me. Each time, however, the doctor would say it was nervous indigestion." Then, as if the death of one son and spending four years not knowing the fate of the other son wasn't stressful enough, just months after the war ended, Gene lost his court reporting job. Judge Guy Kirby retired and Gene was not reappointed to be court reporter for the judge who succeeded him. Gene spent many tense months looking for a new position.

For Gene, the bad news just kept coming: midway through 1947, Gene's brother Ernest, who had been an active member of the Knights of Pythias most of his life, was on his way to a lodge meeting in Los Angeles when he was attacked by would-be robbers and killed. As with Eugene's death, Gene and Lucile never learned more than the barest outline of what happened. Ernest's lodge held funeral services in Los Angeles; Gene made the arrangements for a second service in Bolivar, which Lucile said was "lovely," with most of the Bolivar relatives attending. Although the undertaker in Los Angeles had warned that the casket should not be opened, Gene insisted, and Lucile reported that "he was braced for a pretty trying experience, and you can imagine his vast relief when he found Ernest looked not at all disfigured except for a blue spot on his face." Burial took place in the Upton section of Bolivar's Greenwood Cemetery.[37]

And then, finally, there was some good news. Gene received word he was to be appointed referee for the state Workmen's Compensation Commission, a type of job, Lucile said, "he wanted badly." The good job news, however, was not enough. The very next night, July 8, 1947, Gene suffered a heart attack during the night and was dead before morning. Lucile always blamed his death on the stress of the war and his worries about his two sons. In Gene's long obituary in the *Leader and Press*, it was noted that "during the war years—when he, of course, heard only sketchily and, for long periods not at all, from his prisoner-son—that court house friends noted his failing health. Nevertheless, he continued his work with the quiet efficiency for which he always was noted."[38]

He and Lucile had been married eleven years.

| 9 |

A VERY INTERESTING YEAR

For Lucile, 1947 was one of those years that simply had to be endured. Gene's death in July obliterated almost everything else, but there was more. In January, Docia had taken a year's leave of absence from Springfield Newspapers to serve as a US War Department editor in Japan. Her departure left a hole in Lucile's life and at the newspaper. When George Olds asked, Lucile agreed to take over editing Docia's daily column, "The Waste Basket," for that year. The column was primarily a collection of short essays, poetry, and general commentary sent in by writers and selected by the column editor. As it turned out, Lucile kept the column even after Docia returned to the newspaper and continued as its editor until her retirement at the end of 1963.[1]

At Olds's urging, Lucile took on "quite a lot" of regular reporting as well, and before the year was out, she was handling the church page, though she was less enthusiastic about that, and she did turn down his suggestion that she add the society page to her responsibilities. By February, she was working at the newspaper office every morning and bringing work home, but, as she wrote Docia in Japan, "I'm sure I am not doing nearly as much reporting as George would like for me to do."[2]

Whenever Lucile sat down at home to write a story, she sat straight-backed and flat-footed at a portable typing table, always with a green eyeshade, typical headgear for deadline-focused journalists in those days of harsh office lighting. She typed at a Royal upright typewriter for years, then replaced it with a small manual portable one. Never, in all the years she wrote, did she ever use an electric typewriter, much less a computer. The fact that she was comfortable working from her home office turned out to be terribly important that year, and not just to fill in for Docia.

VANCE RANDOLPH

In February, her old animosity for Vance Randolph resurfaced. The first book of his much-anticipated four-volume collection of Ozarks folk songs was being published by the State Historical Society of Missouri, and a review copy landed on Lucile's desk. The book had taken a long time to materialize. Randolph had begun his collecting almost as soon as he arrived in the Ozarks, later explaining that in those early days he met mountaineers who "were singing ballads about kings and queens and knights and swords. It was all oddly romantic . . . and I was convinced that, as times were changing in this country, the people would change— and if a record of their folkways was to be preserved, someone had to do it without delay." News of his collecting attracted the Library of Congress and others who were impressed enough with his project to loan him a machine to cut disc records of the Ozarks singers when he visited them to listen and capture the lyrics on paper. The four-volume folk song collection was the result.[3]

The books, and the work, got raves—but not from Lucile. When she received the first one, she vented in a letter to Docia: "I have the book on my hands and I don't know what to do with it. You know what I think of Randolph—ditto ballads! As a matter of fact, the book is a nice thing to look at. The end papers are by [Thomas Hart] Benton and are the nicest thing about it. I can't understand why the Historical Society should want to publish all that blabberdash—and in four volumes; three yet to come! But they've done it and I'm stuck with the necessity to write some sort of review. Randolph has used about four songs 'Contributed by Miss Lucile Morris, who had it from Mrs. Blank Blank.' It burns me up. I didn't contribute anything to that book—didn't even know he was going to publish it. I told him if he ever used any of those songs to write to the person who gave them to me and get their permission, and I'd like to know if he ever did. I bet not!" The first volume of Randolph's collection, which actually had a publication date of 1946, was titled *British Ballads and Songs*. Volume two was *Songs of the South and West*; volume three, *Humorous and Play-Party Songs*, and volume four, which was published in 1950, was titled *Religious Songs and Other Items*. Two more volumes of Randolph's collected songs, originally considered too salacious to print, were edited by G. Legman and issued by the University of Arkansas Press in 1992: *Roll Me in Your Arms, A Collection of "Unprintable" Ozark Folksongs and Folklore* and *Blow the Candle Out, Folk Rhymes and Other Lore*.[4]

Years later, Lucile's feelings for Randolph had not diminished. In a letter to her niece, she mentioned coming across a copy of Randolph's book *Ozark Magic and Folklore*, which she was forwarding. The book, she wrote, had come out originally "at a time when Vance and I were at outs and he tried to get even. He always was one to pick brains of everyone possible. At that time he was making his collection of Ozarks folksongs . . . I was doing a page on ballads once a week for the paper (under protest— for I feared copyright trouble and finally proved I was right in doing so). He literally demanded that I turn over the original of contributions I received, to him for the books. Once he drove up here on Sunday and before I could collect my wits took a big wad of the songs, which he used. About that time I married and he still demanded songs and I swore I lost them in the move from my apartment. He was sore as could be . . ." She went on to relate another aggravation with Randolph, but finished, by saying, "The funny thing is he loves me now—writes to me and sends word about how much he always appreciated me. . . ."[5]

NEWSPAPER FIRE

Circumstances kept Lucile from having to write the dreaded review, or if she wrote it, kept it from being published. In the early hours of March 27, her life was again upset by a fire in a printing company. This time, the fire destroyed the newspaper. Lucile heard about the fire on her way to work; it was the bus driver who told her: the bus route was shifted that morning because the *News and Leader* building was on fire. She wasn't alone in her surprise: the whole morning staff was blindsided.

"When I got there," she wrote to Docia a few days later, "they had it out (they thought) and people were milling around in the inch-deep water in the business office . . . It was cold as whiz! About 9:30 Mr. Olds announced we would publish . . . He sent us to places we could get typewriters and telephones. Jerry Lisenby Hankins and I came out here to my house. We got our stuff all ready and went back over there at 11:30 . . . I came back home after I turned in a bunch of church items. About the time I left, fire, water, etc. started sailing through the ceiling of the society department, executive offices . . . they grabbed their typewriters and a few inconsequential things and ran."[6]

While Lucile and the editorial staff worked on their stories, other employees borrowed resources from across Springfield. They secured the Associated Press wire feed from Bixby-owned radio station KGBX, developed photos of the fire in the police department's darkroom, got an engraving plant in nearby Aurora to make the photo engravings, and borrowed printing presses where they could find them. That evening, as promised, there was a newspaper. It carried a giant front-page headline: NEWS-LEADER BUILDING, EQUIPMENT LOST IN FIRE, and a story that told of how "fire roared through the plant of Springfield Newspapers, Inc. at six o'clock this morning, completely destroying the building except for the business office." The whole paper was only four pages, but it came out, complete with photos. And it kept coming out, every day for many months, as the newspaper struggled back toward normalcy.

The day following the fire, a more sober front-page article, signed jointly by owners T. W. Duvall and Tams Bixby Jr., promised that the newspapers "although they will be operating under something of a handicap for some time—will continue publication." The papers, sans advertising, would be printed at the Bixby-owned Oklahoma Press Publishing Company in Muskogee and sent back on a train for morning distribution. Readers would be served. And they were: not a day was missed, even though finding interim office space took a couple of months, and several of the editors relocated temporarily to Tulsa or Muskogee to coordinate printing. By the end of May, there was an advertising supplement. On June 23, the composing room had relocated back to Springfield and the company began producing two daily newspapers once again. Then, as the company recovered, a used press was found at the *Chicago Tribune* and construction of new offices got underway on Boonville Avenue.[7]

Given the seat-of-the-pants publishing process, Lucile had some problems with "The Waste Basket" column. She had to send the items piecemeal to editors who compiled and then forwarded them to the makeup team—the people who actually put the pages together—to get the column ready for printing. From time to time, parts of the column were reordered or left out, but, given the conditions everyone was working under, as she wrote to Docia, "I think they are doing wonderful . . . I don't know how they get out such a good paper under the circumstances." When complications in Muskogee temporarily furloughed "The Waste Basket," readers complained. Once the column was reinstated, Lucile warned her contributors that many of their items had been lost in the fire. She asked them to resubmit, "only please shorten as much as possible for now we have less space."[8]

As the year continued, so did the surprises. Near the end of May, Lucile received word from the Caxton Press that her book, *Bald Knobbers*, would be permanently out of print—certainly a blow to a proud author. Almost immediately, though, she transferred the copyright to her name and began searching for a second publisher, which she eventually found at the School of the Ozarks—but not until 1971.[9]

LETTERS TO DOCIA

At the end of July, about three weeks after Gene's fatal heart attack, and two weeks after Lucile had returned to her newspaper columns, Docia sent her a long comforting letter. Docia wrote that she hoped Lucile would "find a satisfying pattern for your new life . . ." Lucile had no trouble doing that. Her "new life" was going to revolve around the same things, except for Gene, as her old life had: the newspaper, her strong interest in Ozarks history, a bit of teaching, and her family. Throughout that year, she kept

Docia apprised of what was happening in Springfield, and Docia, fascinated with Japan, responded in kind. Their steady stream of communication established a pattern that would continue until the ends of their long lives. In June, Lucile shared family news with Docia: all of the Morris property in Dadeville, including the farm that had been in the family since before the Civil War, had been sold. Historian that she was, Lucile was of two minds about losing the property, but she doubted any member of the family would ever live there again. Veda was living in Springfield with Lucile. Etna was in Jefferson City, now serving as the state's first director of revenue, the department created at L. E. Meador's prompting during the state constitution rewrite, and George had received a promotion to head all the state's fish hatcheries and was moving to Springfield with his wife and son.[10]

Her columns, the weekly "The Good Old Days" and daily "The Waste Basket," took up most of Lucile's time, especially "The Waste Basket." "The Waste Basket" had begun years before Docia's editorship as two separate columns: May Kennedy McCord's "Hillbilly Heartbeats," which ran in the *Daily News*, and the "Old Timer," a regular feature by Dan Kennedy, son of the founder of *The Leader*. Kennedy retired about the same time McCord left the *Daily News* to host a "Hillbilly Heartbeats" radio program for St. Louis station KWK in 1942. The offspring of those two columns was named "The Waste Basket—into which are often tossed things worth while . . ." Docia edited the new column and, like McCord had done in "Hillbilly Heartbeats," and Lucile continued, she made it a reader-written column.

The content varied, but it nearly always included a poem, possibly some reminisces, observations on nature, fan mail for one or more of the contributors, and, while Lucile was editor, a dose of Ozarks history.

"THE WASTE BASKET"

When Lucile took over "The Waste Basket" she made it a point to become personally acquainted with the men and women who sent her their poetry and essays along with news of their communities and, sometimes, of their families. She didn't insert herself into the published column nearly as much as McCord did when it was "Hillbilly Heartbeats," but even in those pre-email days, she responded to each submission, rejecting things that didn't work for the column or making suggestions for improvements. Some of her contributors became famous, including nationally acclaimed Arkansas poet Edsel Ford and Arkansas Poet Laureate Rosa Zagnoni Marinoni. Others, like Mary Elizabeth Mahnkey and Mary Scott Hair, also known as Samantha (or Samanthy), were regional favorites.[11]

Mahnkey's column-in-a-column, called "In the Hills," was full of her observations and an occasional poem about life in her little community. In July 1947 she wrote of raising their old flag on the Fourth, "now getting pretty thin and frail. For almost forty years I've kept this flag. I said something about this, but CP [her husband] said, '. . . the stars are still there,'" so the flag stayed. She wrote about CP's growing deafness being hard for her to bear, and when she was ill, a bit about that, but mostly she shared her love of her garden and her natural surroundings. She wasn't above sharing other observations, either, as in March of 1948, when she wrote, "Of early mornings an opalescent mist marks the course of White River, and I wonder just what changes will be made in this favorite view, when Bull Shoals dam backs these streams up?"[12]

Mary Scott Hair/Samanthy wrote regularly for Lucile's column. She is shown here one day after she took Lucile and Betty Love out "greenin'" for wild edibles. *Springfield Newspapers. Photo by Betty Love. Local History Collection, Springfield-Greene County Library Center. © Springfield News-Leader—USA TODAY NETWORK.*

If a person chose to read "The Waste Basket" every day—it ran five days per week—they would find that it was almost a club, with recognizable contributors, questions and commentary from readers, and letters of concern when a favorite poet or essayist stopped sending material.

In September, one contributor sent memories of riding from Oklahoma to Missouri in a covered wagon, to which Lucile noted: "This editor is completely thrilled by some of the pioneers it has been my privilege to print in the 'Waste Basket,'" then she named several other contributors of pioneer childhood memories, which she of course encouraged. A contributor from Great Bend, Kansas, sent in a note about a trip she had taken into Missouri specifically to meet several other "Waste Basket regulars" at a picnic in Republic, noting, "Many of them looked about as I had pictured them in my mind." She had also stopped to meet Mahnkey: "I could see all about her how she gathers the material for her lovely work. She has only to sit on her front porch and all nature gathers eagerly around her, offering delightedly the beautiful things she writes. The modern world, too, passes continuously by her door, as the highway is only just off there."[13]

In the spring, "The Waste Basket" was full of verses about flowers and gardens. One spring, Mahnkey sang of

The lovely Rose of Sharon by the gate
Looked out upon White River and the hills,
Cow Bells sounded when the hour was late
And sweet the even' song of whip-poor-wills . . .[14]

Years later, when poet Edsel Ford was a regular contributor, he wrote about very early spring:

The wind in the dark
made a cutting remark
last night as I went to my chores.
Now daffodils peep
Through snow an inch deep;
I'll bet they wish THEY were indoors![15]

When "The Waste Basket" was temporarily suspended during the disarray following the fire, Lucile's regulars vied to be included when it started up again. "Yesterday Samantha sent a good column," Lucile wrote to Docia. "Today I got one from Mrs. Mahnkey. Both Mrs. M. and Samantha wanted to be in the first revived column, but they can't be." Of course, they were both published shortly afterward. Mahnkey—she was always "Mrs. Mahnkey" to Lucile and her peers—had been a column regular for years, and before that, she had sent her poetry and reports on daily life in rural Taney County to "Hillbilly Heartbeats."

Samantha/Mary Scott Hair had furnished pieces to "Hillbilly Heartbeats" in the 1930s, and she also had a regular column in her local *Crane Chronicle* called "Much in a Basket." Hair's contributions to Lucile's "The Waste Basket" were published under the heading "By the Sheep Gate," which, she explained, was a barrier set up to prevent her bottle-fed lamb, Niblet, from going into the living room from his nursery in the kitchen. Hair eventually wrote for a variety of Ozarks publications, including Otto Rayburn's *Ozark Guide* magazine and *Ozarks Mountaineer*, for which she contributed a variety of articles and recipes, along with other publications like *Capper's Weekly*, the *Missouri Ruralist* and *The Echo*, which came out of Kansas. She was even regularly quoted in the "Country Correspondent" column of *Country Gentleman* magazine.[16]

Like McCord, Hair, who was part of Stone County's Short clan and first cousin to Congressman Dewey Short, was more educated than many of her neighbors. There had been no high school in the rural community of Hurley when she needed one, so she rode the train to Springfield every week, lived at the YMCA, and attended high school there. When she was seventeen, she quit school to marry a just-returned veteran of World War I and start a family, but when her daughter was six years old, she enrolled in Hurley's new high school and earned her diploma. She went on to study journalism by long distance through University of Missouri correspondence classes and took courses in business, history, and geography at a WPA-sponsored night school. Among other things, she learned to type, and with that skill she took on a variety of jobs, including one as secretary to a couple of state legislators.[17]

"OVER THE OZARKS"

Around 1950, Lucile's column name was changed from "The Waste Basket" to "The Ozarks Wastebasket." In 1956, the name changed again, this time to "Over the Ozarks, with our historians, writers, and poets." About the time it became "The Ozarks Wastebasket," Lucile gave a speech to the Missouri Writers Guild about the column. She told the crowd of writers that editing her five-days-a-week column for nearly ten years had taught her that newspaper publishers "are overlooking a source of vast reader interest if they fail to have a place in their papers for poetry, reminiscences, historical sketches, and personal observations." The "Wastebasket," she continued, was essentially written by readers. Most of them, but not all, were from the Ozarks. Many were elderly folk who saw an opportunity to reminisce or tell it "like it was." Many were poets of various sorts and levels of professionalism. Over the years, Lucile said, she had developed her own philosophy about her contributors: "It little behooves me to be supercilious about literary efforts of any human if the writing has been done with sincerity of purpose. The crudest phrases in prose or poetry may tell the story of a significant personal adventure or aspiration."[18]

About the same time as Lucile's speech, Hair penned an article about the column—and Lucile—for the *Ozarks Mountaineer* magazine. Since Lucile had become editor, Hair wrote, about five hundred people had contributed to the column. Two hundred of them were regulars, including "teachers, farmers, ministers, artists, housewives, a poet laureate, song writers, retired businessmen, a retired actor, and a number of writers who regularly sell material to other publications." In January 1955 alone, "The Ozarks Wastebasket" appeared twenty-eight times in the *Daily News*, the *Leader*, and Sunday *News-Leader*; it included 183 contributions from 66 different writers, 133 poems, and 50 articles, mostly about Ozarks traditions and ways of life. Years later, when Lucile died, Hair devoted part of her column in the *Crane Chronicle/Stone County Republican* to "The Wastebasket" and to Lucile. "Always," Hair wrote, "I have given Lucile Morris Upton credit for my interest in journalism, and her column, 'Over the Ozarks,' was a sounding board for more than one amateur writer."[19]

During the more than twenty years that she edited the column, a bond of loyalty grew between and among Lucile and her contributors. "This editing a column can be a strange business," she wrote to readers one Christmas. "Through the years—and it has been almost five years since I took the column over—I feel that I have come to know many of you contributors as close friends. Yet, actually, I have personally met only a few of you." She was quick to promote good news about her contributors, as when Edsel Ford was honored by the Arkansas Poets Roundtable as the Poet of the Present in 1957, and when frequent contributor Jack Salsman of Camdenton won a blue ribbon for western paintings at the Clearwater County Fair in Orofino, Idaho. When a contributor wrote that he had sold three poems to the *Denver Post*, she shared that news, too. At Christmastime, she ran pictures of her dog, Little Man, and cat, Christopher, and printed good wishes to—and from—the contributors and readers.[20]

She also passed on personal news about her contributors. When well-known author and entertainer Thomas Elmore Lucy was in Ellis Fischel Cancer Hospital in Columbia, she ran his message to readers updating them on his treatments. When Lucy died, she was bombarded with notes from her contributors wanting to memorialize him. "Samantha sent me a special delivery letter asking that she be allowed to write the tribute," she wrote to Docia. ". . . Roy Martin brought me a poem that I ran but I got

Merry Christmas to "Over the Ozarks" contributors and friends.
Morris family photos.

Samantha's column in the same paper so I suppose it was all right. Then here came tributes from Mr. Chancellor, Opal Porter . . . and Mrs. Pursley."[21]

When popular contributor Frank M. Sheffer of Humansville, Missouri, died, she shared her "shock and sadness" in the column. She congratulated contributor Elsie Upton (no relation) of Jasper, Arkansas, on the birth of a daughter. A woman from Conway, Missouri, wrote to say she had never gone to school past eighth grade, but "we'll get along if you'll let me join your big family of contributors." Later, the same woman wrote: "PS if you find my poem too long to publish, just discard it . . . But I do so hope you can use it. It will give my poor sick husband a thrill to read it in his hospital room."[22]

Then there was the woman who wrote a personal letter to tell Lucile how the column had given her dignity and status: "Thanks so much for using so many of my little poems. I am seventy-two years old and have lived nearly all kinds of a life from riches to rags and am now on an old age pension . . . I'm a lonely Republican here in Missouri and resent having it thrown in my face—'Roosevelt is all the reason for your pension.' . . . after getting my name in print so many times, I am at last (in Thayer anyhow) a 'person' in my own right and not just another old woman on relief."[23]

Sometimes Lucile heard from readers who felt so strongly about the column that they just wanted to let her know what they thought about how she was doing, like the unsigned postcard she received in 1951: "Mrs. Upton: Really do you HAVE to print some of those dreadful POEMS?" Lucile didn't. Nor did she print everything she received. If she wasn't certain about something, she didn't just discard it, either, as when she got back in touch with one potential contributor: "Thank you for the poem which I received this morning for the Wastebasket column. However, the poem is of more serious nature than I often publish in the column and I would like to know a bit more about it . . ." By return mail, the woman wrote, "Just one year after my older son was buried, my baby son (16) was killed suddenly on a motorcycle . . . if you do not care to publish it, it is OK. It was a very trying ordeal . . . I used to write several articles for the Wastebasket years ago, but use your own judgment . . ." According to Ann Fair, Lucile was devoted to the people who wrote for her column. "She always wrote back and knew people all over the region. Nobody really appreciated the value of that."[24]

BACK TO TEACHING

Like so many other people who experience loss, one of Lucile's reactions to Gene's death was to fill up as much of her time as she could with work and other activities. The fact that she was taking on more and more newspaper assignments, even while she was busy settling details of Gene's estate and trying to decide what to do about the big house, apparently wasn't enough. She was a reporter, and as the contributors to her column well knew, she was an editor, but she had been a teacher first, and that September, she began teaching in Drury College's new evening adult education program, which featured well-known professional people from around the town to teach the noncredit classes. Initially, she agreed to teach part-time to help out O. K. Armstrong's creative writing class when he had to be away. Then she was asked to teach a class of her own on composition and rhetoric. "I liked the idea especially for it will take up an evening—and I do get lonesome in the evenings," she wrote to Docia. It didn't take long for the regular Drury College administration to learn she might be available and asked her to teach a regular daytime college course in newswriting. She turned that down because "I just felt . . . that if I had any extra day-time hours I should give them to the newspaper, so I declined."[25]

By late autumn of 1947, Lucile was working almost full-time at the newspaper, teaching three nights a week, and grading seventy-seven student papers many of the other evenings. Two of the nights were for Armstrong's class, which had attracted so many students it was divided into two sections. On top of that, those two classes had become almost all hers, between Armstrong being called away to Europe, returning just before his wife died of cancer. The third class was her own composition and rhetoric class, of which she said, "A lot of hardboiled nurses and GIs from O'Reilly in it sit there and look at me as if they wondered where I got the idea I could teach them anything."[26]

The oddities of 1947 continued for Lucile. In September, as she stepped off a bus on the way to teach one of her first classes, she twisted and broke her foot: "Sometimes I think even the crippled foot has been a good thing for me. It has hurt so bad I haven't been able to think of much else—except how I was going to get over to three classes a week, to the office once a day, to special story assignments . . ."[27]

HISTORY IN THE MAKING

During this period Lucile also gained an ally in her crusade to preserve local history. John K. Hulston, a Springfield attorney seventeen years her junior, authored an article in the *Missouri Historical Review*, titled "Daniel Boone's Sons in Missouri." Hulston had grown up in Nathan Boone's community of Ash Grove, but he had been born in Dade County near where Lucile grew up. Despite past dealings between their two families, and the fact that both families were resolute Democrats in Republican strongholds, the two had never met. However, while he was working on his article, Hulston later recalled, "I hunted up Lucile, she having participated in an article on the Boones. She encouraged me, and she and I decided the 380-acre homestead should be a state park." Going forward, Hulston became her friend, her attorney, and fellow champion of memorializing local history. For years, they worked together to achieve recognition for the Nathan Boone homestead and also for the Wilson's Creek battlefield. "She adopted me," Hulston later said, "because of the Nathan Boone connection."[28]

In October, there was more family news: Etna had decided to run for state treasurer the following year. "I'm not for it," Lucile wrote to a cousin, "but I guess if he insists, I'll vote for him! I just don't think he ought to continue in politics. He could get a big job with a bank and I think he should take it." Etna did run, Lucile did vote for him, and he won the state treasurer job in 1948. Later, he was elected to two more nonconsecutive terms as state treasurer—in 1956 and 1964—serving as state director of revenue in the interim years.[29]

In November, it was Betty Love who made the news. Love and the courthouse reporter Joe Cody were waiting in the anteroom of the Greene County jail in hopes of getting a photo when US Marshal Fred Canfil, a Kansas Citian and good friend of President Truman, brought bank robbery suspect "Duke" Petty past their waiting place. When Love started to take the picture, Canfil demurred. Then Cody pointed out that as a newspaper photographer, Love had a constitutional right to take the photo, to which Canfil shouted, "The Constitution be damned!" An uncowed Love did take a photo; it showed the accused and another man being hustled out of the jail under a blanket. Perhaps more important, Cody reported the exchange in the newspaper and Canfil's statement reverberated in newspapers across the country. It became bigger news than the bank robber whose picture Love was trying to take.[30]

As news of Canfil's outburst spread, Missouri's Republican Senator Forrest Donnell called on Truman to fire Canfil, and Grover Dalton, chair of the state Republican committee, also called for Canfil's removal, calling the outburst "one of the most reprehensible statements ever made by a public servant . . . Mr. Canfil's monumental arrogance is not surprising. It is the arrogance of the notorious Pendergast machine, which lists the President as a dues-paying member." Despite the criticism, President Truman stood fast. Ultimately, the incident made Love famous in the photojournalism world, but it cooled her relationship with Truman for some time.[31]

Eventually, according to former *Springfield Leader and Press* city editor Mike O'Brien, "During several visits to southwest Missouri in following years, Truman did his best to hold his hat in front of his face or otherwise spoil attempts by Betty to shoot his photo. Finally, Betty's artist friend Thomas Hart Benton coaxed his longtime buddy Truman into making peace with Betty, and she obtained a memorable portrait of the two together at an area event."[32]

By December, Lucile's busy life was falling into place. She had decided to sell her and Gene's big house and had found a small giraffe-stone house south of downtown for herself, Veda, Little Man, and Christopher. At Christmastime, she took a train to San Francisco to visit her niece, June, June's husband, and their baby daughter. "The trip was a lifesaver to me," she reported. "It was the first time since Gene's death that I was able to forget my troubles and start getting myself together. I came home in SO much better shape and am really beginning to reconstruct my life now."[33]

| 10 |

WOMEN OF THE PRESS

By the years immediately following World War II, a comfortable, if unspo-ken, agreement had come to exist among businesses, outdoor promoters, and the newspapers that the region's future depended on taking advan-tage of, and ballyhooing, the Ozarks' unsullied beauty, hunting and fishing opportunities, and even—up to a point—its hillbillies and lakes. As far as the lakes were concerned, there was still pushback from sportsmen and river lovers like Lucile's brother George, who saw the dams as destruc-tive to the natural beauty and a killer of popular White River float trips. However, the White River had flooded too many times and destroyed too many farms, businesses, and Ozarks communities for the opposition to get much of a toehold. Clear-eyed businesspeople and politicians pushed for Bull Shoals and Table Rock Dams as being key to economic development and the alleviation of at least some of the rural poverty. Hillbillies and dam arguments notwithstanding, everyone wanted people to visit the Ozarks.

BOLIVAR STATUE DEDICATION

In those years, it wasn't only fishing and tourism that brought people to the region. The fact that a Missourian sat in the White House added to the crowds on a number of occasions. In 1946, President Harry Truman invited former British Prime Minister Winston Churchill to Westminster College in Fulton, Missouri, just north of the Ozarks, to present a lecture. "This is a wonderful school in my home state," he scrawled at the bottom of the university's formal letter of invitation to Churchill. "If you come, I will introduce you. Hope you can do it." Churchill did come, and on that day (March 5, 1946) the whole world listened as he described "an Iron Curtain [that] has descended across the Continent" of Europe and warned of the Soviet Union's avaricious greed for lands and people.[1]

Two years later, in early July of 1948, Truman came to the Ozarks—and he brought a guest with him. This time, thousands of visitors streamed into the town of Bolivar, about thirty miles north of Springfield, to see President Truman and Venezuelan President Romulo Gallegos pledge hemispheric friendship and dedicate a seven-foot bronze statue of the town's South American namesake, Simon Bolivar. In the early 1800s, Señor Bolivar had led revolutions against the Spanish Empire to liberate what became the countries of not only Venezuela but also Bolivia, Colombia, Ecuador, Peru, and Panama. Some called Bolivar the George Washington of South America. It was happenstance that Bolivar, Missouri, was the largest of several American towns named for the South American liberator and, therefore, chosen to receive the statue, which was a gift from the people of Venezuela, but it was probably no accident when the selection was made that the chosen Bolivar was in Truman's home state, which meant the statue dedication promised to be an international news event.

Lucile, along with Docia and Betty Love, were part of a contingent of thirteen of Springfield's newspaper staffers among at least a hundred more reporters from across the country who came to Bolivar that day. It was July 5, the 137th anniversary of Venezuelan independence from Spain, a day after the US's 172nd birthday, and—typical for Missouri in July—more than ninety degrees in the shade. The crowd was estimated at more than fifteen thousand—a huge influx for a remote rural town of 3,500.

When Truman and his Bolivian guest stepped off the presidential train—distinguished in their light suits, ties, and straw fedoras—they were accompanied by representatives of other American republics, various ambassadors, and a good number of US officials. The band from Truman's World War I division welcomed the two presidents, who, over the course of that very hot day, were treated to a twenty-one-gun salute, a ham-and-cheese sandwich picnic on the lawn of Southwest Baptist College (now Southwest Baptist University), the national anthem sung by Missouri-born Metropolitan Opera mezzo-soprano Gladys Swarthout, a 150-plane military flyover, and a mile-long parade. When it came time to make the speeches and dedicate the statue, Gallegos spoke briefly, then Truman talked to the crowd about Pan-American cooperation and unity, saying that "Simon Bolivar stands out far, for his . . . clear vision of the eventual solidarity of the American family of nations," and called the day a "celebration that will go down in the history of Missouri."[2]

Following the parade, the concerts, the picnic, and the speeches, the two officials shook hands with members of the crowd and departed. Gallegos flew to New York on the presidential plane *Independence*, and Truman climbed back on the presidential train bound for Washington. Truman's train stopped briefly in Springfield so he could greet the 2,500 well-wishers who waited at the station and shake hands with a few friends, including, as reported by the *Chicago Daily Tribune*, Fred Canfil, "US

Marshal for western Missouri and personal friend of the President." Canfil was the "Constitution be damned!" official who had gotten into the brouhaha with Betty Love over taking the photo of a prisoner the year before. After leaving Springfield, the train stopped again in Lebanon, home of then-Missouri Governor Phil M. Donnelly, where another cheering crowd was waiting.[3]

For her part, besides hobnobbing with the gaggle of national press representatives who had come to the Ozarks, Lucile wrote several stories for the next day's paper: one about how the town of Bolivar would soon be home to a library of Venezuelan literature, and another about the crowds and the terrible Missouri heat that felled dozens of people, including Missouri's governor. She described the long, colorful parade in detail and highlighted a pair of Missouri mules that caught Truman's attention. She even penned a story about the newspaper team that had been sent to Bolivar from Springfield. Although she didn't mention it in any of her articles, Lucile would have known the town was only indirectly named after Simon Bolivar. It had actually been named for Bolivar, Tennessee, which was the burial place of Ezekiel Polk, a Continental Army colonel in the US Revolution, grandfather to President James K. Polk, and cousin of Ozarks pioneer John Polk Campbell. Bolivar, Tennessee, on the other hand, was named for the South American liberator.

Betty, who was one of several photographers assigned to the day, took dozens of photos of everything from the opera diva to the two leaders, the seven-foot-tall statue, the crowds, and the military salute. Docia wrote several pre-event articles plus the next morning's front-page story about Truman's speech. Back in Springfield, Ann Fair had been on hand to report on Truman's impromptu rally with the crowd at the railroad station. Her reports did not mention Canfil.[4]

OZARKS NEWS

The presidential visit to Bolivar-in-the-Ozarks made a big splash on the national scene for a day or two. On the other hand, what held the American people's long-term attention was the Ozarks' own promotional "news" about the region itself. Like the rest of the newspaper staff, Lucile was adept at producing the kind of stories an urban public would expect and, having spent six busy years covering the jail, courthouse, and the worst the Missouri Ozarks had to offer, followed by a decade of war and the loss of her husband, she settled comfortably into pursuing her own interests in Ozarks history and taking on mostly feature assignments from editor George Olds. Some of the stories were not unlike the sob sister stuff she had covered in Denver. She interviewed hundred-year-old women, Civil War widows, retiring professors, and reunited families; she confirmed the identity of three Springfieldians painted into a Thomas Hart Benton mural; wrote a half-page feature on the popularity of parakeets; did the occasional fashion story; described an itinerant family hoping to trade their dog for a car; and edited the church page. Also, as she had in Denver, she managed to put the spotlight on accomplished women when she could. An article about probate judge and ex-officio magistrate judge Ida Bobbitt in Camdenton noted that "Judge Bobbitt is not at all impressed by the fact that she is one of the few women holding the office of probate judge in Missouri. It all seems very usual to her . . ."[5]

Docia and some of Lucile's other colleagues urged her to turn her talents to more serious things, or to leave the newspaper altogether. However, as she explained to Docia, "Hughie Call [a mutual writer friend in Eureka Springs] talks to me just the way you do about all this trivial, routine blah I'm doing at the office. I keep promising to quit it, but I don't . . . I wonder myself, sometimes, but by and large they are paying me fairly well now and I do enjoy it . . ." After all, she had predicted as much in that pro-woman-reporter newspaper column she wrote back in 1932.[6]

Lucile always made it clear she loved newspaper work. She wasn't alone. By 1950, newspaperwomen who had long been featured characters in hit movies were appearing in comic books, and they joined the funny papers in the person of Brenda Starr in mid-1940. The US Census reported a significant, but not surprising, increase in female reporters and editors between 1940 and 1950, up from twenty-five percent of the total before World War II to thirty-two percent afterward. In other words, 28,500 out of 89,070 working editors and reporters in 1950 were women. A lot of newspapers still preferred to hire women only for society and women's pages, but it was no longer any kind of surprise to see women routinely covering politics, crime, and other city desk assignments.[7]

The movies and the comics made heroes of newspaperwomen, but they didn't show all of the real-life goings-on in the newspaper world. In 1949, for example, Docia again left the newspaper, and this time, she departed for good. Not many months later, Olds wrote an insulting piece about an executive at Bixby-owned radio station KGBX and was fired. After that, he started his own weekly newssheet, the *BIAS*, borrowing the name from his Springfield Newspapers column. His name and Docia's had been linked romantically for years—one reporter even swore to having found a marriage license at the courthouse in Hartville —but no one was ever sure whether they were married or not. Either way, the romance apparently was never serious enough to interfere with Docia's career.[8]

TYPESETTERS ON STRIKE

Aside from the major staff shake-ups caused by Docia's and Olds's departures, Springfield's newspaper people had to weather another crisis that year. Even before everything was back to normal after the fire, the typesetters went on strike—in a big way. Someone set off a bomb on the north side of the newspaper building where the presses were located. No one was hurt and there wasn't much damage, but it got the community's attention. Historically, Springfield had been a labor town and had endured a number of serious strikes before World War II—from a successful streetcar strike in 1916 to a failed strike at the Frisco shops in the 1920s—and from what Lucile wrote to Docia, the typesetters had been discontented for some time, and the newspaper's other unions were sympathetic. "Strike," Lucile wrote to Docia. "The printers are out picketing and an assorted array of non-union printers, office typists, etc. are getting out the paper. The stereotypers and pressmen so far haven't walked out, but the last I heard they were on the verge . . . The paper has been awful. The WORST typographical mistakes. It was some better today and came out fairly well on time. They can't get nearly all the copy printed, and everybody just kills time. My poor old 'Waste Basket' hasn't been in since Monday. Some of the editorial people have been helping out in the composing room and the printers yell 'Rat!' when they come to the door. They haven't yet yelled 'Rat!' at me, but they've quit speaking until I speak first . . ."[9]

A week later, she wrote again: "The strike continues. You should see the array of people they have in the composing room, I don't know where they recruited them . . . They have been feeding the crew (about forty-five) noon and midnight in the fine executive kitchen-dining room. . . . Betty [and two others have] borne the brunt of meal serving . . . I went over one night but got there too late to do anything except dry dishes. Betty acted as though she disapproved of me . . . Betty's tongue is one to be feared, but somehow, I don't give a durn . . . By the way, speaking of Betty—*The American Magazine* recently paid her $75 plus $11 expenses for a picture she took of Dr. Good [president and longtime leader] at the School of the Ozarks . . . I don't know what to think about this strike. One minute I feel sorry for the men and the next I want to kick them in the pants . . . I like a lot of those men . . ."[10]

When the strike began, Dale Freeman had just come on board as a young reporter. "They dynamited, they threatened, they put tacks in the driveways," Freeman remembered, "but the ironic part of it is, about half these guys who were walking the line, I was playing ball with at night." It lasted more than two years, but in the end, the strike "just went up into the ether," remembered Freeman. Springfield's newspapers survived.[11]

LUCILE AND BETTY

Also in 1949, Ann Fair left the paper to marry Ray Dodson, her fiancé. This put more pressure on Lucile to return to the office full-time, which she would do the following year. She wrote to Docia, catching her up on gossip and local news: "They are giving Betty more picture taking to do so she is much happier . . . haven't heard anything about Ann Fair since she quit. Betty said she was so happy to get away from the paper; she had settled down and was staying home . . ." Lucile also added that now-famous-author Laura Ingalls Wilder's husband, Almanzo, had died at the age of ninety-two.[12]

Toward the end of that year, Lucile and Betty began working together. As Lucile had written to Docia, Betty's tongue was one to be feared: if she chose, Betty could swear like a sailor, and in a confrontation, she was known to take no prisoners. Lucile, on the other hand, was a bit prim, but she was steely when it came to getting her way. They often bickered when they were sent on assignments, they were certainly not best friends, but they knew each other very well, and they greatly respected each other's work.

In October 1949, Lucile and Betty spent nearly a week exploring Eureka Springs, the old Arkansas mountain spa-town-turned-intellectual-hideaway and Ozarks show village. They were there to promote Ozarks tourism and cover Eureka's second annual Ozarks Folk Festival. For Lucile, whether she was reporting on an Ozarks festival, a community centennial, a new business in town, or, as she would do in 1954, interviewing incoming Governor Orval Faubus of Arkansas—her work reflected either the Ozarks' past, the change that was coming to the Ozarks, or both.

The Eureka Springs trip definitely was about the folklife of the region, but also it was about the virtues of visiting Eureka Springs, and incidentally, to highlight Eureka's community of writers and artists. A few months earlier, Pulitzer Prize–winning poet John Gould Fletcher and Vance Randolph, who had left Galena and moved to Eureka in 1947, organized the Ozark Folklore Society to collect material "pertinent to the rich traditional culture of the Ozarks." Such local literary luminaries as Marge Lyon, Cora Pinkley Call, Otto Ernest Rayburn, Charley May Simon, and artists Louis and Elsie Freund all joined, and they sponsored their own daylong folk festival at the University of Arkansas in Fayetteville, about forty-five circuitous miles from Eureka. Several of them were also involved in the Ozark Folk Festival that had brought Lucile and Betty to town.[13]

Lucile wrote that people from twenty states found their way to Arkansas's "Little Switzerland" to watch square dancers and listen to balladeers, guitar and banjo playing, group singing, and fiddling, including the fiddle music of George Baize of Reeds Spring, who had been at it for sixty-three years. As often happened with Ozarks gatherings, many of the "usual suspects" were part of the event. Lyon was in charge of the last day of the program, and special guest May Kennedy McCord was mistress of ceremonies. While they were in town, Lucile and Betty managed to highlight things for tourists to see, like Hatchet Hall (the retirement home of fiery temperance reformer Carrie Nation), the gracious Crescent Hotel, and shops full of "typically Ozarkian" treasurers like hickory-nut dolls and dogwood flower jewelry. Lucile also noted that "Eureka Springs expects to keep telling the world it is in the Ozarks."[14]

The following Sunday's *Leader and Press* showcased Lucile's story and more than a half-dozen of Betty's photographs of Eureka Springs and the festival. Obviously, someone at the newspaper thought promoting Ozarks carryings-on was a good idea. Yet, on the editorial page of that same day's newspaper, an item observed that while tourism was bringing in $90 million annually to the one-hundred square miles surrounding Springfield, the city was providing less-than-enthusiastic support to the region's primary tourism group, the Ozarks Playground Association. Despite the newspaper's efforts to publicize the region, it appeared that some of the city leaders still had reservations about hillbillies.[15]

ORVAL FAUBUS INTERVIEW

Lucile's interview with Arkansas Governor Orval Faubus a few years later also reflected the inconsistent feelings about the image of the Ozarks people. As far as Lucile was concerned when she interviewed the just-elected Faubus in 1954, he was an Ozarks newspaper publisher who had won statewide office. It was the first time Arkansas had elected a governor from Madison County, and the local citizens were so elated that they presented him with a "sleek, new Mercury automobile . . . as a token of their friendship." Although he didn't talk about it during his campaign, Faubus had come from a true rural Ozarks family. His father was a farmer and timber worker, and Faubus, who was one of seven children, grew up farming, working in timber, and building rail fences. (His father was also a socialist and had given his son the middle name Eugene after socialist politician Eugene Debs.) Faubus told Lucile that local people knew about his background, but the rest of the state would have thought he was "trying to be another Abe Lincoln," had he campaigned using his past.[16]

Faubus's rags-to-riches story included teaching school to finance a few months of college, election as circuit clerk and recorder in Madison County, and several years overseas in the US Army. Once he was discharged from the military, he came home and bought the *Madison County Record* newspaper. His wife, Alta, became editor and publisher of the *Record*, and Faubus used it as a bully pulpit to agitate for good roads, better health care, and better education in Arkansas. That led to an appointment as district highway commissioner in 1949 and, in 1952, being named state highway director in Arkansas. Finally, registering his view on the changing Ozarks, Faubus told Lucile that dams on the White River "are one of the greatest things that ever came to this section." There was little indication at that time that Faubus would become a national figure three years later, when he squared off against President Dwight Eisenhower to prevent African American children from entering all-white Central High School.[17]

Even though Faubus didn't want to talk about his rail-fence background, Lucile's "Good Old Days" column in that same Sunday newspaper was all about the old Ozarks' "days of simplicity." "Celia's" news of 1904 included a lookback to the time when "hickory chairs, bedsteads with their bed covers, and puncheon floors served well the purposes of the modern upholstered furniture, hardwood interiors, and other twentieth century accessories. Hand-woven linseys for the women folk and butternut and blue-dyed jeans for the men and boys were as satisfactory and productive of vanity as the best imported fabrics of today."[18]

DAMMING THE WHITE RIVER

During these years, while many Ozarkers, often including Lucile, were seeking to lure tourists by hyping the "old ways," the region was modernizing: a person didn't need to live like a hillbilly to sell the image to outsiders, and there was general acceptance that anything that could bring the Ozarks out of poverty was probably okay. One of the biggest engines of change was the US Army Corps of Engineers' dedication to building dams, especially on the White River. It was a love-hate situation: before each project, there would be some controversy and a series of hearings. Then it would be determined that despite horrendous floods over the past century, dams would be unacceptable without hydroelectric generation, which would bring electricity, and progress, to the Ozarks. Then the planning would be interrupted by outside forces like the Great Depression or a world war.

In 1936, the Federal Power Commission gave conditional approval for a hydroelectric project at the White River's Wildcat Shoals, just down the river from Bull Shoals, which was later deemed to be a better construction site. In 1939, newly elected Arkansas Congressman Clyde T. Ellis led the fight to make Bull Shoals a dual-purpose dam, with flood control and also power generation, with power to be marketed by the government primarily to public entities. Construction of Bull Shoals Dam had to wait until 1947; it was completed in 1952 and dedicated with much fanfare during another Ozarks visit by President Truman. Table Rock Dam, which had been talked about almost since Powersite Dam was built in 1912, was called for, even by Congressman Dewey Short, as early as 1929, when he announced he would do "all in his power" to ensure federal licensing for the project. Sidelined by the stock market crash and the Great Depression, Table Rock was finally authorized under the Flood Control Act of 1941, but was again delayed because of World War II and the Korean War.[19]

Finally, in 1954, at hearings before the Appropriations Subcommittee of the US Senate, Ozarkers—at least some of them—had their way. The hearings were chaired by Arkansas Senator John McClellan, and testimony in favor of the dam was presented by Missouri Senators Stuart Symington and Thomas C. Hennings Jr.; Congressman Short; tourism boosters like Ben Parnell, who would soon head the People's Bank of Branson; and Springfield civic leader L. E. Meador, plus presidents of the Missouri Federation of Labor, the Missouri Farmers Association, and others. The pro-fishing-and-wildlife Missouri Conservation Commission was even behind the building of Table Rock Dam, although no one from the commission testified that day.[20]

Symington led off the testimony by explaining that "the people of the Ozarks, Mr. Chairman, are not wealthy people, but they are proud people. They only ask that their government . . . give them a fighting chance to improve their low living standard by carrying out the promise to complete this partially finished edifice." Congressman Short—despite his opposition to the New Deal and big government—declared, ". . . many of our people are out of work and need employment, so now is the ideal time to start work on this project . . . Ninety percent of people in the area are for it. Only a small vocal vociferous group, mostly sportsmen, are opposing the construction of Table Rock Dam." And then, had there been any hope by the sports-minded opposition, he squelched it with one sentence: "Anyone with a thimbleful of brains knows there is more fish in a big pond than in a little pond . . ."[21]

The testimony was eloquent and sincere. Congress authorized the appropriation, and construction began almost immediately. Table Rock Dam was completed in 1956, backing up water from not only the White River but also the smaller James River, long known as a popular floating stream. It is telling that even the nationally famous float-trip promoter Jim Owen supported the dam. Owen had sent a statement to Washington the day of the hearing, in which he noted that he had outfitted and led "the famous Ozark float trips" for more than twenty years, but "the building of the dams and the creation of the lakes greatly increases the available fishing waters, makes wonderful lake fishing and boating . . . available to a much greater class of people." He added, "The streams just cannot keep up a sufficient fish supply to offset the yearly increase in fishing pressure" and concluded by acknowledging, "My float business, which is the biggest in the world, will suffer, but even so, Table Rock will mean far more to us all than any one form of fishing or any one individual idea or enterprise."[22]

PHILIBERT CEMETERY STORY

The lake was extremely important, but like all things of this type, its construction had unintended consequences. One night in 1956, as water from the White and James Rivers was in the process of forming Table Rock Lake, a speaker at the Greene County Historical Society meeting told listeners that the historic Philibert Cemetery on the banks of the James River was about to disappear under the waters of the new lake. Lucile, who was in the audience, was concerned. When she went to work the next morning, she wrangled an assignment from the city desk to send her and Betty to visit the cemetery and do a story.

To get her story, Lucile waded across the James River. *Springfield Newspapers. Photo by Betty Love. Local History Collection, Springfield-Greene County Library Center.* © *Springfield News-Leader—USA TODAY NETWORK.*

Lucile and Betty's trip to Eureka Springs several years before probably was the first time that the two were paired up for a major assignment, but it hadn't taken long for newspaper management to recognize a good thing. Over the next dozen years, the two middle-aged women (in 1950 Lucile was fifty-two and Betty was forty) covered a variety of stories together, from bank robberies, to Ozarks centennials, to reports on industrial growth, to tornadoes. As often as not, the reports about what it took for the two women to get their story were at least as interesting as what was published in the newspapers. One of the most well-known of those escapades—and one that was described in detail in Lucile's subsequent article—was driven by that lecture at the Greene County Historical Society, Lucile's passion for regional history, and the rising waters of Table Rock Lake.

Lucile knew that Joseph Philibert, a French fur trader, was one of the first white settlers in that part of the Ozarks. As Lucile explained in her article, Philibert built a log cabin and established a trading post about three-quarters of a mile above the White River on the James, near the site of the old cemetery. He and his wife, Peniniah Yoachum, had seven children. One son, Edward, was buried with them in in the Philibert Cemetery. Philibert's grave and cemetery were certainly worth seeing, photographing, and writing about.

Lucile and Betty's guide for the adventure was Marvin E. Tong Jr., the man who had spoken about the cemetery at the historical society. Besides being a director of the Missouri Archaeological Society and an executive with the region's Boy Scouts organization, Tong was a founding member of the historical society and a friend of Lucile's. Lucile and Betty set a date to meet Tong for the trip to the cemetery, then made preparations. As Lucile wrote to readers, "I'd had enough experience with pioneer cemeteries to arm myself with some new-fangled tick and chigger repellent . . . and to take along heavy shoes. Betty also had extra shoes and slacks." This was still the era when working women wore dresses, so Betty's slacks were worth mentioning. On the appointed day, the two women rendezvoused with Tong, parked their car, and climbed into his vehicle for the rest of the trip. To reach the cemetery, Tong drove them over a rocky, hilly road past three peaks named for Joseph Philibert: "Naked Joe, Bald Joe, and Timbered Joe," according to Lucile. Then the car lurched down a rocky slope to the James River. When Tong pulled up to the river's edge, Lucile and Betty could see the cemetery across the river, but they couldn't get there. The bridge was gone, washed out during a recent storm.

Faced with limited time and a very long drive around to reach the cemetery by car, the reporter and photographer took the suggestion of a local fisherman on the riverbank: they decided to wade across the river. "The shallow water was at least the distance of a city block upstream and to get to it we'd have to wade weeds, then go down a slippery mud bank. But that's exactly what we did," Lucile wrote, "because Betty was determined to get the picture." There was little doubt that Lucile was as interested in getting to the cemetery as Betty was, so she took off her shoes, hiked up her skirt, and headed across. As she waded deeper and deeper, her skirt floated out around her on the river's surface. Almost immediately, Betty snapped a photo of Lucile surrounded by her floating skirt, her "handbag full of notebooks, pencils and junk," and her own small camera on a strap around her neck. Of course, as soon as Betty was in the water, which reached well above her knees, Lucile took her own picture of Betty. Both photos were later printed along with the story and other pictures of the Philibert Cemetery.

Once across, the two women waded up the bank dripping wet but otherwise little worse for wear. Lucile took notes, describing the twenty-two graves in the small cemetery, including that of Joseph Philibert, whose gravestone proclaimed he "was bornd February the 11:18:3 and died February the 4, 1884." Notes and photos in hand, the two women made ready to step back into the river, but with far less enthusiasm than earlier. Then, as Lucile wrote, "just like a movie when rescue comes at the desperate moment," a boat appeared around the bend. Lucile and Betty waved at the young couple in the boat and called for help. The boat slowed, and then—also just like in the movies—the young woman called out, "You're Betty Love, aren't you?"

Lucile and Betty were both fairly well-known in the Ozarks, but Lucile's followers tended to be older: history buffs, contributors to, and readers of, her columns, those who had heard her speak, and people she had interviewed. Betty, on the other hand, took people's pictures, which was something very personal, and something they never forgot. It turned out that Betty had taken the young woman's photo when she won a scholarship several years before. They were saved. The two still-very-damp women climbed into the boat among a pile of camping gear, and their new friends ferried them to the other side of the river. Two men fishing on the riverbank helped them out onto the rocky shore. Betty then took a picture of the couple in the boat, which later appeared in the newspaper. Lucile wrote the story of Philibert and the cemetery, including details of their experience. Given her passion for local history, she ended the article with her observation that "the washed-out highway bridge will not be replaced, neither can historical remnants of the Ozarks that are allowed to be submerged." Fortunately, time proved Lucile wrong. The little Philibert Cemetery, along with nineteen others, was relocated by the Army Corps of Engineers to a single burial ground near Kimberling City, also named the Philibert Cemetery, in 1957.[23]

FURTHER ADVENTURES OF LUCILE AND BETTY

The adventure of the Philibert Cemetery was a history lesson; many of Lucile and Betty's joint assignments dealt with history, but not all. One time, for example, the two women were called away from a party to cover a thwarted robbery at the Farmers State Bank in nearby Republic. A woman who had been at the party that afternoon described what happened: "The call came in to Betty. They [the newspaper city editor] said 'You and Lucile go over and get the story.' Lucile said, 'We may get shot, but we're off.' " When Lucile and Betty arrived outside the bank, police had everything under control; the two actual robbers were in custody, and an extremely drunk getaway driver was handcuffed in the back seat of the car. As Lucile spoke with the police, Betty leaned into the car with her camera. The would-be robber looked her over, gave her a big smile, and said something to this effect: "Hello Betty! Did you come to take my picture?" The other two robbers, incidentally, went to jail. The fellow who recognized Betty made for entertaining reading in the news stories about their arraignment and other court appearances, but because he was so drunk that he couldn't remember anything about the robbery, including whether or not he drove the car, he was set free.[24]

The newspaper story of the arraignment on May 27, 1959, said it all:

> Three sobered amateurs who could write a book on how not to rob a bank were formally charged here today with the $7,676 holdup of the Farmers State Bank of Republic . . . It could have ended differently except—Their getaway car wouldn't start. One of the three was too drunk to run. They failed in efforts to lock four women employees of the bank in a vault. Several persons saw two of the robbers flee into a nearby wheat field where they were caught.[25]

It all happened in the course of thirty minutes. Neither Lucile nor Betty received a byline in the newspaper for articles or photos, but the story-of-the-story remained evergreen with members of the *News and Leader* staff for many years.[26]

Another time, as Lucile told it, "They hollered across the newsroom and said a boy had killed his father. It was out old [US] 65. Betty, [who drove,] said, 'We don't even know where we're going,' then as we rounded the curve she said, 'Oh there it is, I see the body out in the yard.' Well, the father and the boy lived together there in that little house. And the father got his paycheck and went out and got drunk and then came home and started shooting and killed the boy." The women got their story and made it back to the newspaper office unscathed.[27]

Over the years, the two often, but not always, were sent on assignments that would result in Sunday spreads of Betty's pictures and Lucile's stories. Given that many Ozarks communities had been settled during the years just prior to the Civil War, in the 1950s and early 1960s a good many of their assignments involved small-town centennials. These stories offered opportunities for Lucile to share regional history and gave them a chance to rub shoulders with that core group of semiprofessional Ozarkers and politicians who seemed always to be around to promote the region. At the Marionville, Missouri, centennial in June, 1954, Lucile's old friends Meador and McCord, as well as Congressman Short, were on hand for the pageant, "brush arbor choir," beard contest, ballad singing, and queen crowning. Another time, McCord led an old-time sing at the Howell County Centennial in Mountain View when Lucile and Betty were present.[28]

New industry growing up outside Springfield was another subject for the two. The city desk sent them to Arkansas when an old Arkansas mine near Fayetteville was turned into underground cold storage for large food companies. In all, about four acres of the mine were excavated, the floor of the cavernous space paved, lights installed, and offices built. Another trip, this one to Neosho, focused on how postwar industries like the Rocketdyne rocket engine manufacturing plant, the Southwest Lime Company, and a warehouse in a former limestone quarry were benefiting the flower-box town.[29]

One of Lucile's "industry stories," which may or may not have included Betty's pictures (the photos were not bylined), had to do with fish—but not the kind of fish her brother George was raising so successfully as head of the state's hatcheries. In 1925, a Tulsa oilman had purchased land not far from the Lake of the Ozarks to raise trout, but he soon switched gears. When Lucile visited in 1958, Ozark Hatcheries was the largest goldfish hatchery in the world. In telling that story, Lucile, not surprisingly, managed to include more than fish in her article. The historic property was built around three springs and originally was an Osage tribe's summer campground. Later, the spot became a pioneer stopping place and, in the years before the Civil War, a local entrepreneur built the Wet Au Glaize Mill near one of the springs to grind corn for settlers.[30]

Lucile's two brothers, who were already in the news—Etna as a state official and politician, and George as a pioneer fish culturist—were also subjects for occasional stories by Lucile and Betty. On various trips to Jefferson City, Lucile and Betty put together photo-essays on High School Sophomore Day at the capitol, on the newly decorated governor's mansion, and the "Magnificent Showplace of the Show Me State Center of Interest . . . That's Missouri's Beautiful Capitol." Later, the two women were guests at, and did a story on, the secluded Bull Shoals cove where George, the fisherman, had a homebuilt houseboat that included a trapdoor in the living room floor so he could fish in any weather.

After a tornado hit a small town northeast of Springfield, Lucile and Betty drove over to report on the aftermath. This story was good news: six months after much of the community of Grovespring, Missouri, had been destroyed, Lucile and Betty talked to the residents who, even in the face of disaster, had remained in town and were working hard to return to life as usual. Many had memories they were delighted to share with Lucile—"the little amusing things about the tornado the residents like to recall now as they talk over the horrible moment when the terrifying cloud stretched over them." The men and women Lucile visited with didn't dwell on the homes and businesses—including the community's only café—that were destroyed, but talked instead about gathering together in storm cellars, speeding out of the way of the funnel cloud, and a truck at the feed exchange that was turned completely around by the swirling wind and filled with concrete blocks. They told her that a day after the tornado, when the Red Cross canteen tent was blown down, the women of the town took over a building where the Odd Fellows and Rebekah lodges met so they could provide food for everyone in town. The women of the Rebekahs, Lucile wrote, were still serving lunch six months later, providing the likes of chicken and noodles, corn bread, green beans, slaw, dressing, and pie—all for sixty cents, and the money they were making from their post-tornado meals was being saved to build a new hall. Betty's pictures reflected the upbeat tone of Lucile's words: smiling men gathered around a woodstove in the local MFA lumberyard, men and women standing in front of already-completed new homes, and the lunch crowd at the Rebekahs' temporary cafeteria. Lucile probably saw it as a bonus that on the one-year anniversary of the tornado a Grovespring resident told his/her own story of the tornado in Lucile's "Over the Ozarks" column, reporting that of eighteen buildings destroyed or badly damaged, "fifteen have been built back as good or better than new."[31]

About six months after she wrote about Grovespring's recovery, Lucile penned a long article about another tornado, describing "The Tragic Day the Tornado Battered Springfield." That one, which occurred in 1883, demolished forty Springfield homes, damaged sixty more, destroyed J. W. Puller's icehouse, and blew away the upper story of the woolen mill though no employees were badly hurt. It also destroyed a canary's cage in a home on Pacific Street but left the bird uninjured.[32]

Another Betty-and-Lucile story long told by their colleagues was about their ride, on an icy March day in 1960, on the second-to-last day of Missouri Pacific passenger service between Pleasant Hill, Missouri, and Newport, Arkansas. The article, like the situation, was a bittersweet one; Lucile interviewed passengers and traveling railroad executives who told her about past train rides, and one even told of watching crews lay the tracks when he was a small boy. But the article and the photos were also about the gorgeous winter scenery as the train moved south through the snowy Ozarks hills and through five railroad tunnels. Betty's photos were spectacular, especially one of the big diesel engine emerging from a 3,260-foot railroad tunnel through a curtain of gleaming icicles.[33]

In a later interview, Lucile shed light on how Betty was able to get the photo. She told the interviewer that "Missouri Pacific would have its last run of the White River extension and everybody said, 'OK send Betty and Lucile!' so we got up to go down there, and there was ice all over every-

The engineer of the last passenger run of the Missouri Pacific White River Line stopped the train just as it came through the tunnel so Betty Love could get her picture. *Springfield Newspapers. Photo by Betty Love. Local History Collection, Springfield-Greene County Library Center. © Springfield News-Leader—USA TODAY NETWORK.*

thing and all over the roads. Betty, [who was driving,] got upset and said, 'What do they think they're doing, sending us out like this?'

"I didn't think we'd ever make it in all that ice [but we arrived] ahead of the train. The Division manager jumped off and welcomed us. About a dozen people were on the train but they were especially glad to have us. It had rained and when we got down past Branson there were lots of tunnels with long sparkling icicles across the openings. Betty wanted to take the pictures, so they went slow and let her out, and then she shot a picture of the train coming through the tunnel with the icicles hanging across it." Lucile thought the railroad personnel were wonderfully cooperative. Betty's and her colleagues at the newspaper, on the other hand, were aghast, but probably not surprised. The way they saw it was: "Betty actually got the engineer to stop the train so she could get her picture!"[34]

NATHAN BOONE HOMESTEAD

During those years while Lucile and Betty were touring the Ozarks and keeping their newspaper colleagues entertained, Lucile was still doing what she could to educate readers on Springfield history and encourage support for the Nathan Boone home. In 1959, she submitted a proposal to the University of Missouri Press for a Boone biography and received an enthusiastic go-ahead from press director William Peden. She worked on and off for years, but ultimately the manuscript seemed as elusive as recognition for the Ash Grove property, and was never written. Then slowly, over the next twenty years, interest in saving the Boone homestead began to build. In 1963, she did what she could to publicize an Ash Grove Chamber of Commerce initiative to save the big Boone log home, the family cemetery, the cemetery of the family's enslaved people, and the surrounding farmland. The chamber had an option to buy the Boone property from local longtime owner Grace Buckner and offered part of it to the state park board as a monument to a leading pioneer. The move was endorsed by Lucile and her colleagues at the Greene County Historical Society, and when the state park board's advisory council came to town for their official inspection of the Boone homestead, Lucile, along with Meador, John K. Hulston, and Springfield Chamber of Commerce executive director Lou Reps, met with them to talk about the site and answer questions. Following their visit to the Ash Grove acreage, the Park Board Advisory Council did recommend buying it but, ultimately, the purchase failed over the issue of funding. However, there was some good news that year: the site was listed in the Missouri Historic Sites catalog.[35]

Two years later, in 1965, another serious, but again unsuccessful, push was made in the state legislature to appropriate funds. When the site was listed on the National Register of Historic Places in 1969, it brought recognition for the Boone house, but the property still was in private hands. Boone fans like Lucile, Hulston, and the rest worried about deterioration of the property, and with good reason. While the house had been weatherboarded in the 1940s and some of the fireplace had been sealed over, little to nothing else had been done.[36]

More failed attempts followed in the 1970s, then in 1984, Lucile's early writing was front and center when, in a fit of enthusiasm, the community of Ash Grove invited all the Boone descendants they could find and kicked off what became an annual festival, the Nathan Boone Rendezvous. Thanks to Lucile's and Hulston's past work, and an enthusiastic local writer who combined their articles into a book, festivalgoers had a chance to purchase a new volume on Boone that was primarily a compilation of Lucile's 1931 newspaper series with an introductory chapter by Hulston: *Nathan Boone, the Neglected Hero, From Writings by Lucile Morris Upton and John K. Hulston*. The Boone Rendezvous attracted three hundred Boone relatives and descendants and was a big success locally.[37]

The next year, 1985, the Boone home got another boost when it was recognized by the Greene County Historic Sites Board. Five years after that, Lucile's long campaign of article writing, public speaking, and general agitation began to bear serious fruit: the state purchased the property in 1991, and in 2000 the Nathan and Olive Boone Homestead State Historic Site was finally open to visitors.

| 11 |

THE BATTLE FOR WILSON'S CREEK

About the time Lucile came back to work in the newspaper office full-time, her own longtime involvement with Ozarks history began to mesh with a growing national interest in commemorating the past. The country was only eleven years short of the Civil War centennial, and twenty-six years away from the nation's bicentennial. In her work as a reporter, Lucile was interested in the ramification of those events in the Ozarks, but she was even more interested in doing what she could to safeguard the Wilson's Creek Civil War battlefield. Preserving battle sites certainly wasn't a new idea. President Benjamin Harrison, himself a Union veteran, signed legislation in 1890 making the Chickamauga and Chattanooga Battlefield the country's first national military park. Sixteen years later, the National Park Service was created, and other history-focused legislation followed. During the Great Depression, the Historic American Buildings Survey (1933) provided jobs for out-of-work photographers, architects, and draftsmen—and turned a spotlight on close-to-home historic structures. That legislation was followed in 1935 by the Historic Sites Act, which put a national historic preservation policy in place. The National Trust for Historic Preservation came into being after World War II, and in 1966 Congress passed the National Historic Preservation Act, which inaugurated the National Register of Historic Places.[1]

By 1950, Lucile and her history-buff allies had spent long years urging local and state leaders to recognize the historical significance of "her" two Greene County sites: the Nathan Boone homestead and the Wilson's Creek battlefield. Unlike the small but devoted group that finally achieved recognition for the Boone property, the battle to make Wilson's Creek a national park involved civic leaders, state officials, strong public support, members of Congress, and even former President Truman in the background.

Their cause certainly had merit: fought about three weeks after the Battle of Manassas, Wilson's Creek was the first major conflict to take place in the Trans-Mississippi West. At dawn on August 10, 1861, following a series of smaller battles, Brigadier General Nathaniel Lyon led 5,400 Union troops to surprise General Benjamin McCullough's much larger Confederate army of eleven thousand soldiers in rolling farmland about ten miles southwest of Springfield. The battle, which lasted only six hours, was a bloody one. General Lyon was killed—shot off his horse—and all but one of the Union officers above the rank of captain were either wounded or killed as well. Although the battle was initially seen as a Confederate victory, as Lucile wrote in a special centennial supplement to the *Springfield Leader-Press*, "The Confederate Army was so stunned by its losses [1,095 killed, wounded, or missing] it stayed in camp until the next day, then occupied Springfield for a brief period, never regaining sufficient strength to take Missouri with its important supplies and strategic location."

Men and boys from six states fought and died there, and Missourians swelled the ranks of both armies. Lyon's troops hailed from Iowa and Kansas—and Missouri. McCulloch commanded Confederate forces from Texas, Oklahoma, and Arkansas, plus Missourians and a contingent of Native Americans. After Wilson's Creek, other conflicts took place across Missouri and the Ozarks, but it was a decisive Union victory at Pea Ridge, Arkansas, in March 1862, that made it a certainty that Missouri, as well as her rivers, railroads, industry, store of armaments, and other sources of supplies, would remain in the Union. And her men—Missouri was more populous than any of the southern states and had more white men who could be called up to be soldiers.[2]

REUNION AND RECONCILIATION

The battle to secure national recognition for the place where the six-hour Civil War battle had been fought took generations instead of hours, but it, too, succeeded. Here's the story:

For years, the Wilson's Creek battlefield remained pretty much as it had been on that hot, bloody August day. The Ray home, where the family had cowered in a cellar while the battle raged outside, and where General Lyon's body was first taken, was recognized as an important part of history and cared for accordingly by the family for nearly a century. Also for nearly a century, veterans groups and Ozarks leadership gathered on the battlefield and talked of making at least the thirty-seven-and-a-half acres of so-called "Bloody Hill" where Lyon fell a permanent memorial and part of the US National Park System.

Premier historians of the Wilson's Creek battle William Piston and Richard W. Hatcher have noted that army loyalty during the Civil War focused more on hometowns than it did on regiments. In the Ozarks, that seemed to be true after the war as well. Since Missouri hometowns sent relatives and neighbors to both sides of the conflict, and since Ozarkers were known to identify more with their personal surroundings than with larger geographic or political divisions, almost as soon as General Lee

surrendered at Appomattox, Ozarkers from both sides set out to preserve memories of the conflict—but not, unfortunately, as pointed out
by historian David Blight, to address the needs of the region's formerly
enslaved people. Similarly, historian Amy Fluker suggests that despite
Confederates' loyalty to their "Lost Cause," Missourians and Ozarkers held
a "reconciliationist" memory of the battle that concentrated more on brav-
ery and personal accomplishments of the former soldiers than on political
or philosophical issues. This, Fluker says, was in large part a result of the
Ozarks people's relatively strong sense of shared local identity. Missouri's
physical separation from the bulk of the Civil War may also have had an
effect on the way veterans reconciled with their experiences.[3]

Whatever the reason, reunions of Wilson's Creek survivors began a short
time after the war, and as John Hulston described it, "Veterans both North
and South gathered on the Bloody Hill battlefield site, at the place Lyon fell
dead from his horse. They agreed to lay aside differences, evidenced by their
joint expression of interest to preserve the ground upon which each had
fought for what he believed or was told he should believe." By 1878, veterans
were asking Congress to turn the battlefield into a national park.[4]

A national (i.e., federal) cemetery had opened in Springfield in 1867;
four years later, amid growing concern about how weather was beginning to expose bones from shallow and hastily dug Confederate graves,
a formal Confederate burial ground was opened abutting the cemetery.
In 1887, to finance upkeep of that cemetery, former Confederate General
John Sappington Marmaduke successfully urged his fellow Missourians
that "these dead belong to Missouri" and should be "taken care of by
the people of the entire state." Donations came not only from former
Confederates but also from GAR (Grand Army of the Republic, a federal
veterans' organization) posts. In 1901, funded partially by federal veterans, a Confederate monument was erected at the cemetery, and in 1911,
through an act of Congress, the Confederate cemetery officially became
part of the national cemetery. In another act of reconciliation, this one for
the war's survivors, the Missouri legislature voted in 1897 to take financial responsibility for all of her (white) veterans and provide support to
both the Missouri Confederate Home in Lafayette County and the Federal
Soldiers Home in Phelps County.[5]

A decade after Marmaduke sought financial support for the
Confederate cemetery, the thirty-sixth anniversary of the Battle of
Wilson's Creek in 1897 drew hundreds of veterans and thousands of
others. At the time, a *Cape Girardeau Democrat* reporter who joined the
crowds wrote that "two points came out with great distinctness in the
reunion. One is that the veterans are getting to be old men . . . average
of the men who fought at Wilson's Creek was twenty-three. Now it is sixty

. . . The other point . . . is the complete fraternization of the Union and Confederate soldiers. They have reached a time when they mingle together as comrades . . . regardless of having been on opposite sides . . ." A *St. Louis Globe-Democrat* newspaperman also attending the reunion reported that two hundred veterans of the battle had registered that day and were given souvenir badges to identify themselves among the thousands who crowded into the battlefield. The *Globe* also reported that ex-Confederates outnumbered Union veterans nearly two-to-one, probably because of the battlefield's southwest Missouri location. Relations among the participants that day were cordial, he wrote, and described conversations between and among blue and gray veterans concerning the geography of the battlefield and particulars of the day. He did, however, note that a squabble during the planning of the event had caused hard feelings when the decision came down that Confederate veterans could not carry the flag of their lost cause in the opening parade. Historian Fluker and others also note that by 1900, other white Americans were beginning to embrace a "reconcialist memory" of the Civil War.[6]

After 1900, it was not unusual for members of Congress from southwest Missouri to introduce bills seeking to commemorate the battlefield but, unfortunately, none of the bills was taken seriously until shortly after Lucile returned to the Ozarks from El Paso. That was in 1926, when Congressman Sam A. Major took his turn, introducing an appropriation bill for Wilson's Creek. This time, the Wilson's Creek enthusiasts sought endorsements from across the state and forwarded them to Washington to show support for the bill. The Shepherd of the Hills Association, a Springfield-based Ozarks-improvement group led by businessman and highway promoter John T. Woodruff, spearheaded the statewide campaign to garner support. With a $2,000 donation from the Springfield Chamber of Commerce to help finance the campaign and $2,500 for the Wilson's Creek park fund, the group managed to get endorsements from organizations as varied and far-flung as the Joplin Ministerial Alliance, Probate Judges Association of Missouri, Kansas City Real Estate Board, and the WCTU of Missouri. A statement from the St. Louis Rotary probably went to the heart of the matter for many of those involved: "Since Missouri is rapidly building good roads, it means that we will have an ever-increasing number of tourists, and since our Ozarks contain spots of natural beauty, unsurpassed by any state, we believe that this movement started by the Shepherd of the Hills Association, is a most worthy and patriotic one."[7]

Congress appropriated funds for a battlefield survey. L. E. Meador, who, like so many Missourians in those years, had family members who fought in the war—his father served in the Union Army—worked with mapmakers and wrote a detailed statement, referencing forty-three official reports about the battle, that was forwarded to the War Department. Later, when a West Point historian was sent to Springfield to do a survey, Meador spent several days showing him the battlefield, following old roads, drawing attention to the Ray House, the hilltop where Lyon had fallen, and other key sites, then comparing points on the battlefield map. As a result of that visit, and probably with support from Missouri Senator Champ Clark, the War Department changed its assessment of the Wilson's Creek battle from Class D—relatively unimportant—to Class C—influential in the campaign. About a third of the Civil War battle sites had C ratings, which made the hope for a national park designation much more likely, although it did not promise federal funding. In 1928, buoyed by the uptick in interest in the site, Springfield's University Club erected a marker—the first—on the spot where Lyon was shot.[8]

This was about the time Lucile first saw the battlefield. During the summer of 1929, the newspaper's city desk assigned her to help cover the veterans' reunion on the sixty-eighth anniversary of the battle. For three days, she listened to formal speeches, paid attention to reminisces by some of the, by then, elderly soldiers who took part in the battle, watched a fiddle contest judged by Leon and Frank Weaver of the Weaver Brothers vaudeville troupe, and was entertained by a group sing and a performance by Springfield's Boy Scouts band. Afterward, she wrote, "All my life I have heard of Wilson Creek . . . There were stories related of my great uncle who was killed in the battle—vague accounts because this was unwritten history, that have become almost myths to my generation of the family. Yet, somehow, I did not go to the place where all this transpired. Then I saw the battleground—and was completely awed at the thought of what it stood for."[9]

Among the people she met at that reunion were several women who had lived nearby during the battle, including an eighty-one-year-old who remembered her mother and other women being told to leave when the fighting started because their lives were endangered, and who told Lucile, "The roar of the cannon rings in my ears yet." Another woman told her how the battle surged completely around her parents' house, that she had seen many soldiers shot, and about one body that was brought to her home. Speakers on the program during those three August days included Meador, Woodruff, and former Democratic Congressman James Ruffin. Over the next twenty years this core group, supported by Lucile's reporting, would work together to see Wilson's Creek classified and celebrated as a national battlefield.[10]

The 1929 veterans' reunion marked Lucile's first trip to Wilson's Creek, but Springfield's newspapers had been reporting on the battlefield for decades, publicizing reunions and printing letters from living veterans and, ultimately, their obituaries. As time passed, these old newspaper records would find their way into Lucile's articles and appear in her "Good Old Days" column, reminding readers of what had taken place a half century before. During most of those years, however, Washington pretty much ignored the Ozarks battle site.[11]

In 1938, about a decade after Lucile first visited Wilson's Creek, Meador, along with other civic leaders, convinced the Missouri state legislature to appropriate $60,000 to purchase land at the battlefield. The legislature did appropriate the money, but in that Depression year Governor Lloyd Stark vetoed the bill for lack of available funds. Then, during World War II, when most activities of this type came to a standstill, Meador, assisted by Lucile, made an end run to get battlefield acres. While he was serving as a delegate to the state constitutional convention, he managed to include wording that gave the state park board power of condemnation for historic sites. The power of condemnation did become part of the new constitution, but the idea backfired when the state attorney general declared the state could acquire parkland that way, but not "memorial parks." It would take a new law to do that.[12]

L. E. Meador points out the spot where General Nathaniel Lyon fell during the battle of Wilson's Creek to a group of visitors. Note Lucile, busy reporting on the visit, at the far side of the photo. March 26, 1951. © *Springfield News-Leader—USA TODAY NETWORK.*

Regardless of her other duties as a reporter and columnist, Lucile remained an active chronicler of all things Wilson's Creek. About the time she returned to work following the death of her husband, Hulston became the attorney for the newspaper. He recalled, "I was in the office once or twice a week. I always stopped to see Lucile, and she would conspire with me on some business like the Nathan Boone Park or Wilson's Creek. She always was in on the meetings, but always refused to serve on committees." In other words, Lucile was interested, and her presence at any gathering ensured newspaper articles. Probably, though, as she had said about joining the equal rights movement back in Denver, she believed that being an actual part of one of those groups would cast suspicion of bias on her job as a reporter. "She was thoroughly objective," Hulston continued. "When she was a city councilwoman even her best friends wouldn't have lobbied her. They wouldn't have dared." Lucile later confirmed that when she told a group of Springfield teachers, "I believe that it is the business of a newspaper reporter to give unbiased reports of happenings and not to be involved in the mechanics of it."[13]

WILSON'S CREEK BATTLEFIELD FOUNDATION

Lucile's support for the Wilson's Creek campaign was front and center in 1950, when Hulston was president of Springfield's Chamber of Commerce. That year, Hulston, along with Meador, Chamber Executive Lou Reps, Lester Cox, and other civic leaders, organized a Wilson's Creek Battlefield Foundation to raise money from across the community to purchase the thirty-seven and a half acres of Bloody Hill. To support the foundation, Lucile wrote a series of seven articles on "one of the Civil War's most important clashes." The articles ran for a week in the newspaper, then finished with a final piece describing what citizens were doing to memorialize the battleground and kick off the new foundation's fund drive.

By calling forth a "Penny Brigade," the foundation generated interest in the battlefield—and donations—from all parts of the community, including schoolchildren. The fund drive was a success, and the foundation raised enough money to purchase Bloody Hill from Mr. and Mrs. Robert McClure, who were descendants of the Ray family and, like the rest of the community, anxious to see the land turned into a park. Next, the foundation decided to try Washington one more time. Meador headed a steering committee to "plan for and guide" an effort to get a national park. To further boost interest, the foundation reprinted Lucile's series of newspaper stories about Wilson's Creek in a booklet and made it available to the public.[14]

GREENE COUNTY HISTORICAL SOCIETY

Over the next few years, as the upcoming Civil War centennial began to loom large in the American consciousness, things began to happen. In 1954 a group of history-minded stalwarts including Hulston and Meador organized a new Greene County Historical Society, reborn from the old historical society of the 1930s. Lucile joined as a charter member. She was a ready participant in historical society meetings that first year, updating members in September on the coming centennial of the Butterfield Overland Mail line in 1959, making a report in October about the chronological history of Springfield over its past 125 years, which she had compiled for the newspaper, and she was at that November meeting when Marvin E. Tong Jr. alerted the group that the Philibert Cemetery would soon be under the waters of Table Rock Lake. The first president of the new historical society was Springfield's superintendent of schools, C. Benton Manley, another serious student of the Wilson's Creek battle. Over the next dozen or more years, the historical society would be a staunch supporting player in the campaign to make Wilson's Creek a national park.[15]

In 1958, the historical society created a Civil War Centennial Committee with Hulston as chair, and Lucile, Meador, and Tong among the other members. Shortly after that, then-Governor James T. Blair Jr. named Hulston to the Missouri State Civil War Centennial Commission. In the mid-1950s, Missouri Senator Thomas Hennings and Congressman Short introduced Wilson's Creek bills in the Senate and House respectively, and a serendipitous National Park Service survey of the White River Basin recommended that Wilson's Creek battlefield be preserved as a national monument. In 1956, Short lost his reelection bid to Springfieldian Charles Brown, an advertising and television executive, and in 1957 Brown joined Hennings in introducing new bills for Wilson's Creek. Perhaps sensing success, the Wilson's Creek Foundation asked Hennings to offer their battlefield land acres to the federal government as the beginning of a park.[16]

A few months later, when happenstance brought National Park Service director Conrad L. Wirth and other NPS officials to a meeting at Roaring River State Park, about an hour south of Wilson's Creek, they agreed to visit the battlefield. Hulston, Lucile, and Springfield Newspapers' managing editor C. W. "Johnny" Johnson met the NPS group and escorted them to the site. "We showed him [Wirth] where the Wilson's Creek National Battlefield should be," Hulston recalled later, "and even got permission to take him on private property there."[17]

The newspaper articles reporting on Wirth's visit asserted that the NPS director and his fellows "were quite interested" in the battlefield site. Once more, though, things didn't work out: back in Washington, the NPS people wrote a report that concluded Wilson's Creek was a secondary engagement that lacked national significance. Adding insult to injury, the NPS also suggested that the Pea Ridge battlefield, which had become a national park the year before, would serve to commemorate both battles. Perhaps it was the suggestion about Pea Ridge that did it, but after sitting by since the 1890s and watching as a dozen bills were introduced in the US House, plus two in the Senate, the proponents of a Wilson's Creek battlefield park could take no more. Congressman Brown and Senator Hennings announced that hearings on their bills would continue, regardless of the NPS's and Department of the Interior's opinions.[18]

The next salvo was Lucile's. She wrote a long, passionate article about Wilson's Creek that outlined "96 Years of Neglect," pointed out that bills were pending in both the Senate and House to make Wilson's Creek a national park, and described what her fellow Missourians would see when they visited the national-park-to-be: they would see 800 to 1,200 acres of "scenic hills and valleys" that had remained "amazingly unchanged" since the battle. She went into detail about the prickly pear that blooms on Bloody Hill and scrub oak that still grows on the rocky slopes. She told readers about the one house on the site, "in as nearly its original state as possible." She wrote that "now as the one hundredth anniversary of the battle approaches, renewed effort is being made to give the historic site its long overdue honor." To give the story special attention, the newspaper's city desk blasted it over the Associated Press wire to all the newspapers in the state. The article was picked up by the *Kansas City Star*, among others, and played large, with several photos.[19]

By this time, Lucile had written so much about the battle that she was becoming known as a Wilson's Creek expert. The editor of *Civil War Times* magazine got in touch and asked her to write a piece. Her article, "The Battle that Saved Missouri for the Union," resulted in letters from several descendants of soldiers, including one from a woman who wrote that her grandfather and two others had caught General Lyon's body as he fell from his horse. Lucile also began to hear from people with treasured letters and diaries of soldiers that they wanted to share or find safe homes for.[20]

CONGRESSMAN BROWN'S HEARING
AND NATIONAL PARK RECOGNITION

Senator Hennings's health prevented any activity on the bill to take place until 1959, but when the bills were reintroduced that year, this time also with support from Missouri's junior Senator Stuart Symington, Congressman Brown was serious about getting results. When the Wilson's Creek bills were assigned to the Interior and Insular Affairs Committees of the House and Senate, he invited members to a hearing, not in Washington, but in Springfield, and then to a tour of the battlefield. A special subcommittee for the bill took Brown up on his request: congressmen Ed Edmondson from Oklahoma, J. Edgar Chenowith of Colorado, and William Randall from Independence, Missouri, who happened to be a protégé of former President Truman. When the visiting congressmen arrived at Springfield's federal courtroom for Brown's hearing, they were greeted by seemingly half the people in town—a high school history class, businessmen, members of the historical society, state parks director Joe Jaeger, three members of the Missouri Civil War Centennial Commission, the mayor, Greene County's presiding judge, and members of the press. Meador, who was also chair of the Wilson's Creek Foundation, formally offered the Bloody Hill acres to the federal government and then told the visiting congressmen how, shortly after the Civil War, veterans from both sides had agreed the Wilson's Creek site should become a national park.

John K. Hulston (at left), chair of the Wilson's Creek Foundation steering committee, presents the deed to the acres on Bloody Hill to Howard Baker, Omaha regional director of the National Park Service. About 3,500 people were on hand for that August 1961 ceremony at the battlefield. © *Springfield News-Leader—USA TODAY NETWORK.*

Hulston showed the congressmen a map of the battlefield. Manley discussed the troops that had fought there, and Reps reported on travelers from all over the country who came to visit. Following the presentations, the subcommittee, plus the committee's consultant from Washington, Brown, members of the press, and a number of others, climbed onto a bus provided by the Frisco Railroad and were taken to their personal tour of the battlefield.[21]

Although she did not have her name attached to any of the newspaper reports on the committee activities, it was probably more than coincidence that Lucile's "Over the Ozarks" column that same week highlighted an item by a contributor who called out "the 'foot draggin' on the Wilson's Creek Battlefield Monument.'" There, indeed, had been "foot draggin'," for many years, but this time, the hearing and battlefield tour seemed to make a difference. Ten days after their visit, the Interior Subcommittee voted approval of Congressman Brown's bill. A few months after that, during the anniversary week of the battle, Lucile reminded readers that "with only two years remaining until the Civil War Centennial, a renewed effort is being made to get a national park at Wilson's Creek." In December, the National Park Service sent researchers to southwest Missouri to gather data. Finally, almost ninety-nine years after the fact, both houses of Congress passed the Wilson's Creek bills and, on April 22, 1960, although most of the battlefield property had yet to be amassed, President Dwight Eisenhower signed HR 725 into Public Law 86-434 "to provide for the establishment of the Wilson's Creek Battlefield National Park in the State of Missouri."[22]

And so, on August 10, 1961, one hundred years after the six-hour battle, thousands of people came to Springfield for a blowout celebration of the national-park-to-be, including four representatives of the American Hungarian Federation who brought a portrait of Major Charles Zagonyi, leader of a federal charge into Springfield two months after the Wilson's Creek battle. Lucile, along with Hulston and others, was listed in the big red, white, and blue program that highlighted a welcome by Meador, dedication by Senator Symington, speech by Governor John M. Dalton, a gala parade, an army band concert, four military flyovers, including the Blue Angels, multiple history exhibits set up around town, a display of replicas of the *Mercury* space capsules, and special attention for descendants of those who fought. Everyone who attended the celebration at the battlefield received a sixteen-page newspaper supplement Lucile had written for the occasion, entitled the "Wilson's Creek Story." Illustrated by longtime newspaper cartoonist Bob Palmer, Lucile's articles not only described the battle from the ground and from a historical perspective but also portrayed the leading officers on both sides, included an article about Springfield in 1861, had a short piece on a lengthy disagreement as to whether it should be "Wilsons" Creek or "Wilson's" Creek, another on "The Fight That Lasted 100 Years" to secure the battlefield as part of the country's National Park System, and a map of the site. Probably because Lucile was so well-known, and because she regularly heard from readers of her "Over the Ozarks" column on all sorts of topics, the supplement featured comments and notes from descendants of soldiers who fought in the battle, and snippets of letters and diaries of the soldiers themselves. Many of these diaries and letters would eventually find their way to the new park's John and Ruth Hulston Civil War Research Library, which would be created in 1985. As a mark of her behind-the-scenes role in making it all happen, Lucile's editor added a prominent box in the centennial supplement: "Lucile Morris Upton . . . probably has written more about the Battle of Wilson's Creek than any other person. Her research on, and promotion of, the historic Civil War engagement is credited by many with playing a major role in final establishment of the national battlefield park."[23]

Years later, Hulston looked back at the community-wide effort to secure federal protection for Wilson's Creek, noting Lucile's participation in the endeavor: "She reported on every action of the committee and persuaded newspaper managing editor Johnny Johnson to support it." Hulston also provided a few other insights regarding the machinations and connections that finally turned a patch of rolling farmland into a national battlefield park: "Congressman Charlie Brown was friendly with Harry Truman, studied under Dr. Meador at Drury, had been manager of KY3 television [in Springfield], worked in advertising and radio, and defeated Dewey Short. Sam Rayburn [then-speaker of the US House of Representatives] had his eye out for young fresh Democratic congressmen. Charlie made wonderful speeches and persuaded Rayburn to put Wilson's Creek on the calendar. It was voted through during his second term. Senator Tom Hennings [who died from abdominal cancer before the centennial celebration] ramrodded it through the Senate. Symington pushed too—his grandfather, a Confederate officer, had fought his wife's grandfather, a Union officer, at Gettysburg, and he became a regular nut about Wilson's Creek."[24]

WILSON'S CREEK AFTER ONE HUNDRED YEARS

Lucile retired from Springfield Newspapers at the end of 1963, but she stayed interested and involved in the evolution of the battlefield. After all, the story was not yet over. In May 1965, the Wilson's Creek Foundation gave an additional 1,009 acres of land to the federal government, which brought the park up to a size that suited the National Park Service and allowed for it to improve existing roads and build new ones, construct "employee accommodations," destroy all "non-historic" structures on the property, and add parking lots. As part of the improvements, a trailer was put in place to serve as a visitors center. Management of the park, however, was set at the George Washington Carver National Monument, about sixty miles southwest, and park staff was limited to one person. That same year, Lucile donated the first of many personal documents to the park, including several of her original articles, letters from her "Over the Ozarks" readers and others regarding ancestors who had fought in the battle, plus historic handbills, clippings from the 1890s, several military medals, insignia, epaulets, and a Civil War–era box that held the items.[25]

In late 1966, the battlefield was among the first sites listed on the new National Register of Historic Places. The following year, more than forty-one thousand people came to see where the first major Civil War battle west of the Mississippi had been fought. Then, thanks in large part to hard lobbying of the state legislature by leading businessman Lester Cox, and support from Missouri House Speaker Tom Graham, more state funds were appropriated, and more land purchased. On August 10, 1968, Lucile was part of another stem-winder celebration at the battlefield. Both the current governor, Warren E. Hearnes, and former Governor Dalton were there; their two administrations had appropriated funds to purchase the battlefield land, and during the ceremony that day, Hearnes presented deeds to National Park Service director George B. Hartzog Jr. to complete the acquisition of 1,727 acres of land for the battlefield. Hulston, Meador, and others were recognized for their long-lasting belief in the project. Springfield's Glendale High School's band opened and closed the program.[26]

Even after the 1968 celebration, the Wilson's Creek battlefield was a work in progress, and still managed from the Carver National Monument. As the years passed, and the park moved toward more permanent footing, Lucile remained interested, occasionally wrote newspaper stories, and continued to be honored as Springfield's Wilson's Creek historian. She also contacted the School of the Ozarks about writing a book about Wilson's Creek, and Townsend Godsey, then vice president of the school, with responsibility for its publications, was enthusiastic about the prospect. In 1970, the Wilson's Creek acreage was redesignated as a national battlefield (rather than a battlefield park), and in 1972, Lucile was on the platform again, with Hulston, Meador, and other notables when Wilson's Creek National Battlefield was "formally established" at a ceremony arranged by the National Park Service. In 1976, as the nation celebrated its two-hundredth birthday, more than fifty-three thousand visitors came to Wilson's Creek. That year, administration of the park was finally moved from the Carver National Monument to the battlefield.[27]

In the following years, Lucile served as a member of the advisory council for a reborn Wilson's Creek National Battlefield Foundation. A nine-thousand-square-foot visitors center was dedicated in 1982, replacing the trailer that had served in that capacity for twenty-one years, and restoration was completed on the Ray House. In 1985, a year when almost 177,000 people visited the park, the John K. and Ruth Hulston Civil War Research Library opened with three thousand bound volumes and more than one thousand journals and magazines.[28]

By the late 1980s, Lucile was no longer active in park activities, but the battlefield, and the public's interest in it, continued to grow. A new, larger library was dedicated in 2003, and in 2005, the Wilson's Creek Foundation, with help from the National Park Service, purchased General Sweeny's Civil War Museum, a private collection of nearly ten thousand artifacts, primarily from the Trans-Mississippi West, that became the core of the Wilson's Creek Museum collection. In 2019, a grand total of 233,000 people visited the battlefield, and on Memorial Day 2021, an expanded museum and updated visitors center opened to the pubic. As of this writing (2022), the 1,750-acre Wilson's Creek National Battlefield is one of seventeen Civil War battle sites that are cared for by the National Park Service.[29]

| 12 |

THE HONORABLE—AND MEMORABLE—LMU

When President Dwight Eisenhower signed the bill to make Wilson's Creek a national battlefield park in April of 1960, heritage tourism—the practice of going on vacation to visit historic places—was on the upswing. Tourism in general was booming and, with a quarter of the country's people within a day's drive of the Ozarks, the region was a natural destination and ready for more company. Not that the Ozarks hadn't already been welcoming company for a while. In 1960, when the Ozarks Playground Association celebrated its fortieth anniversary, it estimated that tourist spending in the region had risen from $200,000 in 1920 to an anticipated $215 million in 1960. The organization went on to predict a "really golden" future ahead.[1]

As tourism increased in the Ozarks, so did tourism promotion, especially the homegrown variety. Probably the biggest and most successful of these efforts was at Marvel Cave. In 1950, when the Lynch sisters leased the cave to Chicagoans Hugo and Mary Herschend, the Herschends immediately went to work to bring in more visitors. They replaced rickety stairs and walkways with concrete, added electric lights to make the interior more tourist-friendly, and built a little train to bring people from the cave's depths to the surface. While the Herschends spent money on safety, their initial promotional efforts tended to be creative rather than costly, as when they sponsored a national square dance festival that attracted attention from coast to coast.

Hugo Herschend died in 1955. After that, his widow, Mary, and their two sons, Jack and Peter, took over cave management, and in less than a decade, they turned their regional show cave into a national tourist attraction. In 1959, to give people something to do while they waited for their cavern tour, Mary helped design and oversaw construction of five small buildings on a short "main street" near the cave entrance that was to become the beginning of an "Ozark Mountain Village." Main Street boasted an ice-cream shop, blacksmith forge, and craft shops, and it also had a lively cast of actors, including a hillbilly sheriff, ongoing Hatfield-McCoy feud, musicians, and a variety of local characters. They named the little village "Silver Dollar City."[2]

Lucile knew Mary Herschend and her sons, and she was so enthusiastic about the goings-on outside the cave that when her niece, June, brought her family for a visit, Lucile took them there. As the group was strolling along the main street of Silver Dollar City, a "Daisy May" lookalike scampered up and made eyes at June's husband, only to be followed almost instantly by a belligerent and bearded older man in overalls, waving a shotgun. The bearded fellow insisted on—what else?—a "shotgun wedding" between Daisy May and June's husband, complete with horseshoe nail rings that he provided, a hillbilly preacher, and musicians. Lucile's relations loved the hillbilly street theater and loved being part of the entertainment. It didn't take long before the hillbilly characters, music performances, craftspeople, and shops at Silver Dollar City outdrew the cave in popularity. In 1950, as an example, 6,500 people visited Marvel Cave. In 1962, more than one hundred thousand people toured the cave, but five times that many visited Silver Dollar City. In 1964, Silver Dollar City welcomed 790,000 visitors.[3]

MORE HILLBILLIES

During those years, not only the Ozarks, but Vance Randolph's classic Ozarks people—hillbillies—were attracting more attention than ever. At one point, Lucile told a group of listeners that "the outside world thinks—or at least hopes—that this is a land of bewhiskered men and tired old clay-pipe smoking women," adding, "I am not sure we Ozarkers haven't encouraged this view. We have enjoyed telling big whoppers to credulous people." She also noted, "There was a time when we natives resented tourists saying, 'So you're a hillbilly.' But no more. It has become good box office to be a hillbilly and a lot of us have tried to get into that act." Lucile's participation, it goes without saying, was strictly from the outside, via talking and writing. She never would have sung a folk song, smoked a pipe, or pieced a quilt—and rarely even went fishing.[4]

By 1960, the hillbillies in Al Capp's long-running (1934–1977) Li'l Abner comic strip had been joined by hillbilly families on the nation's television screens. In 1955, Springfield radio and TV impresario Si Siman, with Ralph Foster, John B. Mahaffey, and financial backer Lester Cox, launched Ozark Jubilee, the first successful national network television program to feature top country music performers. Hosted by hugely popular country music star Red Foley, the Jubilee showcased the likes of Wanda Jackson,

Slim Wilson, Floyd "Goo-Goo" Rutledge, the Foggy River Boys, and future stars like Porter Wagoner and Brenda Lee. A few years later, hillbillies invaded the world of television sitcoms beginning with *The Real McCoys*, starring Walter Brennan and Richard Crenna (1957–1963), and the Darlings characters on *The Andy Griffith Show* (1960–1969), which was set in a rural North Carolina town. *The Beverly Hillbillies* (1962–1971), *Petticoat Junction* (1963–1970), and *Green Acres* (1965–1971), were all created by Missouri native Paul Henning.

If all of that wasn't confirmation enough that hillbillies and hillbillyism were "in," a Missouri Court of Appeals judge in Springfield made national headlines when he revoked a 1960 divorce over the definition of the word "hillbilly." A fellow named Lowell Moore had filed for divorce in part because his wife, Minnie, was "bossy and domineering, interfered with his fishing and stock trading—and called his relatives hillbillies." A lower court judge had granted the divorce, but when Minnie appealed, Springfield Court of Appeals Judge Justin Ruark reversed the decision. Ruark declared that "in Southern Missouri the appellation 'hillbilly' is not generally an insult or indignity; it is an expression of envy." Therefore, Moore's wife had not been insulting his relatives, and Moore had to remain married. The judge also acknowledged, however, that a husband does have a right to go fishing without interference from his wife. The story about the revoked divorce and benefit of being called a hillbilly was picked up in newspapers across the country, including Lucile's old *El Paso Times*. Hillbillies were good copy.[5]

REPORTING HISTORY

By the 1960s, Lucile rarely covered "hard" news stories anymore. She was a well-known columnist with contributors and readers from as far away as both coasts. Her interest in history was beginning to overshadow everything else—except the features that she did with Betty Love. She and Betty were still producing major spreads on anything from a homecoming celebration in Neosho for native son artist Thomas Hart Benton to the annual Democratic Jackson Day conclave in Springfield. They reported on progress at the new Corps of Engineers Pomme de Terre Dam that was under construction north of Springfield, and they continued to use their talents to showcase Ozarks folkways and history. In the fall of 1961, Lucile penned a long story about the best places to see fall colors and described some of the most popular fall festivals. The next year, she and Betty documented the colorful Glade Top Trail through twenty-seven miles of the Mark Twain National Forest near Ava—and let people know about the free guides and chicken barbecue for visitors on a designated Sunday. Lucile, of course, had to put at least a bit of history in her article and regaled readers with a tale about "The Pinnacle," a very steep place on the trail where Ozarkers once came the first Sunday of May for special outdoor religious services. There was a tradition that anyone who dug for gold on the Pinnacle would find it, but many had tried with no luck. According to Lucile's article, on one of those May mornings a "Mrs. Murray" prayed aloud, "O Lord, strike this peak lightly and break it open so we can find gold," but as she prayed, an old man in the crowd realized that such a strike would kill the people at the service, so he prayed, also aloud, "O Lord, DON'T strike this peak!" Suddenly, according to the tale, there was a huge clap of thunder, a heavy downpour, and almost as suddenly, the crowd dispersed. In the end, there was no gold, but there were no bodies, either.[6]

A month later, in October 1962, Lucile and Betty took in the popular War Eagle Crafts Fair, centered at a 130-year-old farmhouse near Rogers, Arkansas. It was a place, Lucile wrote, where "a century ago, oxen tramped the road past the house, pulling wagons loaded with grain to the nearby grist mill. Now, in three days' time, 20,000 persons ride down the dusty road in their shiny automobiles and delight in . . . displays of Ozarks-made items." Since 1962 was a centennial year for the Civil War, she added a side story about the war in that corner of Arkansas: how Confederates had burned the War Eagle Mill to prevent the Union Army from grinding grain there to augment their food supply and how a commemorative plaque was coming to War Eagle. Betty's eye-catching images of wood-carvers, painters, doll makers, leatherworkers, and the crowds took up almost two full pages of that Sunday's *News and Leader*.[7]

During those Civil War Centennial years (1961–1965), Lucile nearly always included details about the war in the Ozarks in her feature stories whenever it was appropriate. She also wrote straight historical articles, as she did on January 8, 1961, when the newspaper launched her series on the American Civil War in the Ozarks, beginning with a list of battles and a detailed description of the January 8, 1863, Battle of Springfield, during which Federal Brigadier General Egbert Brown and his troops held off Confederate General Marmaduke's army, which was aiming to destroy the Union supply line between Rolla and Springfield.[8]

In May 1963, Lucile and Betty drove back to northwest Arkansas to do what was probably their last major photo feature together. Their subject was the soon-to-be-dedicated 4,210-acre Pea Ridge National Military Park. Although it was designated as a park by law in 1956, Pea Ridge, like Wilson's Creek a few years later, had to wait until a proper acreage was in place before it could receive the formal blessing of the National Park Service. In her article, Lucile described the park's new visitors center,

discussed its new Civil War research library, and recounted the story of
the battle, which had taken place about seven months after the battle of
Wilson's Creek.[9]

RETIRED

Lucile turned sixty-five a couple of months after the Pea Ridge article
appeared, and when she announced that she would retire at the end of the
year (December 31, 1963), the newspaper did her proud. Ann Fair Dodson
interviewed her for a major feature about her long career as a journalist in
the West and in the Ozarks. Church editor Mary Ritchie hosted an open
house in her honor, and, on the first Sunday in January 1964, a *News and
Leader* editorial titled "All of Us Will Miss Lucile" described her as "an
editor's dream of a newspaperwoman, the reporter who can do everything
and anything, and do it well . . . To every story she contributed enthusiasm,
knowledge and the painstaking thoroughness of the good reporter. With
great understanding and good will, she edited the contributions of hundreds
of present and former residents of these Ozark hills to 'Over the Ozarks,' and
conscientiously handled the tremendous volume of correspondence which
the column evoked." At the end, the author wished her a pleasant retirement, but noted, "She'll not be inactive—for she doesn't know how!"[10]

The editorial was correct. She retired from the newspaper and took
leave of her friends and hundreds of "Over the Ozarks" pen pals, but she
kept her "Good Old Days" column, which continued to appear every
Sunday, and she carried on with her series on the Civil War in and around
Springfield. On occasion, she would show up in the newsroom with other
articles she had written on things she felt deserved attention. Most of those
stories, not surprisingly, involved developments at the Wilson's Creek
battlefield, Nathan Boone Homestead, or the Greene County Historical
Society. As her time became her own, she focused more and more on the
region's history. Sometime during those years, she also created "Pastime,"
snippets of local history facts that editors could slot into the paper wherever there was space.

Once she was no longer legally bound to the newspaper, she was free
to actively support Democratic politics, and while she never took a leadership role, she was more than willing to lend her talents to the cause.
In the fall of 1964, she moderated an event in Springfield with Muriel
Humphrey, wife of vice-presidential candidate Hubert Humphrey. Early
in January 1965, she was on the platform at the state capitol when Etna
was sworn in for his third term as Missouri state treasurer. She had been a
popular member of the newspaper staff and she was still very photogenic,
so in both of those cases, as in much else she did during her "retirement

years," her old colleagues made sure her activities—and her picture—got plenty of attention on the pages of the morning *Daily News* and afternoon *Leader and Press*.[11]

Part of Lucile's retirement, of course, involved her family. Veda, who had lived with her in the little giraffe-stone house where she moved following Gene's death, had died in 1960, but Lucile stayed close to her two brothers and their families as well as her two stepchildren, Rosemary in Houston, Texas, and JB and his family in St. Louis. George, by this time, was living in Springfield and was something of a celebrity in the fish world. He was credited with developing the state's highly successful catfish propagation program, which still continues today. In the 1930s and 1940s, he had been a successful buffer and peacemaker between the influx of professional biologists and the conservation department's highly skilled but not-professionally-educated hatchery folk. In the 1950s, he had worked with scientists at (then) Ralston-Purina to develop one of the earliest dry diets for hatchery trout, replacing raw liver as their feed. What's more, he had become a prolific author himself, writing about fish and fishing for both general and technical audiences. His family and friends particularly loved to tell the story about what happened when he applied to attend a federal Department of Agriculture–sponsored hatchery school in the mid-1960s: he was only reluctantly accepted to the class because, like his siblings, he lacked a college degree. However, just as his siblings generally did in strained circumstances, George won the day: it turned out he had written a part of the class textbook.[12]

Lucile also took time out to travel. She was a regular guest at George's houseboat on Lake Bull Shoals. She frequently visited Etna in Jefferson City and went to Europe several times, once writing to Etna that Paris was far from her favorite stop on a multicountry tour. Another time she spent a month in Rome, which she quite liked. Later still, she went with a group to England and Wales.[13]

Leisure time, however, was never Lucile's preference. She always had been a willing speaker, a role she continued into her retirement, talking to groups about her career as a reporter, about local history, and about the old Ozarks, hillbillies and all. As time passed, despite her assertions to the contrary, many of her talks had a feminist edge to them, whether she was talking about her own newspaper career or singing the praises of women she had known. She participated in and organized writing seminars, turned out historic pieces for the newspaper and the occasional magazine, and in 1967, she took on a new teaching gig, this one as part of the Women's Daytime Program at Drury College. Lucile's class, Creative Writing for Fun and Profit, was popular: more than forty students arrived for the first session, even though officially, the class size was limited to thirty.

George, Veda, Lucile, and Etna in front of Lucile and Veda's home in Springfield. *Morris family photos.*

SPRINGFIELD CITY COUNCIL

A couple of months after she started teaching again, Lucile attended a dinner with a large group of her friends and, as she told it, "They said, 'You know about city government, you've been covering these offices so long' . . . Before it (the dinner) was over I'd promised them if they'd circulate a petition I'd let them use my name as a candidate for City Council. I never asked anyone for a vote, and as for putting up money . . ." The lone woman member of the council, Dr. Souter Smith, had announced her retirement after fourteen years, and as Lucile said, "They needed a woman candidate." She ran, took no donations, and was elected a Springfield City Council member-at-large. "I enjoyed it," she later told a public television interviewer. "I'm glad I did it, but it was their idea."[14]

Running for city council may have been her friends' idea, but her newspaper family, as always, treated her as their own special celebrity, beginning in the month prior to the election. She ran unopposed, but at the last minute there was pushback on her candidacy. A retired insurance executive, C. Belton Hembree, offered himself as a write-in opponent to Lucile, objecting to her association with Drury College—Drury Vice President Carl Stillwell was already on the council—and with the newspaper. Hembree should have considered whom he was up against; the *Sunday News and Leader* came to Lucile's defense in a long editorial that concluded, "She is in no way obligated to Drury nor likely to favor it over Southwest Missouri State, Evangel, or any other institution of higher learning—not that college affairs very often come to the council's attention anyway." The editorial also pointed out that Lucile was retired from the newspaper except for contributing her "Good Old Days" column and that her "interest in Greene County and Missouri history makes her a valued consultant and occasional contributor in this field." Finally, it said, "These newspapers could not influence Mrs. Upton's position on municipal affairs even if they would—and we consider it regrettable if employment with Springfield Newspapers or with other Springfield news media should forever bar an individual from government service."[15]

Election day was April 4. On April 5, the *Daily News* headline proclaimed: "Incumbents on Council Stay, Upton Is Added." She led the vote-getting among the at-large candidates with 4,182 votes. Hembree, the write-in, received 439. Not only had the newspaper family championed her candidacy, but also, during that election week, her picture was in the paper twice, she was written up in two different articles about the new city council, and the newspaper published two history-related articles she had authored. On Tuesday, April 4, election day, the *Leader and Press* carried a long article by Lucile on "The Hundred-Year History of Springfield Newspapers." Since she hadn't yet been elected and was still a private citizen at that point, she was identified to readers as "a longtime former staff member." Two days later, the afternoon paper ran another article by Lucile, this one about the beginning of World War I. By this time, however, she was an elected city official, so the newspaper labeled her only as a "Special Correspondent of the *Leader and Press*." As much as they loved showing her off, her editors apparently decided that since she was now a working politician, she needed an arm's-length relationship with the paper.[16]

THE CITY'S BUSINESS

As a member of Springfield City Council, Lucile did what most members of city councils do: She dealt with zoning issues and with expanding public utilities in underserved parts of town. She worked alongside other council members on budgets, taxes, and concerns over city employees; and she debated new places to spend money—or not. She questioned just how much land the state college should be taking over in the community, and whether Baptist Bible College really needed to assume ownership of a street right-of-way. She voted for a zoo master plan, championed an urban beautification program, sponsored a bill to give the city condemnation power for parks, and sat out a vote on whether the city should purchase land where a sinkhole had appeared. She called for a study on the anchoring of mobile homes, sponsored a bill to open an alcohol treatment center, and was appointed to a committee to improve communication between the council and Springfield citizens. All the while, she continued her long-time campaigns for improvements at the jail and for the community to pay attention to its past. However, she also kept an eye out for issues she could affect that would help Springfield people. Sometimes she was successful, but as always is true in politics, sometimes she was not.

"We all on the City Council had our pet interests," she said later. "I felt greatly concerned about certain housing fire hazards. I argued about these until I succeeded in getting an ordinance requiring that second floor apartments must have two outlets to the outside. I failed to get a requirement of fire walls between rows of dwelling units, as in town houses or large apartment complexes . . . Also I failed to get an ordinance to require that mobile homes be tied down to give at least some protection in windstorms. Today you will notice most of our mobile home parks still have trailers propped up on blocks waiting for the first high wind to topple them over."[17]

By the time Lucile became a councilwoman, the old jail built by the WPA in 1936 had seen better days. Whether the newspaper agreed with her or not, the concerns she voiced in a council meeting were duly

reported in the local media, as when she pointed out the need to correct
the jail's unsanitary and crowded conditions and, further, that since city,
county, state, and federal prisoners were housed at the jail, none of those
governmental units should be "parties to operating a torture chamber."
Conditions at the jail, she said, "can cause great damage to the community
in disease, in the spread of crime . . . if something isn't done." She may have
been eloquent, but she was unsuccessful. The next Greene County Jail was
not built until 2001.[18]

HISTORIC SITES

As far as historic preservation was concerned, the results of her efforts
were much more positive. Early in her four-year term, Lucile attended
a National League of Cities meeting in San Diego. When the organizers
learned she was interested in local history, they called the head of the
San Diego historic sites board to meet with her. Serendipitously, the man
turned out to be a former Missourian. "I knew him quite well," Lucile
said. "He asked if I would like to see some of their local historic sites, and
asked if we had a Historical Sites Board in Springfield." When she said
"yes" to the tour but "no" regarding a historic sites board, he showed her
around and offered to send her a copy of San Diego's ordinance. Back
home, she sponsored a bill for a similar program in Springfield, and in
January 1970, the council voted in favor of creating a historic sites board
"to advise city agencies on preservation and restoration of sites, buildings,
and landmarks significant in Springfield history." The council appointed
nine board members and assigned Lucile to meet with them and "assist
in their organization."[19]

About a year after the board was created, Springfield had its first three
official historic sites: the 1875 Day House on South Avenue, which had
been built by brickmaker and former mayor George Sale Day; the Landers
Theater; and, ironically, given Lucile's opinion of the city's past jails, the
Old Calaboose. The twenty-six-by-twenty-six-foot Calaboose, which still
stands a couple of blocks southwest of Springfield's Park Central Square,
was one of the city's earliest jails and looks like a prop out of a western
movie. Built in the early 1890s, the foreboding little building with its heavy
dark bars across each window opening was described as a "sturdy structure of hand-pressed brick on a native stone foundation." It was named
to the National Registry of Historic Places in 1980 and became a police
museum that is regularly open to the public.[20]

Lucile's council term ended in 1971. After that, she joined the sites
board for real. One of her first projects was to develop a booklet showing a "City Center Historic Walk" of notable places in the vicinity of Park

Central Square. She continued her relationship with the University Club to have historic markers placed around the city, and in the mid-1970s, as the nation celebrated its two-hundredth birthday, she kicked off the first Bicentennial Historical Bus Tour, providing commentary to passengers in her role as "Springfield historian."

It's possible that serving on city council had opened her eyes—or at least made her more sympathetic—to privacy issues from the government side. It's also possible that she was simply more conservative than even she knew. She had never particularly been a "progressive," and eschewed the feminist movement (though she benefited from the movement's results), but she had always spoken up—or written about—things that didn't suit her, and just a few months after leaving city council, she took on a national issue. The foment of the 1960s and 1970s really did not sit well with Lucile. On June 13, 1971, when the *New York Times* published the first of seven articles on the Pentagon Papers, showing how the federal military had misled the American people about the Vietnam War, she wrote about her concerns to *Times* publisher Arthur Ochs Sulzberger Sr. In her "not for publication" letter she told Sulzberger that she was a longtime journalist and told him, "You are jeopardizing our country." Sulzberger actually wrote back, declaring, "While I obviously disagree with your point of view, I appreciate your having taken the time to write to me." She saved the letter.[21]

Also in 1971, following years of negotiations, the School of the Ozarks Press finally reprinted *Bald Knobbers*. When the new edition appeared, Lucile learned that the out-of-print Caxton Press edition had a become a collector's item, which the newspaper said could be priced "as high as thirty-five dollars."[22]

After Lucile's city council years, her friends at the newspaper began to retire. Betty Love retired in 1975, after becoming a nationally known photojournalist and a pioneer in color newspaper photography. She died in 1984. Ann Fair Dodson retired in 1979, then lived twenty-five years more, dying in 2004, the same year that John K. Hulston died, both of them at age eighty-nine. May Kennedy McCord, who had been in a nursing home several years, died in 1979, and Vance Randolph followed in 1980. Docia, long retired in the San Francisco area, held on almost as long as Lucile: she died in 1989. Lucile's brother George died in 1985, and Etna in 1988.

Lucile continued to produce her "Good Old Days" column for the Sunday newspaper until 1982, filling it with chatty news reports of early-days Springfield. To do that, she also continued her yearslong visits to Springfield's central library, which archived old issues of the newspaper. She had been a regular visitor for so long that everyone at the library knew her, but in those years, she wasn't just "the retired reporter doing research."

She became "the woman with the dog in her handbag." Lucile had always been fond of dogs, and when she was editor of "Over the Ozarks" she had printed her dog's picture at Christmastime to show readers. That dog, a long-lived miniature pinscher named Little Man, had stayed at home. About the time Lucile joined city council, Little Man passed on, and Etna gave her a new dog: a white toy poodle named Caesar. Cesar was a gentleman, and not a barker. What's more, he was just the size to fit comfortably in the large black purse Lucile carried over her arm to the library, along with pens, pencils, and notebooks. That made him a good library companion; while she read and took notes from old microfilm, the little poodle would settle down and snooze in his "cave" until she had gathered enough historic information for the next column and it was time to go home. In time, Caesar was followed by a black purse-poodle named Gigi, who was followed by a small rescue pooch named Inky. Unlike Caesar and Gigi, Inky did not go to the library.

Lucile loved doing the column, and over the years, she heard from generations of Ozarkers who said they learned their local history from "The Good Old Days." As she later told a television interviewer, she was glad that she could share her knowledge of Springfield history, but it wasn't just the facts of what had happened; she tried hard to put events in context. "I consciously have tried to use as many parallel events as I can in the column," she said. "It's amazing how many things that happened fifty years ago are happening in a different form right now. I enjoy doing that." Her city council experience had probably shown her how many citizen concerns recur over and over again, despite efforts to solve those problems.[23]

Sometimes peculiar things resurfaced in "The Good Old Days." In 1951, and again in 1960, the column news was about madstones, no doubt reflecting Lucile's memories of the days when her grandparents would be called out to minister with her family's madstone. In August 1951's "Good Old Days," the apocryphal Celia wrote to her aunt (in 1901) that it was the season for hydrophobia, and therefore there was a need for madstones. In her October 9, 1960 "Good Old Days" column, the news of 1910 concerned the brother of a Texas County politician who had been badly bitten by a pet cat and made his way to Springfield by horseback and rail to be treated with a madstone. Other times, the column simply described historic goings-on that were important to Lucile, such as the June 27, 1971, column, which lingered on news of seven new historic markers unveiled in 1921, commemorating, among others, Springfield's first store, first grist mill, and the site of Ozarks explorer Henry Schoolcraft's camp.

Once she finished writing the week's column, Lucile would take it to the newspaper office and personally hand a copy to cartoonist Bob Palmer to create an illustration, and then she would carry the original to the Sunday editor. One of the young editors who worked with Lucile and her column during those years was Mike O'Brien, later a city editor for the paper, and a journalism instructor at both Missouri State University and Drury College. "In the early 1970s, when I was Sunday editor," he remembered, "I had to deal with her over the 'Good Old Days.' She was *very unhappy* if so much as a syllable was changed in her copy! And *hellfire* rained down if an item had to be cut altogether! Lucile scared me," O'Brien continued, "but at the same time I was fascinated by her love of Ozarks history. Eventually she recognized that, and she helped me with research on a couple of stories. It remained an uneasy truce, however, as long as I was Sunday editor with responsibility for getting her column published exactly as she wrote it."[24]

CELEBRATING LUCILE

Besides being known for her newspaper work and as a champion of the Ozarks' past, Lucile became a bona fide local celebrity in the years following her retirement. A variety of civic groups and at least one history-focused organization made her an honorary lifelong member, and she was feted at several awards ceremonies. The newspaper reported on each of her awards and applauded the honors given to a member of the newspaper family. In late 1967, when she was named Springfield Woman of Achievement by the Women's Division of the Chamber of Commerce, the newspaper proudly reported: "Woman of the Year: Our 'Celia' " and described her as a "teacher, newspaper reporter and columnist, wife and mother, author, historian, lecturer, and member of City Council." The surprise announcement came at a banquet at the local Lamplighter motel ballroom. Lucile had rushed out of a council meeting to get to the annual civic dinner, and when the master of ceremonies began his windup to reveal that year's honoree, Lucile later told friends: "I knew it was me when they started talking about Wilson's Creek."[25]

Around that time, she received another sort of honor from a totally different direction. *Bald Knobbers* was turned into an opera. Written by longtime New York radio organist and Springfield native, Bert Buhrman, the "folk opera" premiered at the School of the Ozarks and was performed several times in 1968 in Springfield and elsewhere in Missouri—but never made it to New York.[26]

That same year, she was honored at a dinner sponsored by the community Business and Professional Women's Club. Her after-dinner speech, like many she would give during those years, was about opportunities for women. Since she had not been a suffragist and had not been an equal rights activist—although she had promoted both through her writing—

her attitude and her advice were that women should—and could—make their own success. "In my personal opinion, no woman of any age can lack the opportunity of accomplishing a good life for herself today," she told the group, and pointed to Betty Love and Ann Fair Dodson at the newspaper, as well as to a number of successful Springfield women, including a US Commissioner, the Drury adult education director, the chair of the Springfield Park Board, and the county welfare director. The city's first businesswoman, she noted, was Postmaster Permilla Stephens, who was appointed to that position in 1867. Independent sort that she was, Lucile concluded, "It's doubtful that equal opportunity laws for women help very much. It depends on the woman and what she wants to make of herself."[27]

Another time when she was talking to a group of women she told them that "the fact that I am a woman has not been detrimental to my doing what I wanted to do if I had the talent and energy to do it," and that "only once was I certain I was discriminated on salary because I was a woman. That was when the Depression hit and we all received pay cuts. Mine was $2.50, more than an unmarried man doing the same type of work I was doing. I was furious, and when I protested, the publisher explained that it took more for a man to live because he had to pay for dates. It happened that this man and I each maintained an apartment. We each had a small, inexpensive car. We often ate together at the same restaurant and each paid his own bill. I still resent that, but it did not drive me to the Woman's Lib."[28]

In 1978, the Museum of the Ozarks (today's History Museum on the Square in Springfield) conferred its Heritage Award on Lucile for outstanding contributions "to the study of Ozarks History." *News-Leader* executive editor Dale Freeman, who presented the award, said he was "completely biased and totally prejudiced" in giving the award to Lucile, noting she had spent "many years as a valuable and lovable employee of Springfield Newspapers." He called her a "walking encyclopedia of Ozarks history." About four hundred people were at that banquet, and they gave her a standing ovation when she told them, "It is a privilege to live in the Ozarks, where one can have such wonderful friends."[29]

In 1980, the School of the Ozarks at Point Lookout named her to its Ozarks Hall of Fame along with retired Congressman Durward G. Hall. Many friends, former colleagues, and her whole family—except George, who was sick—came from across the state to attend the event. Freeman, by this time also retired from Springfield Newspapers and teaching at what is now Missouri State University, was again on hand to introduce her. He told the attending crowd, "She holds great love for her heritage and has engaged in a lifelong love affair with her native Ozarks." He added, "She has served her land and her people well."[30]

Lucile receives the 1978 Ozarks Heritage Award from Springfield Newspapers managing editor Dale Freeman. © *Springfield News-Leader—USA TODAY NETWORK.*

Lucile stopped writing "The Good Old Days" in 1982, but she did not stop writing for the newspaper. In 1983, for the county's sesquicentennial celebration, she put together a chronology of Greene County historical events that the newspaper turned into a special section. That same year, the Greene County Court named her Official Historian of Greene County, and in 1988, in recognition of her upcoming ninetieth birthday, her friends funded a scholarship in her name for history students at Evangel University.[31]

IN APPRECIATION

Lucile relished the public recognition that came her way, but what she really treasured was the love and appreciation of her friends and her long-time fans, as well as the many letters from her column faithfuls—both writers and readers—like the June 1987 letter to the editor of the *News-Leader* from a "Miz Parsons" that said, "I keep watching . . . for a return of the longtime favorite *'Over the Ozarks'* column. I know it will be hard to find a really good person like Lucile Morris Upton who used to encourage the old writers . . ." There were dear letters from her far-flung friends like Docia, in San Francisco, and Goldie Smith in Tulsa who wrote, "Your friendship is one of the most treasured things that ever happened to me."[32]

By this time, Lucile's life had narrowed considerably. She rarely went out, hired a woman to fix her breakfast every morning, and welcomed Meals on Wheels volunteers who brought her dinners. She continued to read, but she needed a handheld magnifying glass to see the words of books and magazines. People dropped in regularly, from family members, to old newspaper friends, to others curious to learn what she knew.

During this period, she began to plan for the future. In a letter to George's son, Allan, she gave instructions for the funeral director (Ralph Thieme) and her funeral service (at Springfield's First Congregational Church). Obituary material, she told him, would be available in *Who's Who of the Midwest*, *Who's Who among American Women*, or *Foremost Women in Communication*, but, she wrote, "They have all about me at the office"—"the office," of course, being Springfield Newspapers. Further, she instructed Allan, "I want to be buried in the Dadeville lot of the Masonic Cemetery next to my grandparents," and "if anyone wants to know why I'm not to be buried beside Gene, the Upton lot in Bolivar is full." In other words, she preferred to finish up where she had begun: in Dadeville with her family.[33]

She had a bad fall in 1988, and her family moved her into a nursing home. After that, her friends began remembering her to the world. Ella Mae Tucker, who wrote cookbooks and an "Out Our Way" column for the *News and Leader*, told readers about "the first attempt I ever made of getting something I wrote published. It was a poem about strawberries, and was published in Lucile Morris Upton's column 'Over the Ozarks' . . . I kept that paper for ages, and each time I ran into it, I popped my buttons, I was that proud."[34]

O'Brien remembered Lucile to the newspaper reading public in a 1989 column: "Lucile Morris Upton, like Betty Love, strode boldly into male-dominated newsrooms and survived and thrived . . . However, she is unique as . . . a chronicler of the settlement and development of Springfield and much of the Ozarks. Frail with her ninety years, Lucile resides at Primrose Place [the nursing home]. After a recent visit, I called a friend who shares my admiration for her. 'I know of no writer who has contributed more to the future generations of Springfieldians than Lucile,' he said. 'Long after the rest of us are forgotten, they'll be reading Lucile's articles and books to find out how things *really* came to pass around her in the 19th and 20th centuries.' "[35]

Perhaps most telling of all was a letter she had received in 1984 from water pollution expert Ralph Fuhrman in Washington, DC. A native of

Kansas City, Furhman had lived in Springfield during the 1930s, then moved to DC for the rest of his busy and productive life. He began his letter by writing, "I almost addressed you as 'dear Celia' as my acquaintance with you and your fine work goes back to when your nom-de-plume was Celia Ray." Furhman, like so many people across the Ozarks, had been reading her words and learning about Ozarks history for more than fifty years.[36]

As Lucile herself had said back in 1935, "There is a lot of satisfaction, it seems to me, to be gleaned from delving into the history of our Ozarks. It is filled with romance and color, progress, and adventure. I wish that much more of it had been written in the past and were being intelligently preserved at this time."[37]

Lucile certainly did her part.

And the Morris madstone? Following Lucile's death, her family donated it to the Ralph Foster Museum at the newly named College of the Ozarks.

ABBREVIATIONS

LMU—Lucile Morris Upton

SHSMO—State Historical Society of Missouri

SGCLC—Springfield-Greene County Local History Department, Springfield, Missouri

LMU-SHSMO—Lucile Morris Upton Papers (C3869), State Historical Society of Missouri

LMU-SGCLC—Lucile Morris Upton Collection, Local History Department, Springfield-
   Greene County Library Center, Springfield, Missouri

Morris Family Photos—part of Lucile Morris Upton Collection, Local History Department,
   Springfield-Greene County Library, Center, Springfield, Missouri

Upton Collection—Lucile Morris Upton Collection, Wilson's Creek National Battlefield

AUTHOR NOTE

In the century that has passed since Lucile Morris joined the staff of the *Denver Express*, new technology has been developed, new information has become available, and historians have acquired new perspectives on historical events. While Lucile's work was deemed accurate at the time, and even today researchers respect her careful attention to detail, her writings about the Bald Knobbers, Young Brothers Massacre, Nathan Boone, and the Battle of Wilson's Creek have been augmented considerably by the work of those who came later.

For further reading, the following is recommended:

BALD KNOBBERS

Hernando, Matthew J. *Faces Like Devils: The Bald Knobber Vigilantes in the Ozarks*. Columbia: University of Missouri Press, 2015.

YOUNG BROTHERS MASSACRE

Barrett, Paul W. and Mary H. Barrett. *Young Brothers Massacre*. Columbia: University of Missouri Press, 1988.

NATHAN BOONE

Hurt, R. Douglas. *Nathan Boone and the American Frontier*. Columbia: University of Missouri Press, 2000.

BATTLE OF WILSON'S CREEK

Phillips, Christopher. *Damned Yankee: The Life of General Nathaniel Lyon*. Columbia: University of Missouri Press, 1990, reissued by Louisiana State University Press, 1996.

Piston, Garrett and Richard W. Hatcher III. *Wilson's Creek: The Second Battle of the Civil War and the Men who Fought It*. Chapel Hill: University of North Carolina Press, 2000.

NOTES

INTRODUCTION

1. Carrie Buchanan, "Sense of Place in the Daily Newspaper," *Aether: The Journal of Media Geography* (Spring, 2009): 62–83, accessed November 27, 2020, https://www .academia.edu/download/58570988/aether_volume_04.pdf#page=68; Karin Wahl-Jorgensen, "News Production, Ethnography, and Power on the Challenges of Newsroom-Centricity," in S. E. Bird ed., *The Anthropology of News and Journalism* (Bloomington, Indiana: Indiana University Press, 2009): 21–35; Douglas A. McIntyre, "Over 2000 American Newspapers Have Closed in Past 15 Years," *24/7 WALL ST*, January 6, 2020, accessed November 25, 2020, https://247wallst.com/media/2019 /07/23/over-2000-american-newspapers-have-closed-in-past-15-years/; Mason Walker, "U.S. Newsroom Employment Has Fallen 26% since 2008," Pew Research Center, July 13, 2021, accessed September 3, 2021, https://www.pewresearch.org /fact-tank/2021/07/13/u-s-newsroom-employment-has-fallen-26-since-2008/; "The Status of Women in the U.S. Media 2019," Women's Media Center, accessed November 25, 2020, https://womensmediacenter.com/reports/the-status-of-women-in-u-s -media-2019; Steve Pokin, Columnist, Springfield Newspapers, Inc., to author, email, November 26, 2020.
2. George Wharton James, *New Mexico, the Land of the Delight Makers* (Boston: Page Company, 1920), 4.
3. Buchanan, "Sense of Place in the Daily Newspaper."

CHAPTER 1

1. Lucile Morris Upton, interview by Carolyn Gerdes, *Spotlight on Women*, KOZK-TV, Springfield, Missouri, March, 1978, Lucile Morris Upton Papers (C3869), State Historical Society of Missouri. (In future references, her historical society papers will appear as LMU-SHSMO.)
2. John K. Hulston to author, interview in his office, Springfield, Missouri, April 11, 1995.
3. LMU, "Madstone," *Three Morris Young-Uns*, compiled by Pam Morris Jones into a spiral-bound booklet (pages not numbered), July 1990, Lucile Morris Upton Collection, Local History Collection, Springfield-Greene County Library Center (hereafter LMU-SGCLC); Diane Wendt, "Surviving Rabies 100 Years Ago," in *O Say Can You See? Stories from the Museum*, National Museum of American History, October 28, 1913, accessed March 18, 2020, https://americanhistory.si.edu/blog/2013 /10/surviving-rabies-100-years-ago.html. Louis Pasteur had developed a treatment for hydrophobia in 1885, but it didn't become available in the US until 1911, when a Philadelphia drug company (H. K. Mulford) developed a treatment kit that could be shipped directly to doctors.

4. For these "cures" and more, see Vance Randolph, *Ozark Superstitions* (New York: Columbia University Press,1947). After Ella was old, she let some people take the madstone home without her attendance. Once, when she loaned it out, it was returned weeks later and had been broken. It was tied together with sewing thread. She looked it over, then turned to Lucile, and said, " 'Huh! I think it's about as good as it ever was.' That's what she said after she'd worked with it all these years . . ." LMU to author, interview, circa 1980.

5. LMU, "The Ozarks Wastebasket," *Springfield Daily News*, May 30,1952, 10; LMU, "Three Morris Young 'Uns," *Three Morris Young-Uns*, LMU-SGCLC. Dadeville had originally been named Melville but the name was changed in 1858.

6. LMU, *Spotlight on Women.*

7. LMU, *Spotlight on Women*; Pam Morris Jones (great-niece to LMU) to author, interview, March 16, 2020.

8. LMU, "The Blue and the Gray," *Three Morris Young-Uns*, LMU-SGCLC.

9. LMU, "The Blue and the Gray," *Three Morris Young-Uns*; "15th Regiment, Missouri Cavalry," Union Missouri Volunteers, Battle Unit Details, Civil War, National Park Service, accessed November 9, 2020, https://www.nps.gov/civilwar/search-battle -units-detail.htm?battleUnitCode=UMO0015RC.

10. Lucile Morris, "Collecting Ozarks History," speech to Greene County Historical Society, January 16, 1936, Box 5, LMU-SGCLC.

11. LMU, "The Blue and the Gray," *Three Morris Young-Uns.*

12. LMU, "Morris," *Three Morris Young-Uns.*

13. *Dade County Advocate*, July 28, 1898, 5.

14. LMU, "The Blue and the Gray," *Three Morris Young-Uns*; John K. Hulston to author, interview, April 11, 1995; LMU, *Spotlight on Women.*

15. For more about the St. Louis World's Fair, see Elana V. Fox, *Inside the World's Fair of 1904*, 2 vols. (First Book Library, 2003).

16. LMU, "Metro Club Speech," April 6, 1935, LMU-SGCLC.

17. LMU, "Three Morris Young-Uns," *Three Morris Young-Uns*; "Greenfield Schools, High School," *Greenfield Vidette*, November 26, 1914, 1.

18. Emily Newell Blair, *Bridging Two Eras, The Autobiography of Emily Newell Blair, 1877–1951*, Virginia Jeans Laas, ed. (Columbia: University of Missouri Press, 1999); Carol Driscoll, "Emily Newell Blair, Missouri's Suffragette," *Missouri Life Magazine*, July 19, 2020; LMU, "What Each One's Life Work Was," My Golden School Days Scrapbook, LMU-SGCLC.

19. "History of Hollister," City of Hollister, Missouri (website), accessed June 13, 2020, http://cityofhollister.com/visitors/history_of_hollister /index.php.

20. LMU, "Metro Club Speech."

21. LMU, "Metro Club Speech."

22. Stephen L. McIntyre, "The Age of Industry, 1870–1945, Introduction," Stephen L. McIntyre, ed., *Springfield's Urban Histories: Essays on the Queen City of the Missouri*

Ozarks (Springfield: Moon City Press, 2012), 81–85; Angela Wingo Miller, "Retail Rivals: Springfield's Commercial Street versus the Public Square, 1870–1945," in *Springfield's Urban Histories*, ed. Stephen L. McIntyre, 99–101. By 1920, Springfield had more than five thousand union members among its population of nearly forty thousand.

23. Lewis E. Meador Papers, 1904–1982 (R0674) SHSMO; John K. Hulston, *Lester E. Cox 1895–1968: He Found Needs and Filled Them* (Cassville, Missouri: Litho Printers, 1992).

24. "Albert G. Morris (Deceased)," *History of Dade County and Her People, Vol. II* (Greenfield, Missouri: Pioneer Historical Company, 1917), 198.

CHAPTER 2

1. "Otterville Mail," *Sedalia Weekly Democrat*, July 14, 1895, 6.

2. Homer Garland, letter to Lucile Morris, May 4, 1917, from Otterville, Missouri, Folder 415, LMU-SHSMO.

3. Homer Garland, letter to Lucile Morris, September 14, 1917, Folder 415, LMU-SHSMO.

4. Homer Garland, letter to Lucile Morris, n.d., Folder 415, LMU-SHSMO; "Do You Know," *Parsons Daily Sun*, December 1, 1917, 4. Lucile pasted the short notice in her School Memories Scrapbook, along with a note: "Drove to Parsons, Kansas. Ruth K, George K, Etna and myself. Thanksgiving holidays 1917."

5. "Uncle George Stories," *Family History*, Sarah Morris Riddick interview with George Morris, CD, LMU-SGCLC.

6. "A Tragedy Interrupts Moving Picture Show," *Greenfield Vedette*, May 31, 1917, 1; Homer Garland, letter to Lucile Morris, May 29, 1917, Folder 415, LMU-SHSMO.

7. "A Tragedy Interrupts Moving Picture Show"; "Jury Acquits Dunaway of Ches Pyle Killing," *Greenfield Vedette*, November 29, 1917, 1; "Brief Term of Circuit Court," *Dade County Advocate*, November 29, 1917, 1.

8. Betty Houchin Winfield, ed., *Journalism 1908: Birth of a Profession* (Columbia: University of Missouri Press, 2008), 3. For more about Arthur Aull, see Chad Stebbins, *All the News Is Fit to Print: Profile of a Country Editor* (Columbia: University of Missouri Press, 1998). Lamar was also the hometown of US president Harry Truman.

9. Homer Garland, letter to Lucile Morris, August (n.d.), 1917, Folder 415, LMU-SHSMO; "Dadeville," Greenfield Vedette, March 14, 1918, 4.

10. "Food Administration Issues New Rulings," *Greenfield Vedette*, March 14, 1918, 1.

11. Mike O'Brien, "COVID-19 Reminds of 1918 Spanish Flu Pandemic," *Ozarks Alive!*, March 31, 2020, accessed November 3, 2021, https://www.ozarksalive.com/stories /covid-19-reminds-of-1918-spanish-flu-pandemic?rq=Mike%20O%27Brien; Helen and Townsend Godsey, *Flight of the Phoenix, a Biography of the School of the Ozarks . . . a Unique American College* (Point Lookout: School of the Ozarks, 1984), 228.

12. Homer Garland, letter to Lucile Morris, n.d., Folder 418, LMU-SHSMO.

13. Newspaper clipping, n.d., in Lucile Morris, School Memories Scrapbook, LMU-SGCLC.

14. Bob Stewart, letter to Lucile Morris, August 6, 1922, Folder 420, LMU-SHSMO; "Jack Hull Colorful Clovis pioneer," *Eastern New Mexico News*, February 14, 2009, accessed March 13, 2021, https://www.easternnewmexiconews.com/story/2009/02/14/publish faith-and-lifestyles/jack-hull-colorful-clovis-pioneer/16165.html; J. R. Hull return address torn from an envelope in Lucile Morris scrapbook, LMU-SGCLC.

15. Homer Garland, letter to Lucile Morris, June 21, 1919, Folder 419, LMU-SHSMO.

16. Homer Garland, letter to Lucile Morris, August 11, 1918, Folder 418, LMU-SHSMO; Homer Garland, letter to Lucile Morris, June 2, 1920, Folder 419, LMU-SHSMO.

17. "Hollister, Missouri Cabins Have Unique Names," clipping pasted in LMU, School Memories Scrapbook, with a handwritten note: "*Kansas City Post*, Sunday July 10, 1921, $1," LMU-SGCLC.

18. "Class of 1915," *Greenfield Vedette*, May 13, 1920, 6.

19. James, *New Mexico, the Land of the Delight Makers*, 4.

20. Pam Morris Jones to author, interview, May 19, 2020; Joseph Miller and Henry G. Alsberg, eds., *New Mexico: A Guide to the Colorful State* (New York: Hastings House, 1953), 347; Warren A. Beck, *New Mexico: A History of Four Centuries* (Norman: University of Oklahoma Press, 1962), 291.

21. Elvis E. Fleming, *Captain Joseph C. Lea, from Confederate Guerilla to New Mexico Patriarch* (Las Cruces: Yucca Tree Press, 2002); "Captain Joseph C. Lea, the Father of Roswell," *Padgett.blogspot.com*, accessed March 25, 2021, http://padgitt.blogspot .com/2012/11/captain-joseph-c-lea-father-of-roswell.html; New Mexico Military Institute, https://www.nmmi.edu. Alumni of the New Mexico Military Institute include hotelier Conrad Hilton, football star Roger Staubach, writer Paul Horgan, and others.

22. Lucile Morris, "Christmas 1922 when I was in Roswell. Spent in El Paso with Dorothy Turner," Folder 423, LMU-SHSMO.

23. Betty Houchin Winfield, *Journalism 1908, Birth of a Profession* (Columbia: University of Missouri Press, 2008), 87.

24. Alice Fahs, *Out on Assignment: Newspaper Women and the Making of Modern Public Space* (Chapel Hill: University of North Carolina Press, 2011), 3, 83.

25. Jean Marie Lutes, *Front-Page Girls, Women Journalists in American Culture and Fiction, 1880–1930* (Ithaca: Cornell University Press, 2006), 9; George Garrigues, *Marguerite Martyn, America's Forgotten Journalist* (Morro Bay, California: City Desk Publishing, 2019).

26. The Atlantic and Pacific Railroad was a predecessor to the Missouri Pacific, among others, and was incorporated by US Congress in 1866 as a transcontinental railroad connecting Springfield, Missouri, and Van Buren, Arkansas, with California. The central portion was never constructed, and the two halves later became parts of the St. Louis–San Francisco Railway (Frisco) and Atchison, Topeka and Santa Fe Railway systems, now both merged into the BNSF Railway. Donald A. Ritchie, *Reporting from Washington: The History of the Washington Press Corps* (New York: Oxford University Press, 2005), 161.

27. LMU, "Speech to Business Club," Box 5, LMU-SGCLC.

CHAPTER 3

1. Lucile Morris, letter to Veda Morris, June 1923, Folder 422, LMU-SHSMO.

2. Phil Goodstein, *In the Shadow of the Klan: When the KKK Ruled Denver, 1920–1926* (Denver: New Social Publications, 2006), 80–81.

3. Sherilyn Cox Bennion, *Equal to the Occasion, Women Editors of the Nineteenth-Century West* (Reno: University of Nevada Press, 1990), 10–11.

4. Bennion, *Equal to the Occasion,* 84–92.

5. "Helen Ring Robinson," *Colorado Encyclopedia* (website), accessed April 4, 2020, https://coloradoencyclopedia.org/article/helen-ring-robinson.

6. Dolores Plested, "Minnie Reynolds: A Nineteenth Century Woman of Today," *Colorado Encyclopedia* (website), adapted from *Colorado Heritage Magazine* 4, no. 1 (1984), accessed April 29, 2020, https://coloradoencyclopedia.org/article/minnie-reynolds -scalabrino.

7. Lutes, *Front-Page Girls,* 65–93.

8. LMU, "Speech to Reed Junior High School Girls," April 30, 1938, Box 5, LMU-SGCLC.

9. LMU, "Speech to Business Club."

10. Following the church service, and a speech that evening, Harding continued west and became the first president to visit Alaska. After he returned to California, he died in San Francisco on August 3, 1923.

11. Lucille Morris, "President and Wife Attend Services at First Baptist Church," *Denver Express,* June 25, 1923, Scrapbook Series, Volume 1, LMU-SHSMO.

12. LMU, "Women in Journalism," speech to Saturday Club, September 28, 1940, Folder 550, LMU-SHSMO.

13. Lucile Morris, letter to Veda Morris, 1923, Folder 422, LMU-SHSMO.

14. Commentary and quotes about Lucile's newspaper career in Denver in this chapter come from undated clippings in her scrapbooks, which are on microfilm, vols. 1–3, LMU-SHSMO.

15. LMU, "Speech to Business Club."

16. Cynthia Grey columns, *Denver Express,* 1923–1924, undated clippings, vols. 1–3, LMU-SHSMO.

17. LMU, "Speech to Teachers Sorority [Alpha Delta Kappa]," April 10, 1973, Folder 550, LMU-SHSMO.

18. Wilda M. Smith and Eleanor A. Bogart, introduction to *The Wars of Peggy Hull: The Life and Times of a War Correspondent* (El Paso: Texas Western Press, 1991).

19. Cynthia Grey columns, vols. 1–3, LMU-SHSMO; LMU, "Speech to Teachers Sorority."

20. The Equal Rights Amendment seeks to guarantee equality under the law regardless of sex. It was introduced into Congress in 1923 in the wake of the Nineteenth Amendment, but despite deadline extensions, as of 2023 it had not been ratified by enough states to become part of the US Constitution. ("*Section 1. Equality of rights under the law shall not be denied or abridged by the United States or by any State on*

account of sex. Section 2. The Congress shall have the power to enforce, by appropriate legislation, the provisions of this article. Section 3. This amendment shall take effect two years after the date of ratification.")

21. Lucile Morris, Scrapbooks, 1923–1924, vols. 1–3, LMU-SGCLC.

22. LMU, "Speech to Business Club."

23. LMU, "Speech to Business Club."

24. Grace Long, "The Anglo-American Occupation of the El Paso District" (master's thesis, University of Texas at Austin, 1931), 39, UT Electronic Theses and Dissertations, accessed May 16, 2020, https://repositories.lib.utexas.edu/handle/2152/73742.

25. Owen P. White, *The Autobiography of a Durable Sinner* (New York: G. P. Putnam's Sons, 1942), 59–60; Garna L. Christian, "Always in His Heart: Owen Payne White and Old El Paso," *Southwestern Historical Quarterly* 112, no. 2 (2008): 172–90, accessed May 17, 2020, www.jstor.org/stable/30239622.

26. "History," *The Woman's Club of El Paso*, Woman's Club of El Paso records, 1857, 1895–2016, MS 576, C. L. Sonnichsen Special Collections Department, University of Texas at El Paso Library, accessed May 17, 2020, https://www.utep.edu/library/_Files/docs/special-collections/finding-aids/MS576_womens.pdf.

27. LMU, Speeches, Box 5, LMU-SGCLC.

28. Smith and Bogart, *The Wars of Peggy Hull*, 70–131.

29. LMU, "Speech to Business Club."

30. LMU, "Speech to Reed Junior High School Girls"; "Evelyn S. Stewart, Free Press Reporter," *Detroit Free Press*, March 29, 1978, 12.

31. Kenneth Stewart, *News Is What We Make It, a Running Story of the Working Press* (Boston: Houghton Mifflin Company, 1943), 29.

32. Stewart, *News Is What We Make It*, 114.

33. LMU "Speech to Businesswomen," Box 5, LMU-SGCLC.

34. Lucile Morris, "El Pasoans Soon Will See 'Leviathian of the Air,' Giant US Fighting Ship," *El Paso Times*, October 5, 1924, 40.

35. LMU, "Possibilities in Business are Unlimited for American Girls, Says Clara Hawkins," *El Paso Times*, March 5, 1925, 7.

CHAPTER 4

1. Brooks Blevins, *A History of the Ozarks, Volume 1: The Old Ozarks* (Urbana: University of Illinois Press, 2018), 2.

2. According to noted Ozarks geographer Milton Rafferty, the Ozarks has several important cultural traits:

   1. Rural.

   2. Heritage springs from the Upper South Hill Country—semi-arrested frontier.

   3. An uncommon sense of place: "This consciousness of place and the liking for naming things is a primitive trait. There are no names without people, and with people there are names. High density of place names seems to coincide most often with a cultural background in agriculture."

4. Relative stability of the social system compared with the fluidity of social relations typical of the rest of the US.

Milton D. Rafferty, *The Ozarks: Land and Life* (Fayetteville: University of Arkansas Press, 2001), 2–6.

3. LMU, "Metro Club Speech."

4. LMU, *Spotlight on Women*; Paul Green, Editor Mail Edition, *St. Louis Post-Dispatch*, to Lucile Morris in Everton, Missouri, October 16, 1925, Folder 27, LMU-SHSMO.

5. "Monument to Characters in 'Shepherd of Hills,' " special to the *St. Louis Post-Dispatch*, October 5, 1925, 17.

6. "Uncle Ike's Job Is Taken," *Kansas City Times*, October 22, 1925, 15.

7. Brooks Blevins, "Region, Religion, and Competing Visions of Mountain Mission Education in the Ozarks," *Journal of Southern History*, 82, no. 1 (February 2016): 78–79.

8. "Woman Has Driven Autos for Hire for Seven Years," *St. Louis Post-Dispatch*, n.d. 1925, Scrapbook Series, vol. 6, LMU-SHSMO; Lynn Morrow and Linda Myers-Phinney, *Shepherd of the Hills Country, Tourism Transforms the Ozarks, 1880s–1930s* (Fayetteville: The University of Arkansas Press, 1999), 212.

9. Alden Evans, City Editor, *El Paso Times*, to LMU, July 25, 1925, Folder 427, LMU-SHSMO; Josh Wilson, *Denver Express*, to LMU, n.d., 1925, Folder 427, LMU-SHSMO; LMU, Speech, Box 5, LMU-SGCLC.

10. Kathleen A. Cairns, *Front Page Woman Journalists, 1920–1950* (Lincoln: University of Nebraska Press, 2003), 20.

11. Edna Ferber, quoted in Fahs, *Out on Assignment*, 9.

12. Louise Kiernan, "Murder She Wrote," *Chicago Tribune*, July 16, 1997, 51. *Chicago* was made into another movie in the 1940s starring Ginger Rogers. In the 1990s, it was revived on Broadway and also made into an Oscar-winning film.

13. F. A. Behymer, "Sister Act on a Missouri Newspaper," *St. Louis Post-Dispatch*, June 26, 1942, 29.

14. "Maud Duncan's Linotype Machine," *OzarksWatch Magazine*, Spring/Summer 2020, 48.

15. Margaret H. Welch, "Is Newspaper Work Healthful for Women?," *Journal of Social Science* (November 1894): 113. Quoted in Fahs, *Out on Assignment*, 7.

16. Mike Sears, "She's Seen Library Crowd Aging Quarters," *Springfield Daily News*, December 2, 1970, 28.

17. Lucile Morris, "Leader Girl Reporter at Fast, Bumpy Ride with Tour," *Leader*, October 16, 1929, 1. Wiley Post also helped develop pressure suits and discovered the jet stream. He died in an airplane crash with his passenger and good friend Will Rogers in Point Barrow, Alaska, in 1935.

18. LMU, *Spotlight on Women*. Harry Jewell got back into the newspaper business in March 1929 when he started the *Springfield Press*. The *Press* merged with the other Bixby newspapers during the Great Depression.

19. Morrow and Myers-Phinney, *Shepherd of the Hills Country*, 181; Susan Croce Kelly, *Father of Route 66: the Story of Cy Avery* (Norman: University of Oklahoma Press, 2014). While cities in those days generally had at least some kinds of pavement, cross-country

highways were mostly dirt or gravel. In 1909, Wayne County, Michigan, paved a test strip of concrete highway that attracted visits from state highway officials from across the country. After that, paving was possible but had to wait for federal laws in 1916 and 1921 to provide matching funds to get the job done.

20. Morrow and Myers-Phinney, *Shepherd of the Hills Country*, 37–59.

21. Helen Laverty, "Eerie Majesty in Vivid Scene Deep in Cave," *Leader*, July 19, 1929, 1; Dewey Short was widely known for his pithy opinions of Congress, the liberal court, and FDR, one of the most famous being:

> I deeply and sincerely regret that this body has degenerated into a supine, subservient, soporific, superfluous, supercilious, pusillanimous body of nitwits, the greatest ever gathered beneath the dome of our National Capitol, who cowardly abdicate their powers and, in violation of their oaths to protect and defend the Constitution against all of the Nation's enemies, both foreign and domestic, turn over these constitutional prerogatives, not only granted but imposed upon them, to a group of tax-eating, conceited autocratic bureaucrats a bunch of theoretical, intellectual, professorial nincompoops out of Columbia University, at the other end of Pennsylvania Avenue who were never elected by the American people to any office and who are responsible to no constituency. These brain trusters and 'new dealers' are the ones who wrote this resolution, instead of the Members of this House whose duty it is, and whose sole duty it is, to draft legislation.
>
> —Delivered in the US House of Representatives on January 23, 1935.

22. Brooks Blevins to author, note, September 1, 2021.

23. Robert Cochran, *Vance Randolph: An Ozark Life* (Urbana: University of Illinois Press, 1985). Randolph wrote Little Blue Books and other work for E. Haldeman-Julius in Girard, Kansas, the first mass-market paperback enterprise in the United States.

24. Mike O'Brien, "Ted Richmond and the Wilderness Library," *OzarksWatch Magazine*, Fall 2020, 48–51. After Rayburn stopped publishing *Ozark Life* in the early 1930s, Richmond found his way to the Buffalo River Country in Arkansas, where he built up a local free lending library for the area residents.

25. Susan Croce Kelly, "May Kennedy McCord, Hillbilly Sweetheart," *OzarksWatch Magazine*, Spring/Summer 2020, 14–17. See also *Queen of the Hillbillies, Writings of May Kennedy McCord*, edited by Patti McCord and Kristine Sutliff (Fayetteville: University of Arkansas Press, April 2022).

26. "Beth Campbell Assigned by AP to Join Mrs. FDR," *Springfield Daily News*, December 24, 1936, 2; LMU, "Women in Journalism." Harry Jewell started the *Springfield Press* newspaper in 1929 and in 1933 merged with the Bixby newspapers to become president of Springfield Newspapers, Inc. At that time the evening paper became the *Leader and Press*. The *Daily News* remained the morning paper and the Sunday paper was the *Sunday News and Leader*. From "Springfield Newspapers: 150 Years of History," *News-Leader*, January 7, 2017, J2; Obituaries: Fern Elaine Nance Shumate, *News-Leader*, February 16, 2003, 21.

27. Ellen Gray Massey, *A Candle Within Her Soul, Mary Elizabeth Mahnkey and her Ozarks, 1877–1948* (Lebanon, Missouri: Bittersweet, Inc., 1996).

28. Rose Wilder Lane, letter to LMU, Rocky Ridge Farm, Mansfield, Missouri, March 15, 1935, Folder 430, LMU-SHSMO.

29. Caroline Fraser, *Prairie Fires* (New York: Metropolitan Books, 2017), especially 328–52.

30. Dale Freeman to author, interview, August 10, 2017.

31. Lucile Morris, "Collecting Ozarks History."

32. LMU, *Bald Knobbers* (Caldwell, Idaho: Caxton Press, 1939); Lucile Morris, "Collecting Ozarks History."

33. LMU to Marilyn Prosser, interview, November 1982.

34. LMU to Marilyn Prosser, interview.

35. "You and Your Newspaper, Day to Day with the Editor," *Leader*, May 12, 1930, 4, accessed February 6, 2021, https://www.newspapers.com/image/40058867/ ?terms=%22Lucile%20Morris%27%20story%20of%20the%20end%20of%20 the%20Bald%20Knobbers%22&match=1. Three-quarters of a century after Lucile's book, Matthew J. Hernando's *Faces Like Devils, The Bald Knobber Vigilantes in the Ozarks* (Columbia: University of Missouri Press, 2015) became the scholarly standard on the subject.

36. "The Story of a Neglected Hero," advertisement in *Leader*, August 29, 1931, 7.

37. LMU, "The Story of a Neglected Hero: Nathan Boone," *Leader*, August 29, 1931, 7; *Leader*, August 30, 1931, 13; *Leader*, September 1, 1931, 1; *Leader*, September 2, 1931, 4; *Leader*, September 3, 1931, 3; *Leader*, September 1, 1931, 1; *Leader*, September 4, 1931, 28; Albert G. Brackett, *History of the United States Cavalry, from the Formation of the Federal Government to the First of June 1863* (New York: Harper and Brothers, 1865), 130; Lucile Morris Upton and John K. Hulston, *Nathan Boone, the Neglected Hero, From Writings by Lucile Morris Upton and John K. Hulston*, ed. Carole Bills (Republic, Missouri: Western Printing Company, 1984), 58.

38. Lucile Morris, "The Very Idea," *Leader*, April 15, 1932, 16.

39. LMU and Hulston, *Nathan Boone*, 72.

CHAPTER 5

1. "Our History," Branson.com, accessed May 28, 2020, https://www.branson.com /branson/shepherd/history.htm; Morrow and Myers-Phinney, *Shepherd of the Hills Country*, 205. After McDaniel's death in the 1940s, Dr. Bruce and Mary Trimble acquired the property and turned it into the Shepherd of the Hills Farm and Old Mill Theatre, a central attraction in the Branson area.

2. Lucile Morris, "Collecting Ozarks History."

3. LMU, "Collecting Ozarks History."

4. Brooks Blevins, *Hill Folks* (Urbana: University of Illinois Press, 2002), 128; B. Z. Goldberg, "World Today, Haven for Restless," *Brooklyn Daily Eagle*, March 26, 1932, 3.

5. W. Johnson, letter, in "Hillbilly Heartbeats," *Sunday News and Leader*, December 18, 1932, 19.

6. Walter O. Cralle, "Social Change and Isolation in the Ozark Mountain Region of Missouri," *American Journal of Sociology* 41, no. 4 (January 1936); James West (Carl Withers), *Plainville U.S.A.* (New York: Columbia University Press, 1945), book review in *American Journal of Sociology* 51, no. 2 (September 1945); Joseph Jablow, "Carl Withers (James West) 1900–1970," Obituaries, *American Anthropologist* 74, no. 3 (June 1972).

7. Vance Randolph, letter to Lucile Morris, from Gillett Hotel, Manhattan, Kansas, January 17, 1935, Folder 430, LMU-SHSMO; Vance Randolph, "A Word List from the Ozarks," in *Dialect Notes* 5, 1926 (New Haven: Tuttle, Morehouse & Taylor Company, Publication of the American Dialect Society), 397–401; Morrow and Myers-Phinney, *Shepherd of the Hills Country*, 208; Cochran, *Vance Randolph: An Ozark Life*, 13.

8. Celia Ray, "Watchtower," *Springfield Daily News*, May 31, 1930, 10; (no author listed), "The Wastebasket," *Leader*, May 7, 1931, 14.

9. Lucile Morris, "The Very Idea," *Leader*, May 6, 1932, 24.

10. Celia Ray, "Watchtower," *Springfield Daily News*, September 30, 1931, 10; Vance Randolph, *The Ozarks: An American Survival of Primitive Society* (Fayetteville: University of Arkansas Press, 2017), 3.

11. Morrow and Myers-Phinney, 210.

12. Celia Ray, "Ozark 'Dialect'—The Real Thing!—In 'Hills' Film," *Springfield Daily News*, October 9, 1927, 5. Celia Ray, "Ozarks Withered by Awful Blast From Film 'Star,' " *Springfield Daily News*, January 18, 1928, 6.

13. LMU, "Poet Sandburg enjoyed Ozarks pickin', singin . . . ," *News and Leader*, July 9, 1978, 78.

14. "No 'Freak Shows' for Ozarks Fete, Leaders Assert," *Springfield Daily News*, March 20, 1934, 2; "Springfield and the Folk Festival," *St. Louis Post-Dispatch*, March 25, 1934, 49; "Vance Randolph in Defense of Ozarks and Hillbillies," *Kansas City Star*, March 28, 1934, 8.

15. "In the Springtime, Missourians Turn to Hill 'Hoofers,' " *Nashville Banner*, April 2, 1934, 9; Richard Lloyd Jones, *Tulsa Tribune*, reprinted as "An Oklahoma Idea of Advertising the Ozarks," *Leader and Press*, March 26, 1934, 8.

16. "Leaves from a Memory Book: America has 'gone folklore' says Ozarkian Writer," *Thayer News*, March 16, 1934, 8; Associated Press, "Attack Made on Writers on Life in Ozarks Area," *Sedalia Weekly Democrat*, April 20, 1934, 5.

17. May Kennedy McCord, "Hillbilly Heartbeats," *Post Tribune*, April 18, 1934, 4; "National Folk Festival to Glorify the Hill-Billy," *Jefferson City Sunday News and Tribune*, February 25, 1934, 4.

18. " 'C. C. Always for Festival,' Leader Avers," *Leader and Press*, April 19, 1934, 1; "Real Ozarkians Have Grand Time and Join Right In at Folk Festival," *Springfield Daily News*, April 18, 1934, 2. *The Woods Colt*, which was a Book of the Month Club selection, described the downward spiral of an illegitimate child (a "woods colt," in Ozark vernacular) who had grown up shunned and in the course of the book is charged with robbery, murders a US marshal, drinks moonshine, and makes love to his cousin—all things the outside world expected of a hillbilly.

19. May Kennedy McCord, "Hillbilly Heartbeats," *News and Leader*, March 25, 1934, 19; "A Golden Opportunity," *Citizen-Times*, August 4, 1934, 4.

20. Lucile Morris, "Good Ol' Hillbilly . . . ," *University Review, Journal of the University of Kansas City* 4, no. 2 (1937): 188, 190.

CHAPTER 6

1. Missouri Population 1900–1990 (all incorporated places), 18, accessed August 3, 2020, https://mcdc.missouri.edu/population-estimates/historical/cities1900-1990.pdf; Gregory J. Holman, "From *News-Leader* Archives: A Springfield Art Museum Timeline," *News-Leader*, February 20, 2019, accessed September 15, 2020, https:// www.news-leader.com/story/news/local/ozarks/2019/02/20/missouri-springfield -art-museum-timeline/2919045002/; Carlton Whiting, "Planes Give Speedy Time to Two Coasts," *Springfield Press*, October 23, 1930, 6.

2. "Hundreds Praise and Criticize Features of *News and Leader*," *News and Leader*, August 16, 1931, 15; Jerry Siegel, Los Angeles, Letters to the Editor, *Time Magazine*, May 30, 1988, 6–7.

3. "Polk Countians Return to GOP," *Springfield Daily News*, November 8, 1934, 3; James F. Keefe, *The First Fifty Years, Missouri Department of Conservation* (Jefferson City: Missouri Department of Conservation, 1987), 331.

4. Chapman eventually left Springfield for Lincoln, Nebraska, where he covered the statehouse and became an Associated Press reporter, and Rhodes went west, eventually working for the *San Diego Union*.

5. Lucile Morris, "Speech to Missouri Writers Guild," May 1936, Box 5, LMU-SGCLC.

6. Lucile Morris, "Speech to Business Club."

7. LMU, "Speech to Reed Junior High School Girls."

8. LMU, "Speech to Reed Junior High School Girls."

9. LMU, "Speech to Reed Junior High School Girls."

10. LMU, "Speech to Business Club."

11. "First Witness Brands Adams; Slayer Nerved," *Leader and Press*, July 17, 1928, 1.

12. Docia Karell, "Wounds Are Fatal for Zella Sinclair," *News and Leader*, August 12, 1928, 1.

13. "Slayer of Three Cheats Gallows by Taking Poison," *St. Joseph News-Press*, September 10, 1929, 18; Skinker's court reporter during that trial was Eugene V. Upton, a member of one of the first families of Bolivar and Lucile's future husband.

14. "Slayers of Six Officers Elude Posses in Ozarks," *St. Louis Star and Times*, January 4, 1932, 2; "US Agents Into Case," *Kansas City Star*, January 4, 1932, 2; "Reward Offered for Young Trio," *Moberly Monitor-Index*, January 4, 1932, 1.

15. Lucile Morris Upton, "The Day That Six of Greene County's Finest Fell," *Sunday Leader and Press*, January 3, 1960, 37; "Slayers of Six Officers Elude Posses," *St. Louis Star*, January 4, 1932, 1.

16. Celia Ray, "Watchtower," *Springfield Daily News*, January 4, 1932, 6; Lucile Morris, "The Good Old Days," *News and Leader*, January 3, 1982, 58. For more about the

Young Brothers Massacre, see Paul and Mary Barrett, *Young Brothers Massacre* (Columbia: University of Missouri Press, 1991).

17. "Ozark Manhunt Fails. Killer of 6 Still Free," *New York Daily News*, January 4, 1932, 2; "Youngs Die in Trap," *Kansas City Star*, January 5, 1932, 1.

18. Nancy Nance, "Youngest Member of the Young Clan Visits in Springfield," *Springfield Press*, January 4, 1932, 4; Nancy Nance, "Excitement Prevails as News of Youngs' Deaths Is Spread," *Springfield Press*, January 5, 1932, 6; Lon Scott, "Lon Scott Writes of Rescue of Bodies In Farmyard," *Springfield Press*, January 5, 1932, 2; LMU, "Sheriff Good on His Word; There Was Story," in "The Good Old Days," *News and Leader*, January 3, 1982, 58.

19. "Widow of Sheriff to Take His Job," *New York Daily News*, January 4, 1932, 43; Larry Wood, "The Barker Gang and the Murder of Sheriff Kelly," *Daily Journal* online, October 23, 2016, accessed August 2, 2020, https://dailyjournalonline.com/news/the-barker-gang-and-the-murder-of-sheriff-kelly/article_19b62a7f-f301-52d1-bcab-a2d5d9bcc561.html; "Mrs. Kelly Becomes Third Woman Sheriff," *Howell County Gazette*, December 15, 1932, 1; "Texas County Sheriff Dies," *West Plains Journal-Gazette*, December 15, 1932, 1.

20. Lucile Morris, "Speech to Missouri Writers Guild."

21. Lucile Morris, "The Very Idea," *Leader*, March 4, 1932, 12.

22. Lucile Morris, "Speech to Business Club"; Lucile Morris, "The Very Idea," *Leader*, February 12, 1932, 14.

23. Lucile Morris, "Speech to Missouri Writers Guild."

24. Lucile Morris, notes for speech, circa 1933–34, Folder 538, LMU-SHSMO.

25. Lucile Morris, notes for speech, circa 1933–34.

26. Docia Karell, "O'er Peaks, Starry Lights to Alameda, Flight's End," *Leader*, July 11, 1932, 14.

27. Lucile Morris, "The Very Idea," *Leader*, July 15, 1932, 20.

28. "Amelia Beats Ruth's Record," *Leader*, July 13, 1932, 4; Helen Welshimer, "Aviation Is Woman's Game as well as Man's, Says Amelia—And She Has Proved It," *Leader*, July 16, 1932, 3.

29. Lucile Morris, "Lucile Before the Mike," *Leader*, July 18, 1932, 2. Also refers to the three preceding paragraphs.

30. Hank Billings, "Delta Not First Airline to Leave; TWA Once Served Ozarks, Too," *News and Leader*, April 8, 1979, 82.

31. Carlton Whiting, "Planes Give Speedy Time to Two Coasts," *Springfield Press*, October 23, 1930, 6; "32-passenger Planes to Fly Through Here," *Springfield Press*, December 3, 1930, 1; "Air Mail Official Gives City Advice on Port Problem," *News and Leader*, May 15, 1932, 1; "TWA Discontinues Line Through Here as Mail Withdrawn," *Leader and Press*, February 20, 1934, 7; "City to Have Two Airlines," *Leader and Press*, June 13, 1934, 12; "Claim Airlines Trying to Force Paving of Runs," *Springfield Daily News*, June 10, 1935, 1; "US Engineer Will Inspect City's Airport," *Leader and Press*, June 8, 1936, 1; "City Has Field, but Not 'Planes," *Leader and Press*, September 30, 1936, 1.

CHAPTER 7

1. LMU, *Spotlight on Women.*

2. Michael B. Dougan, *Community Diaries, Arkansas Newspapering 1819-2002* (Little Rock: Arkansas Press Association, 2003), 216–18.

3. Mrs. C. P. Mahnkey, "When Roseville Was Young, Reminisces of Pioneer Days in the Ozarks," *Springfield Press*, February 26, 1933, 9.

4. Mrs. C. P. Mahnkey, "When Roseville Was Young, Reminisces of Pioneer Days in the Ozarks," *Springfield Press*, March 19, 1933, 26.

5. "Champion Ozark Scribe Is Home after a Long Trip," *Jefferson City Post Tribune*, July 29, 1935, 3; A. B. MacDonald, "New York: Amazed Mrs. Mahnkey of the Ozarks, But She'd NEVER LIVE THERE," *Kansas City Star*, August 4, 1935, 29; Massey, *A Candle Within Her Soul*, 2.

6. John E. Miller, "Laura Ingalls Wilder: A Perspective from 1932, the Year of Publication of Her First 'Little House' Novel," Southeast Missouri State University Press (website), accessed March 22, 2020, http://www.semopress.com/laura-ingalls-wilder-a-perspective-from-1932-the-year-of-publication-of-her-first-little-house-novel/; Caroline Fraser, *Prairie Fires*, 413–14.

7. John K. Hulston, *An Ozark Boy's Story, 1915-1946* (Point Lookout: School of the Ozarks Press, 1971), 153; "Significant Weather Events of the Century for Missouri," Climate Center, University of Missouri College of Agriculture, Food, and Natural Resources, accessed December 20, 2020, http://climate.missouri.edu/sigwxmo.php.

8. "Club Picnics at Chesapeake," *Leader and Press*, July 9, 1935, 5.

9. John K. Hulston, *A Look at Dade County, Missouri, 1905-1985* (Greenfield, Missouri: Citizens Home Bank, 1985), 75; June Croce, "Powerful Voice, Peculiar Name," *Ozarks Mountaineer*, February 1981, 56–7. The poet William Cullen Bryant's famous meditation on death, "Thanatopsis," ends

> So live, that when thy summons comes to join
> The innumerable caravan, which moves
> To that mysterious realm, where each shall take
> His chamber in the silent halls of death,
> Thou go not, like the quarry-slave at night,
> Scourged to his dungeon, but, sustained and soothed
> By an unfaltering trust, approach thy grave,
> Like one who wraps the drapery of his couch
> About him, and lies down to pleasant dreams.

10. In fact, 1932 was the first year since the Civil War that Camden, Stone, and Christian Counties voted for a Democrat for president. Albert J. Menendez, *The Geography of Presidential Elections in the United States, 1868-2004* (Jefferson, North Carolina: McFarland, 2009), 239–46; "Everton Bank Closed on Monday Morning," *Greenfield*

Vedette, July 16, 1931; "Everton Picnic Last Week a Great Success," *Greenfield Vedette*, August 4, 1932.

11. "Everton," *Greenfield Vedette*, July 26, 1934, 8; "Everton Picnic this Week," *Greenfield Vedette*, July 26, 1934, 1.

12. John K. Hulston, interview by Neil M. Johnson, January 11, 1988, Oral History Collection, Harry S. Truman Library, Independence, Missouri, accessed July 29, 2020, https://www.trumanlibrary.gov/library/oral-histories/hulstonj; John K. Hulston to author, interview, April 11, 1995.

13. John K. Hulston, interview by Neil M. Johnson, January 11, 1988; Hulston, *A Look at Dade County, Missouri, 1905–1985*, 112.

14. "Many Close Contests in County Primary," *Greenfield Vedette*, August 9, 1934, 1; "Etna Morris Re-Elected," *Greenfield Vedette*, November 15, 1934, 1.

15. Dale Freeman to author, interview, November 9, 2018.

16. Tom Uhlenbrock, "Rare Historic Photos Show CCC Crew," *Daily Journal* online, February 24, 2016, updated March 2, 2017, accessed October 23, 2020, https://dailyjournalonline.com/news/local/rare-historic-photos-show-ccc-crew/article_5072b85b-a9cf-5e26-8378-92dfd23b1370.html. See also Brooks Blevins, *A History of the Ozarks, Volume 3: The Ozarkers* (Urbana: University of Illinois Press, 2021), 146–47.

17. Uhlenbrock, "Rare Historic Photos."

18. May Kennedy McCord, "Hillbilly Heartbeats," *News and Leader*, October 23, 1932, 5.

19. Lucile Morris, "The Very Idea," *Leader*, October 21, 1932, 22.

20. "Lucile Morris and Vance Randolph," September 10, 1933, cited in *Busplunge* (blog), November 1, 2006, accessed March 12, 2020, https://bus-plunge.blogspot.com/search?q=Vance+Randolph.

21. LMU to Marilyn Prosser, interview.

22. "The Caxton Press," BYU Special Collections and Archives (website), accessed December 3, 2020, https://byuispecialcollections.wordpress.com/2016/07/01/the-caxton-press/.

23. "Bald Knobbers Gallop Again over Pages of an Ozark Girl's Re-Telling of Whispered Legends of the Hills," *Leader and Press*, April 16, 1939, 4; LMU to Marilyn Prosser, interview.

24. Regarding Gene's brothers: His brother Ben died at age twenty-five of tuberculosis. His brother Joe, who had owned the *Eldorado News* in Eldorado Springs, hanged himself. His brother Maynard, a professional baseball player, died in Houston, Texas, when the walls of a restaurant collapsed on him. His brother Ernest, who had graduated from the University of Missouri law school and served a term as Polk County prosecuting attorney, left the state in 1914, moved to Los Angeles, and was working as a day laborer when Gene and Lucile were married. "Death of Joseph Upton of Polk," *Maryville Republican*, February 13, 1902, 1; "Joe G. Upton," *Hermitage Index*, January 13, 1921, 1; "George Mark Upton," *Springfield Daily News*, February 26, 1937, 24; "Arrests in Connection with Main Street Fire," *Houston Post*, August 24, 1914, 1; "Travel Items," *Leader and Press*, August 24, 1937, 6.

25. Carole Bills, "Two Women Blazed Trails," *Springfield!*, June 1984, 36–7.

26. Megan McDonald Way, *Family Economics and Public Policy, 1800–Present* (New York: Palgrave MacMillan, 2018), 152; Ann Fair Dodson to author, interview, April 12, 1995.

27. LMU, "Women in Journalism."

28. Docia Karell, "Watchtower," *Leader and Press*, April 23, 1939, 22; C. E. Rogers, "Triple Hanging a Half Century Ago Climaxed Reign of Bald Knobbers," *Kansas City Star*, May 16, 1939, 18; "Tea Tuesday for Local Author," *Sunday News and Leader*, April 16, 1939, 9; "Writers Guild Pays Respects to Its Author," *Leader and Press*, April 22, 1939, 5.

29. "Excerpts from reviews," Folder 544, LMU-SHSMO.

30. LMU to Marilyn Prosser, interview. Another reason may have been that a major film had just been made in the Ozarks. Twentieth Century Fox's *Jesse James*, starring Tyrone Power, was filmed in Pineville in 1938. It became the third-highest grossing film of 1939, after *Gone with the Wind* and *Mr. Smith Goes to Washington*.

CHAPTER 8

1. Larry Roberts, "The History of Fort Leonard Wood," *Maneuver Support Magazine* (Summer 2008), 4–6, accessed August 26, 2020, https://web.archive.org/web/20091229132642/http://www.wood.army.mil/engrmag/Maneuver%20Support%20Magazine/PDFs%20for%20Summer%202008/Roberts.pdf.

2. "Cities of Southwest Missouri Organize to Cope with Camps," *Leader and Press*, October 11, 1941, 3; Mike O'Brien, "Radio Signals to Rocket Engines: Camp Crowder," in *TechnOzarks: Essays in Technology, Regional Economy and Culture*, ed. Tom Peters and Paul L. Durham (Springfield: Ozarks Studies Institute of Missouri State University, 2019), 99–112. Camp Crowder was the inspiration for the Beetle Bailey comic strip's Camp Swampy.

3. Docia Karell, "O'Reilly's Finished—But Commander's Job is Just Starting: Formal Opening of Institution Tentatively Set for October," *Springfield Daily News*, August 24, 1941, 26; Michael Glenn, "O'Reilly General Hospital of Springfield, Missouri. About O'Reilly: A Brief Introduction," Local History Collection-SGCLC, accessed September 23, 2020, https://Thelibrary.Org/Lochist/Oreilly/Intro.Cfm.

4. Docia Karell, "Looking Back on One Year (and What a Year!!) In the Ozarks," *Sunday News and Leader*, September 7, 1941, 33.

5. "Briefs," *Springfield Daily News*, November 30, 1943, 4; LMU, letter to George Morris, March 6, 1945, Box 5, LMU-SGCLC.

6. Glenn, "O'Reilly General Hospital of Springfield, Missouri"; John Rutherford, "O'Reilly General Hospital of Springfield, Missouri: Springfield's Hospital with a Soul," reprinted with permission from *Fifty Plus* (February 2002), Local History Collection-SGCLC, accessed September 23, 2020, https://Thelibrary.Org/Lochist/Oreilly/Fiftyplus.Cfm; LMU, letter to "Dear Sister and Brother" (Gene's siblings), March 25, 1945, Box 5, LMU-SGCLC. Six months after it was closed as an army hospital (September 1946), O'Reilly was reopened by the US Veterans Administration for six more years (until

1952). In 1954 the General Council of the Assemblies of God bought the facility to be the location for their new Evangel College.

7. LMU, letter to "Dearest Garnet," June 2, 1945, Box 5, LMU-SGCLC. Doc Savage was a best-selling pulp fiction hero, and Marge Lyon was a former Chicagoan who relocated and wrote a Chicago newspaper column and popular books about her adventures in the Ozarks.

8. LMU, letter to "Dear Sister and Brother."

9. LMU, "At O'Reilly," April 3, 1944, Folder 543, LMU-SHSMO.

10. LMU, "The Good Old Days: WWII to Blame for 40-Year-Old Column," *News and Leader*, January 24, 1982, 62.

11. Anne R. Kenney, " 'She Got to Berlin': Virginia Irwin, *St. Louis Post-Dispatch* War Correspondent," *Missouri Historical Review* 079, no. 4 (July 1985): 456–89.

12. "Dear Readers" and "1945 Fort Leonard Wood, In the Beginning," *Old Settlers Gazette*, January 4, 1945, 14.

13. Nancy Woloch, "Eleanor Roosevelt's White House Press Conferences," National Women's History Museum, September 22, 2017, accessed January 21, 2021, https://www.womenshistory.org/articles/eleanor-roosevelts-white-house-press-conferences.

14. Lucile Morris, "The Good Old Days: WWII to Blame for 40-Year-Old Column," *News-Leader*, January 24, 1982, 62.

15. Lucile Morris, "The Good Old Days," *Leader and Press*, January 25, 1942, 2.

16. Elizabeth McCain to author, interview, Springfield, Missouri, April 12, 1995; "Club Calendar," *Daily Capital News*, May 17, 1939, 2. The painting was titled *Sunday Afternoon.*

17. George Olds, "On the Bias," *Leader and Press*, June 18, 1944, 18; Ann Fair, "Lebanon Political Rivals Battle for Gubernatorial Nominations," *Sunday News and Leader*, June 18, 1944, 15. Donnelly, who had been a state senator for twenty years, won the governorship in November, and again in 1952. He died in 1961. Bradshaw, who ran unsuccessfully for US Senate in 1964, was chairman of the board of Ozark Air Lines. He died in 1970. Bradshaw's son Paul Bradshaw was a Missouri state senator from 1971 until 1984.

18. "For Betty, with Love," *News-Leader*, November 28, 1984, 69; LMU interview, *Springfield Profiles*, KOZK-TV, Springfield, Missouri, May 26, 1981, Gordon McCann Ozarks Folk Music Collection, Special Collections and Archives, Missouri State University Libraries, Missouri State University.

19. John G. Neihardt, letter to LMU, July 17, 1933, Folder F433, LMU-SHSMO.

20. Lurton Blassingame, letter to LMU, July 2, 1942, Folder 432, LMU-SHSMO.

21. Lurton Blassingame and James Zarbuck, letter to LMU, Folder 432; Robert M. McBride and Company, letter to LMU, November 1, 1945, Folder 433, LMU-SHSMO.

22. Rose Wilder Lane, letter to LMU, March 15, 1935, Folder 430, LMU-SHSMO; Vance Randolph, letter to LMU, January 3, 1934, Folder 430, LMU-SHSMO.

23. LMU, letter to Ralph Davis, September 28, 1945, Box 5, LMU-SGCLC.

24. For more on the Missouri Writers Guild, see Folder 399, LMU-SHSMO.

25. "Address to the People of the 1943–44 Constitutional Convention of Missouri," advertisement in the *St. Louis Post-Dispatch*, February 23, 1945, 11; "Con Con Debate Stirs C. of C.: Merit Plan Attacked, Defended," *Leader and Press*, November 21, 1944, 5.

26. I. T. Bode, Director of the Missouri Conservation Department, "Statement to the Committee on Agriculture and Conservation of the Missouri Constitutional Convention," and Sidney Stephens, Chairman of the Missouri Conservation Commission, "Statement," n.d., L. E. Meador Papers (Agriculture, Conservation), State Historical Society of Missouri.

27. Justin Dyer, "Constitutional Revision in Missouri: The Convention of 1943–1944, Show-Me Institute (website), June 2018, accessed March 19, 2020, https://showmeinstitute.org/wp-content/uploads/2018/06/20180424%20-%20Constitutional%20Revision%20in%20Missouri%20-%20Dyer.pdf.

28. LMU, letter to Harvey Allen at Farrar Rinehart, New York, March 1, 1945, Folder 433, LMU-SHSMO.

29. "Upton Receives Card from Son in Jap Camp," *Leader and Press*, August 19, 1943, 7; "Springfield Man Rescued from Japs," *Leader and Press*, February 2, 1945, 1.

30. LMU, letter to "Dear Sister and Brother."

31. "Eugene Upton, Jr., Killed in Action in the Pacific," *Leader and Press*, April 20, 1945, 1; "Springfield Sailor Died on Franklin, Relatives Believe," *Leader and Press*, May 18, 1945, 14.

32. "Sgt. Joseph B. Upton Here on a Furlough," *Leader and Press,* November 8, 1945, 22; "Eugene Upton, Jr., Killed in Action in the Pacific"; LMU to Marilyn Prosser, interview; LMU, letter to Ernest Upton, July 4, 1945, Box 5, LMU-SGCLC.

33. LMU, letters to George Morris, March 25 and April 9, 1945, LMU-SGCLC.

34. Perry Smith, "Hook Line and Sinker," *Leader and Press*, May 20, 1945, 11.

35. George Morris, in "Bench Warmer" column by Perry E. Smith, *News and Leader*, June 15, 1945, 10.

36. Docia Karell, "Upton Recalls How Peace Came to Japanese Prison Camp," *Leader and Press*, November 11, 1945, 1; "Sgt. Joseph B. Upton Here on a Furlough"; "Upton, Joseph B.," *St. Louis Post-Dispatch*, February 12, 1989, 24.

37. "Ernest D. Upton," *News-Leader and Press*, June 6, 1947, 2.

38. LMU, letter to Mrs. Guy A. Reed, February 19, 1948, Box 5, LMU-SGCLC; "Death to Eugene Upton, Longtime Court Reporter," *Leader-Press*, July 9, 1947, 16; LMU, letter to "Dear Stella," June 8, 1947, Box 5, LMU-SGCLC.

CHAPTER 9

1. George Olds, "On the Bias," *News and Leader*, January 5, 1947, 20.

2. LMU, letter to "Dear Mool" (Gene's brother), February 5, 1947, Box 5, LMU-SGCLC; LMU, letter to Docia Karell, February 9, 1947, Box 5, LMU-SGCLC.

3. "The Man Who Made the Photographs—How and Why He Did It," *Sunday News and Leader*, March 17, 1974, 45.

4. LMU, letter to Docia Karell, February 9, 1947, Box 5, LMU-SGCLC. Docia's sister was already in Japan as a civilian army employee, and Sidney Whipple, the Denver editor who had hired Lucile, was also in Japan.

5. LMU, letter to author, December 5, 1976.

6. LMU, letter to Docia Karell, March 29, 1947, Box 5, LMU-SGCLC.

7. "News-Leader Building, Equipment Lost in Fire," *Leader and Press*, March 27, 1947, 1; T. W. Duvall and Tams Bixby Jr., "Statement By Publishers Of Springfield Newspapers, Inc.," *News-Leader*, March 28, 1947, 1; Kaitlyn McConnell, "Behind the Byline: Generations Who Grew Up with the Newspaper," *Ozarks Alive!*, February 4, 2016, accessed December 11, 2020, https://ozarksalive.com/behind-the-byline-generations-who-grew-up-with-the-newspaper/.

8. LMU, letter to Docia Karell, May 16, 1947, Folder 438, LMU-SGCLC; LMU, "The Waste Basket," *News-Leader and Press*, April 17, 1947, 8.

9. Townsend Godsey, letter to LMU, January 13, 1971, Folder 451, LMU-SHSMO. In 1971 the School of the Ozarks contracted with Lucile to reprint *Bald Knobbers* initially for ten years. She renewed the copyright in 1966 for twenty-eight years—coincidentally the rest of her life.

10. LMU, letter to "Dear Friends," June 23, 1947, Box 5, LMU-SGCLC.

11. Mary Scott Hair, "The Ozarks Wastebasket—A Favorite Column," *Ozarks Mountaineer*, April 1955, 6; Larry Wood, "Lucile Morris Upton," *Missouri and Ozarks History* (blog), March 13, 2012, accessed August 2, 2020, http://ozarks-history.blogspot.com/2012/03/lucille-morris-upton.html.

12. Mary Elizabeth Mahnkey, "In the Hills," in "The Waste Basket," *Springfield Daily News*, July 9, 1947, 10; Mahnkey, "In the Hills," March 8, 1948, 6.

13. Bess Poyner, contributor, "The Waste Basket," *Springfield Daily News*, September 19, 1947, 26.

14. Mahnkey, "In the Hills," July 1, 1948, 23.

15. Edsel Ford, "Report from Route 4," in "Over the Ozarks," *Springfield Daily News*, February 25, 1960, 10.

16. Mary Scott Hair, "By the Sheep Gate," in "Over the Ozarks," *Springfield Daily News*, February 1, 1960, 10.

17. Kaitlyn McConnell, "Mary Scott Hair Lives on at the Crane County Museum," *OzarksAlive!*, May 21, 2018, accessed September 6, 2020, https://ozarksalive.com/mary-scott-hair-lives-on-at-stone-county-museum/.

18. LMU, "Over the Ozarks," Journalism Week Speech, April 29–May 5, 1956, Folder 539, LMU-SHSMO.

19. Hair, "The Ozarks Wastebasket—A Favorite Column"; Hank Billings, "Offbeat," *News-Leader*, December 7, 1992, 9.

20. LMU, "The Ozarks Wastebasket," *Daily News*, Christmas 1952, 12; LMU, "Over the Ozarks," *Springfield Daily News*, October 28, 1957, 6.

21. LMU, letter to Docia Karell, June 23, 1947, Folder 438, LMU-SHSMO.

22. Gladys Atkinson, Conway, Missouri, letters to LMU, July 7, 1950, and October 13, 1950, Waste Basket/Over the Ozarks ring binder, LMU-SGCLC.

23. Ethel McCracken, Thayer, Missouri, letter to LMU, February 26, 1951, Folder 539, LMU-SHSMO.

24. Unsigned postcard to the "Ozarks Waste Basket," December 15, 1951, Folder 440, LMU-SHSMO; Beth Lucille Compton, Harrisonville, Missouri, and LMU, correspondence from June 10, 11, and 13, 1952, Waste Basket/Over the Ozarks ring binder, LMU-SGCLC; Ann Fair Dodson to author, interview, April 12, 1995.

25. LMU, letter to Docia Karell, September 14, 1947, Box 5, LMU-SGCLC.

26. LMU, letter to John Morris, October 11, 1947, Box 5, LMU-SGCLC; LMU, letter to Helen (probably her cousin Helen Hower), October 24, 1947, Box 5, LMU-SGCLC.

27. LMU, letter to Helen (Hower), October 24, 1947.

28. John K. Hulston, "Daniel Boone's Sons in Missouri," *Missouri Historical Review* 041, no. 4 (July 1947) 61–72; Hulston to author, interview, April 11, 1995.

29. LMU, letter to Helen (Hower), October 24, 1947. At the time, it was against the law for a Missouri state treasurer to serve consecutive terms. In 1970, the constitution was amended to allow the treasurer to serve two back-to-back terms.

30. "Outburst by Fred Canfil," *Kansas City Star*, November 28, 1947, 1.

31. "GOP Chairman Demands Firing of U.S. Marshal," *News and Leader*, November 30, 1947, 1; "Blast at Canfil," *Kansas City Star*, November 30, 1947, 4.

32. Mike O'Brien, "Betty Love, Photojournalist," *OzarksWatch Magazine*, Fall 2017, 43–44.

33. LMU, letter to Mrs. Guy A. Reed, February 19, 1948, Box 5, LMU-SGCLC.

CHAPTER 10

1. Harry S. Truman, handwritten note on letter from Westminster College President Franc McCluer to Winston Churchill, October 5, 1945, copy at America's National Churchill Museum, Fulton, Missouri.

2. Harry S. Truman, "Address in Bolivar, Missouri, at the Dedication of the Simon Bolivar Memorial Statue, July 5, 1948," American Presidency Project (website), accessed March 6, 2021, https://www.presidency.ucsb.edu/node/232646.

3. Laurence Burd, "Truman Lauds Pan-American Co-Operation," *Chicago Daily Tribune*, July 6, 1948, 1. Burd put the Springfield crowd at about three thousand and the Bolivar Crowd at fifteen thousand.

4. Ann Fair, "Truman Addresses Crowds at Station on Return Journey," *Springfield Daily News*, July 6, 1948, 1.

5. LMU, "Camden County Magistrate Can Be Stern Despite Sex," *News and Leader*, July 17, 1955, 42.

6. LMU, letter to Docia Karell, October 30, 1949, Box 5, LMU-SGCLC.

7. United States Census Bureau, "A Comparison of the Census Occupation and Industry Classifications and Statistics of 1930 and 1940," accessed January 3, 2021, https://www2.census.gov/library/publications/decennial/1940/population-occupation/00312147ch1.pdf; United States Census Bureau, "1950 Census of Population: Volume 4. Special Reports, Table 2–Detailed Occupation of Employed Persons, by Detailed Industry and Sex, for the United States: 1950," accessed January 3, 2021, https://www2.census.gov/library/publications/decennial/1950/population-volume-4/41601751v4p1ch6.pdf.

8. Mike O'Brien and Dale Freeman to author, interviews, August 10, 2017; Dale Freeman to author, phone call, March 4, 2021; "And Then What Happened to Docia Karell?" *News and Leader*, February 21, 1976, 18; LMU, letter to Docia Karell, July 17, 1949, Folder 438, LMU-SHSMO. In 1949, Docia took a research job at the University of Illinois but stayed there only until she managed to get the army to send her back to Japan—continuing a love affair with that country that would last the rest of her career. In all, she would spend nine years in Japan working for the US Army, and sixteen more working for Japan Air Lines (JAL), primarily as editor of their in-flight magazine based in San Francisco.

9. LMU, letter to Docia Karell, July 17, 1949.

10. LMU, letter to Docia Karell, July 24, 1949, Folder 438, LMU-SHSMO.

11. Kaitlyn McConnell, "Behind the Byline"; O'Brien and Freeman to author, interviews; Freeman to author, phone call, March 4, 2021; McIntyre, *Springfield's Urban Histories*, 85.

12. LMU, letter to Docia Karell, October 30, 1949.

13. "Ozark Folklore Society," *Encyclopedia of Arkansas*, accessed December 17, 2020. https://encyclopediaofarkansas.net/entries/ozark-folklore-society-6239/. Directors of the society included Otto Ernest Rayburn; Mary Celestia Parler, a UA folklore professor and later Vance Randolph's wife (1962); Charlie May Simon; May Kennedy McCord; and University of Arkansas English professor Robert Morris. The society held an annual folk festival that hosted performances by Ozark singers and musicians, presentations by professional folklorists, and opportunities for members to get together. The name was changed to Arkansas Folklore Society in 1951.

14. LMU, "Promoting Ozarks Becomes a Science," *News and Leader*, October 23, 1949, 30; "Folk Festival Opens Monday for Ozarkians," *Springfield Daily News*, October 16, 1949, 3; "Square Dancing Enters Finals," *Springfield Daily News*, October 22, 1949, 5; "2500 from 20 States at Eureka Springs," *News and Leader*, October 23, 1949, 10. Temperance crusader Carrie Nation gained national attention around 1900 when she began using a hatchet to destroy saloons. Although she had been arrested (and jailed) several times in Arkansas, she retired to Eureka Springs, and her home, known as Hatchet Hall, was at various times a boarding house, school, and place of refuge for battered women.

15. "Talking Things Over . . ." editorial, *News and Leader*, October 23, 1949, 16. The Ozarks Playground Association was organized in 1919, headquartered in Joplin, and dissolved in 1979. OPA published booklets, maps, and pamphlets to promote tourism in the Missouri, Arkansas, and Oklahoma Ozarks. The fact that the Ozarks Playground Association was based in Joplin may also have contributed to Springfield's lack of interest in providing much financial support to the organization.

16. "Orval Faubus, Segregation's Champion Dies at 84," *New York Times*, December 15, 1994, 1.

17. LMU, "From Ozarks Log Cabin to Governor's Office, Story of Arkansas' Orval Faubus," *News and Leader*, December 26, 1954, 41.

18. LMU, "The Good Old Days," *News and Leader*, December 26, 1954, 29.

19. Glenn Johnson, "The Bull Shoals Dam," chap. 18 in *The History of Marion County, Arkansas*, accessed May 9, 2021, https://www.argenweb.net/marion/history/history -marion-co-ar-18-bull-shoals-dam.html; "Wildcat Dam Seems Likely," *Leader and Press*, December 17, 1936, 6; Floyd Sullivan, "Here's Looking at You," *Springfield Press*, December 19, 1929, 14; "Ozark Power & Water Company Announce Tentative Plans for Developing Additional Projects," *Springfield Republican*, February 19, 1922, 1.

20. Bob Flanders and Lynn Morrow, "The Damnable Current River Dam and Other Topics: A Conversation with Dan Saults, 1982," *OzarksWatch Magazine*, Winter 1992, 67–70.

21. Civil Functions, Department of the Army Appropriations 1955, "Hearings before the Subcommittee of the Committee on Appropriations United States Senate, Eighty- Third Congress Second Session, on H.R. 8367," (Washington, DC: US Government Printing Office, 1954): 1580–98, accessed December 28, 2020, https://books.google. com/books?id=vPYdAAAAMAAJ&pg=PA302&lpg=PA302&d- q=TAble+Rock+Dam-+Hearings+before+the+Subcommittee+of+the+Committee+on +Appropriations+United+States+Senate,+Eighty-Third+Congress+Second+Session, +on+H.R.+8367&source=bl&ots=EMc9bVyN-O&sig=ACfU3U3ilHCtVNGCitjkBiUHe OsAKGE5-A&hl=en&sa=X&ved=2ahUKEwjh15nr6fnyAhWJu54KHcPTBywQ6AF6B AgCEAM#v=onepage&q=TAble%20Rock%20Dam-%20Hearings%20before%20the %20Subcommittee%20of%20the%20Committee%20on%20Appropriations%20 United%20States%20Senate%2C%20Eighty-Third%20Congress%20Second%20 Session%2C%20on%20H.R.%208367&f=false.

22. Civil Functions, Department of the Army Appropriations 1955, "Hearings before the Subcommittee."

23. This and the preceding paragraphs all concern the events written about in LMU, photos by Betty Love, "Grave Hunt Strenuous," *News and Leader*, July 22, 1956, 37. Also see Jo Dunne, "Joseph Philibert Cemetery Located Near Kimberling City, Missouri," accessed January 15, 2021, http://sites.rootsweb.com/~mostone/cemetery /Philibert.html.

24. Elizabeth McCain to author, interview, Springfield, Missouri, April 12, 1995.

25. "Bank Holdup, Plotted in Bar, Proves Fizzle," *Springfield Daily News*, May 27, 1959, 25.

26. Story of the bank robbers told to author by Mike O'Brien, Elizabeth McCain, and Dale Freeman.

27. LMU to author, interview, March 24, 1985.

28. "Nineteenth Century Marionville Lives Again," *News-Leader*, June 20, 1954, 37; LMU, "Mountain View Whoops It Up," *News and Leader*, June 26, 1960, 43; LMU, "Christian County Brothers, Sisters Living it Up," *News and Leader*, June 28, 1959, 43; LMU, "Christian Countians Turn Back Clock to Relive Colorful Past," *News and Leader*, June 28, 1959, 41.

29. LMU, "Convert Limestone Cavern for Storage," *Sunday News and Leader*, January 8, 1956, 43. As of this writing the space provides thirty million cubic feet of controlled-

temperature storage to companies like Cargill, Simmons, Walmart, Tyson, and ConAgra. LMU, " 'Flowerbox Town' of Ozarks Shows Fast, Healthy Growth, Rocketdyne Plant Boosts Neosho's Boom," *News and Leader*, July 7, 1957, 31.

30. LMU, "Stoutland's Bagged Goldfish Scattered Throughout the World," *Sunday News and Leader*, July 13, 1958, 43. As of this writing, Ozark Fisheries still exists and sells ornamental goldfish and koi across North America.

31. LMU, "Village That Went with Wind Rises Anew," *News and Leader*, February 25, 1960, 41; V. O. Kinkade, "Grovespring Tornado," in "Over the Ozarks," *Springfield Daily News*, September 22, 1960, 16.

32. LMU, "The Tragic Day the Tornado Battered Springfield," *News and Leader*, April 24, 1960, 43.

33. LMU, "Last Ride on the White River Line," *Sunday News and Leader*, March 20, 1960, 41.

34. LMU to author, interview, March 24, 1985; Mike O'Brien to author, interview, August 10, 2017.

35. LMU, letter to William Peden, Folder 447, LMU-SHSMO; "State Park Advisors to View Boone Home," *Leader-Press*, November 14, 1963, 5, 13; "Historians Endorse Plan for Park at Boone Home," *Leader-Press*, April 26, 1963, 13; LMU, "Boones of State Visit Homestead," *Springfield Daily News*, October 21, 1963, 11; LMU, "Boone Kin Gather, Boost State Park," *Leader-Press*, October 21, 1963, 17; "Christmas Spirit Misses Some People," *News and Leader*, December 13, 1964, 36. In 1963, the Nathan Boone Homesite was registered in the Missouri Historic Sites Catalog by the State Historical Society of Missouri. See "Nathan Boone House," National Register of Historic Places Inventory nomination form, US Department of the Interior National Park Service, December 1968, accessed May 10, 2021, https://mostateparks.com/sites/mostateparks/files/Boone%2C%20Nathan%2C%20House.pdf.

36. "Nathan Boone House," National Register of Historic Places Inventory—Nomination Form; Charles W. Graham, "Presenting Long-Hidden History of Nathan Boone's Life," *Kansas City Star*, July 21, 1946, 37.

37. Don Mahnken, "Book to Detail Life of Nathan Boone," *Leader and Press*, May 14, 1984, 1; John Hoogesteger, "Relatives of Daniel Boone Celebrate Past in Ash Grove," *News-Leader*, September 22, 1984, 20.

CHAPTER 11

1. "Our first National Military Park," *Hallowed Ground Magazine*, American Battlefield Trust, Fall 2010, accessed August 27, 2020, https://www.battlefields.org/learn/articles/our-first-national-military-park.

2. LMU, "War at a Glance," *Wilson's Creek Story*, *Leader-Press*, August 8, 1961, 16. For the most up-to-date information on, and assessment of, the battle, see William Garrett Piston and Richard W. Hatcher III, *Wilson's Creek, the Second Battle of the Civil War and the Men Who Fought It* (Chapel Hill: University of North Carolina Press, 2000).

3. Piston and Hatcher, *Wilson's Creek*, xv, xvi; Amy Laurel Fluker, *Commonwealth of Compromise: Civil War Commemoration in Missouri* (Columbia: University of

Missouri Press, 2020), 115; David W. Blight, *Race and Reunion* (Cambridge: Belknap Press of Harvard University Press, 2001), 3. Historian Blight's work aims to show that despite the results of the Civil War and the 13th, 14th, and 15th Amendments to the Constitution, justice for formerly enslaved people has yet to be accomplished more than 150 years after slavery was abolished.

4. John K. Hulston, *Lester E. Cox, 1895–1968*, 215; LMU, "The Fight That Lasted 100 years," *Wilson's Creek Story, Leader-Press*, August 8, 1961, 10.

5. Fluker, *Commonwealth of Compromise*, 134–40; Piston and Hatcher, *Wilson's Creek*, xiii–xvi.

6. "Wilson Creek. Reunion of the Blue and the Gray on the Battlefield," *Cape Girardeau Democrat*, August 21, 1897, 3; "Wilson's Creek, Thousands Attend the Reunion on the Historic Battle-Field," *St. Louis Globe-Democrat*, August 11, 1897, 1; Fluker, *Commonwealth of Compromise*, 115; Caroline E. Janney, *Remembering the Civil War* (Chapel Hill: University of North Carolina Press, 2013), 3. There were no reports of any Black veterans at the 1897 reunion, probably for two reasons. At that time, it is doubtful whether a newspaper aimed at a middle-class white audience would have mentioned the presence of Black veterans, but it is also likely that there were few to attend. African American soldiers did not begin to take part in the Civil War until 1862, and then only in small numbers. Black soldiers were a greater presence after the Emancipation Proclamation in 1863.

7. "Statewide Interest Is Being Shown in Proposed Park Plan," *Leader*, January 26, 1927, 12; Thomas A. Peters, *John T. Woodruff of Springfield, Missouri, in the Ozarks: An Encyclopedic Biography* (Springfield: Pie Supper Press, 2016), 96, 212.

8. "Engineers Here to Make Survey of Wilson Creek," *Springfield Daily News*, April 11, 1928, 16; *Civil War Sites Advisory Commission Report on the Nation's Civil War Battlefields* (Washington, DC: Civil War Sites Advisory Commission c/o National Park Service, 1993). See also Connie Langum, "The Battle for Wilson's Creek," American Battlefield Trust, accessed November 18, 2021, https://www.battlefields.org/learn/articles/battle-wilsons-creek.

9. Celia Ray, "Watchtower," *Springfield Daily News*, August 12, 1929, 6.

10. Celia Ray, "Memories of Wilson Creek," *Springfield Daily News*, August 10, 1929, 2.

11. LMU, "The Fight That Lasted 100 years," *Wilson's Creek Story, Leader-Press*, August 8, 1961, 10.

12. LMU, "The Fight that Lasted 100 Years," *Wilson's Creek Story, Leader-Press*, August 8, 1961, 10; LMU, "Battle of Wilson's Creek: Bloodiest of the Civil War," *News and Leader*, Sept 10, 1950, 37.

13. John K. Hulston to author, interview, April 11, 1995; LMU, "Speech to Teachers Sorority."

14. *Wilson's Creek National Battlefield Cultural Landscape Report, Volume 1*, prepared for National Park Service Midwest Regional Office, Omaha, Nebraska, by John Milner Associates, Inc., Charlottesville, Virginia, September 2004, 1–22.

15. "Copy of the Original Minutes of the Organization of the Greene County Historical Society, June 2, 1954," Greene County Historical Society Meeting Minutes 1954–1957,

Box 1/Folder 13, Greene County Historical Society Records (M38), Special Collections and Archives, Meyer Library, Missouri State University. The Ray House was a regular stop for the Butterfield Overland Mail stagecoaches as they went across the country between 1858 and 1861.

16. Greene County Historical Society Meeting Minutes, 1954–1957; "Park Site Gift Offered to US," *Leader-Press*, February 13, 1957, 7.

17. John K. Hulston to author, interview, April 11, 1995. Johnson was also president of the Ozarks Playground Association at that time.

18. "Wilson's Creek Battlefield Viewed by Park Officials," *Leader and Press*, May 8, 1957, 1; "Wilson's Creek Park Hearings Scheduled," *Leader and Press*, July 12, 1957, 1.

19. LMU (AP), "After 96 Years, a Chance to Live," *Kansas City Star*, July 14, 1957, 5.

20. LMU, "Battle of Wilson's Creek," *Civil War Times*, November 1959, 8, LMU Archives, Box 2, Hulston Civil War Research Library, Wilson's Creek National Battlefield, Republic, Missouri. Although the *Civil War Times* was not published as a typical magazine until 1962, it appeared as a tabloid publication for several years before that.

21. "Congressmen Are Given a Complete Report on Importance of Wilson's Creek Battle," *Springfield Daily News*, April 4, 1959, 5.

22. LMU, "Over the Ozarks," *Springfield Daily News*, April 13, 1959, 6; LMU, "Cannon Roared 98 Years Ago Tomorrow at Wilson's Creek," *Leader-Press*, August 9, 1959, 33; Public Law 86–434, April 22, 1960. The law called for the Secretary of the Interior "to acquire, by gift, purchase, condemnation or otherwise, the lands (together with any improvements thereon) comprising the Wilson's Creek Battlefield site . . ."

23. LMU, "Governor Sees Park as Symbol of Valor," *Springfield Daily News*, August 10, 1961, 1; "Parade Starter for Final Day of Centennial," *Springfield Daily News*, August 10, 1961, 15; LMU, "About the Author . . . ," *Wilson's Creek Story*, *Leader-Press*, August 8, 1961, 3.

24. John K. Hulston to author, interview, April 11, 1995. Stuart Symington's wife was also a Civil War descendant; her grandfather was Union Major General James S. Wadsworth, who was fatally wounded at the Battle of the Wilderness in 1864.

25. *Wilson's Creek National Battlefield Cultural Landscape Report, Volume 1*; Langum, "The Battle for Wilson's Creek"; US Department of the Interior National Park Service George Washington Carver National Monument, letters to LMU, August 6, 1965 and April 12, 1965, Folder 449, LMU-SHSMO.

26. Mike North, "90-Year Dream Becomes Reality," *News and Leader*, Aug 11, 1968, 1. LMU, "Ceremony Set at Battlefield for August 10, *News and Leader*, July 28, 1968, 41. The day was marred by the sudden death of Lester Cox from a heart attack, only hours before. Cox had been slated to chair the event.

27. LMU, "Heroic Sacrifices are Memorialized," *News and Leader*, May 28, 1977, 26; Marjorie Moore Armstrong, "Living on the edge of History," *News and Leader*, August 7, 1977, 70; "Closer to Victory," *News and Leader*, October 30, 1977, 29.

28. Ann Fair Dodson, "Residents Should See Battlefield," *Sunday Leader and Press*, May 9, 1982, 48; Brian Levinson, "Visitors' Center at Battlefield Almost Finished," *Leader and*

Press, April 20, 1982, 9; Brian Levinson, "Battlefield Park Chief Is Named," *Leader and Press*, August 9, 1982, 1; "Touching Our Past," *Leader and Press*, March 3, 1982, 10.

29. John and Ruth Hulston donated the core of the library collection's original twelve thousand items, most of which are related to the Civil War period and the Civil War in the Trans-Mississippi West. John K. and Ruth Hulston Civil War Research Library, Wilson's Creek National Battlefield, National Park Service. https://www.nps.gov/wicr /learn/historyculture/hulston-civil-war-research-library.htm. For a contemporary look at General Lyon and the Battle of Wilson's Creek, see Christopher Phillips, *Damned Yankee: The Life of General Nathaniel Lyon* (Columbia: University of Missouri Press, 1990), reissued by Louisiana State University Press, 1996, and Piston and Hatcher, *Wilson's Creek*. This is the current definitive work on Wilson's Creek.

CHAPTER 12

1. "Playground Group to Meet to Celebrate 40th Birthday," *News and Leader*, February 21, 1960, 46.
2. Silver Dollar City was actually named by legendary promotions man Don Richardson, who said "Ozark Mountain Village" is "only three adjectives." He suggested Silver Dollar City as a punchier name, and also suggested that change be given in silver dollars—which of course, caused quite a stir and brought a lot of publicity. Crystal Payton, *The Story of Silver Dollar City* (Springfield: Lens and Pen Press, 1997), 56. Mary Herschend designed Main Street with the help of Russell Pearson, a theme park designer with a circus background. Crystal Payton, *Handcrafted at Silver Dollar City* (Springfield: Lens and Pen Press, 2001), 7–8.
3. Payton, *The Story of Silver Dollar City*, 62. Silver Dollar City's inspired promotion over the years came from Don Richardson, self-described "press agent" for the city. He achieved a major coup when he convinced *Beverly Hillbillies* creator Paul Henning to bring the cast to Silver Dollar City and film several episodes there. See also, Hank Billings, "Area Resorts Get Set for Season," *News and Leader*, April 25, 1965, 45.
4. LMU, "Romance of the Ozarks," speech to Monett Commercial Club, 1951, Box 5, LMU-SGCLC.
5. Moore v. Moore, 337 S.W.2d 781 (Mo. Ct. App. 1960) Casetext, accessed August 20, 2020, https://casetext.com/case/moore-v-moore-221.
6. LMU, "Touring Glade Top Trail," *News and Leader*, October 14, 1962, 41.
7. LMU, "War Eagle Fair One of Top Fall Festivals," *News and Leader*, November 4, 1962, 41. As of this writing, the War Eagle Fair, held the third week in October since 1954, generally attracts more than two hundred craftspeople from across the US, and thirty to fifty thousand visitors, depending on the weather.
8. LMU, "The Civil War in the Ozarks!" *News and Leader*, January 8, 1961, 39.
9. LMU, "Pea Ridge Battlefield Spruced Up for Dedication," *News and Leader*, May 6, 1963, 41.
10. "All of Us Will Miss Lucile," *News and Leader*, January 5, 1964, 22.

11. Mount Etna Morris served three nonconsecutive terms as Missouri state treasurer: 1949–1953, 1957–1961, and 1965–1969.

12. "Trout Hatchery Pioneer A. George Morris Dies," *Springfield Daily News*, December 20, 1985, 10.

13. LMU, letters, Folder 449, LMU-SHSMO.

14. LMU, *Spotlight on Women*.

15. "Was This Delay Really Necessary?" *News and Leader*, March 19, 1967, 30.

16. "Incumbents on Council Stay, Upton Is Added," *Springfield Daily News*, April 5, 1967, 1.

17. LMU, "Speech to Teachers Sorority."

18. "Unauthorized Entry Barred," *Springfield Daily News*, July 14, 1970, 11.

19. "LMU, *Springfield Profiles*; Minutes, Springfield City Council, January 26, 1970 and March 9, 1970, Busch Municipal Building, 840 Boonville Avenue, Springfield, Missouri.

20. "Old Jail Could Become Museum," *Leader-Press*, February 5, 1970, 33.

21. Arthur Ochs Sulzberger Sr., letter to LMU, June 22, 1971, Folder 452, LMU-SHSMO.

22. "Two from School of Ozarks Press," *News and Leader*, February 14, 1971, 48.

23. LMU, *Springfield Profiles*.

24. Mike O'Brien to author, email, August 9, 2017.

25. "Woman of the Year: Our 'Celia," *Leader-Press*, October 10, 1967, 15.

26. "News Over the Ozarks," *Kansas City Star*, April 28, 1968, 4.

27. "Be Positive, Get the Jobs, Women Told," *Springfield Daily News*, March 19, 1968, 22.

28. LMU, "Speech to Teachers Sorority."

29. Mary Sue Price, "Reporter, Historian, Given Heritage Award," *Springfield Daily News*, March 28, 1978, 3.

30. "Hall of Fame Inducts Two," *Leader and Press*, April 28, 1980, 9; "When Credit Is Due," *Leader and Press*, May 1, 1980, 8.

31. "Reagan Proclamation Notes County's Birthday," *Leader and Press*, January 4, 1983, 9; "Another Historical Note," *News-Leader*, May 8, 1988, 61.

32. Goldie (Mrs. Hugh) Smith, Tulsa, Oklahoma, letter to LMU May 5, 1984, Box 2, LMU-SGCLC.

33. LMU, typed letter to "Dear Allan," circa 1985, Box 5, LMU-SGCLC.

34. Ella Mae Tucker, "Out Our Way," *News and Leader*, July 30, 1989, 66.

35. Mike O'Brien, "Some of Life's Best Lessons are Taught Outside Classroom, *News-Leader*, January 19, 1989, 69.

36. Ralph E. Fuhrman, letter to LMU, July 3, 1984, Box 3, Miscellaneous Correspondence, Upton Collection, Wilson's Creek National Battlefield Collection.

37. LMU, "Collecting Ozarks History."

BIBLIOGRAPHY

Balducchi, David E. "Second Battle of Wilson's Creek." *Missouri Historical Review* 105, no. 3 (April 2011): 159–78.

Barrett, Paul and Mary Barrett. *Young Brothers Massacre.* Columbia: University of Missouri Press, 1991.

Beck, Warren A. *New Mexico: A History of Four Centuries.* Norman: University of Oklahoma Press, 1962.

Bennion, Sherilyn Cox. *Equal to the Occasion, Women Editors of the Nineteenth-Century West.* Reno: University of Nevada Press, 1990.

BIAS, a weekly newspaper in Springfield, Missouri 1950–1955. Local History Collection, Springfield-Greene County Library Center.

Bills, Carole. "List of Greene County's Greats." *Springfield!,* July 1983.

———. "Two Women Blazed Trails." *Springfield!,* June 1984.

Blair, Emily Newell. *Bridging Two Eras, The Autobiography of Emily Newell Blair, 1877–1951.* Edited by Virginia Jean Laas. Columbia: University of Missouri Press, 1999.

Blevins, Brooks. *Hill Folks.* Urbana: University of Illinois Press, 2002.

———. *A History of the Ozarks, Volume 1: The Old Ozarks.* Urbana: University of Illinois Press, 2018.

———. *A History of the Ozarks, Volume 2: The Conflicted Ozarks.* Urbana: University of Illinois Press, 2019.

———. *A History of the Ozarks, Volume 3: The Ozarkers.* Urbana: University of Illinois Press, 2021.

———. *Hill Folks.* Urbana: University of Illinois Press, 2002.

———. "Region, Religion, and Competing Visions of Mountain Mission Education in the Ozarks." *Journal of Southern History* 82, no.1 (February 2016): 78–79.

Blight David W. *Race and Reunion.* Cambridge: Belknap Press of Harvard University Press, 2001.

Bode, I. T., Director of the Missouri Conservation Department, "Statement to the Committee on Agriculture and Conservation of the Missouri Constitutional Convention," and Sidney Stephens, Chairman of the Missouri Conservation Commission, "Statement," n.d., L. E. Meador Papers (Agriculture and Conservation), State Historical Society of Missouri.

Brackett, Albert G. *History of the United States Cavalry, from the Formation of the Federal Government to the First of June 1863.* New York: Harper and Brothers, 1865.

Brooklyn (NY) Daily Eagle

Buchanan, Carrie. "Sense of Place in the Daily Newspaper." *Aether: The Journal of Media Geography* (Spring 2009): 62–83.

Busplunge (blog)

Cairns, Kathleen A. *Front Page Woman Journalists, 1920–1950.* Lincoln: University of Nebraska Press, 2003.

Cape Girardeau Democrat (Missouri)

"The Caxton Press," BYU-Idaho Special Collections (website), last updated July 1, 2016.
    https://byuispecialcollections.wordpress.com/2016/07/01/the-caxton-press/.

Chicago Tribune

Christian, Garna L. "Always in His Heart: Owen Payne White and Old El Paso."
    Southwestern Historical Quarterly 112, no. 2 (2008): 172–90. http://www.jstor.org
    /stable/30239622.

Citizen-Times (North Carolina)

Civil War Sites Advisory Commission Report on the Nation's Civil War Battlefields.
    Washington, DC: Civil War Sites Advisory Commission c/o National Park Service, 1993.

Clovis News Journal (New Mexico)

Cochran, Robert. *Vance Randolph: An Ozark Life*. Urbana: University of Illinois Press, 1985.

Connors, Kate. "Mary Roberts Rinehart, Mystery Novelist, Adventure Tourism Pioneer."
    Adventure Journal, September 13, 2018. https://www.Adventure-Journal.Com
    /2018/09/Mary-Roberts-Rinehart-Mystery-Novelist-Adventure-Tourism-Pioneer/.

Cralle, Walter O. "Social Change and Isolation in the Ozark Mountain Region of Missouri."
    American Journal of Sociology 41, no. 4 (January 1936): 435–46. https://doi.org/10
    .1086/217185.

Croce, June. "Powerful Voice, Peculiar Name." *Ozarks Mountaineer*, February 1981, 56–57.

Dade County Advocate (Missouri)

Davis, James H. "Colorado Under the Klan." *Colorado Magazine*, Spring 1965.

"Dear Readers" and "1945 Fort Leonard Wood, In the Beginning." 2020 *Old Settlers Gazette*
    Waynesville, Missouri.

Denver Express

Detroit Free Press

Dougan, Michael B. *Community Diaries, Arkansas Newspapering 1819-2002*. Little Rock:
    Arkansas Press Association, 2003.

Driscoll, Carol. "Emily Newell Blair, Missouri's Suffragette." *Missouri Life Magazine*, July
    19, 2020.

Dyer, Justin. "Constitutional Revision in Missouri: The Convention of 1943–1944."
    Show-Me Institute (website), June 2018. https://showmeinstitute.org/wpcontent
    /uploads/2018/06/20180424%20-%20Constitutional%20Revision%20in%20
    Missouri%20-%20Dyer.pdf.

Eastern New Mexico News

El Paso Times

El Paso Herald

Fahs, Alice. *Out on Assignment: Newspaper Women and the Making of Modern Public
    Space*. Chapel Hill: University of North Carolina Press, 2011.

Flanders, Bob and Lynn Morrow. "The Damnable Current River Dam and Other Topics: A
    Conversation with Dan Saults, 1982." *OzarksWatch Magazine*, Winter 1992.

Fleming, Elvis E. *Captain Joseph C. Lea, from Confederate Guerilla to New Mexico
    Patriarch*. Las Cruces: Yucca Tree Press, 2002.

Fletcher, Mrs. Rockwell. "The Oasis Correspondent." *White River Valley Historical Quarterly* 4, no. 10 (Winter 1972–73): 9–11.

Fluker, Amy Laurel. *Commonwealth of Compromise: Civil War Commemoration in Missouri.* Columbia: University of Missouri Press, 2020.

Fox, Elana V. *Inside the World's Fair of 1904: Exploring the Louisian Purchase Exposition,* 2 vols. First Book Library, 2003.

Fraser, Caroline. *Prairie Fires.* New York: Metropolitan Books, 2017.

Freedman, Estelle B. "The New Woman: Changing Views of Women in the 1920s." *Journal of American History* 61, no. 2 (September 1974): 382. https://www.jstor.org/stable /1903954.

Garrigues, George. *Marguerite Martyn, America's Forgotten Journalist.* Morro Bay, California: City Desk Publishing, 2019.

Gilley, B. H. "A Woman for Women: Eliza Nicholson, Publisher of the New Orleans Daily Picayune." *Louisiana History: The Journal of the Louisiana Historical Association* 30, no. 3 (1989): 233–48. http://www.jstor.org/stable/4232737.

Gilmore, Robert. "A Building Legacy Preserved, the WPA and CCC." *OzarksWatch Magazine,* Spring 1994.

———. *Ozark Baptizings, Hangings, and Other Diversions, Theatrical Folkways of Rural Missouri 1885–1910.* Norman: University of Oklahoma Press, 1984.

Glazier, Robert. "First Ladies of Springfield." *Springfield!,* March 1996.

Glenn, Michael. "O'Reilly General Hospital of Springfield, Missouri. About O'Reilly: A Brief Introduction." Local History Collection, Springfield-Greene County Library Center. https://Thelibrary.Org/Lochist/Oreilly/Intro.Cfm.

Godsey, Helen and Townsend Godsey. *Flight of the Phoenix, a Biography of the School of the Ozarks . . . a Unique American College.* Point Lookout: School of the Ozarks Press, 1984.

Goldberg, Robert A. "Denver: Queen City of the Colorado Realm." In *The Invisible Empire of the West: Toward a New Historical Appraisal of the Ku Klux Klan of the 1920s,* edited by Shawn Lay, 39–67. Champaign: University of Illinois Press, 2004.

Goodstein, Phil. *In the Shadow of the Klan: When the KKK Ruled Denver, 1920–1926.* Denver: New Social Publications, 2006.

Gordon McCann Ozarks Folk Music Collection. Special Collections and Archives, Meyer Library, Missouri State University.

Greene County Historical Society Records (M38). Special Collections and Archives, Meyer Library, Missouri State University.

Greenfield Vedette (Missouri)

Grosenbaugh, Richard. "Celia's Magnificent Time Machine." *Springfield!,* February 1980.

Hair, Mary Scott. "The Ozarks Wastebasket—A Favorite Column." *Ozarks Mountaineer,* April 1955.

Hammon, Neal O., ed. *My Father, Daniel Boone: The Draper Interviews with Nathan Boone.* Lexington: University Press of Kentucky, 1999. Reissued in 2012.

"Hearings before the Subcommittee of the Committee on Appropriations United States Senate, Eighty-Third Congress Second Session, on H.R. 8367," in *Civil Functions,*

Department of the Army Appropriations 1955, 1580–98. Washington, DC: US
Government Printing Office, 1954.

"Helen Ring Robinson," *Colorado Encyclopedia* (website). https://coloradoencyclopedia.org
/article/helen-ring-robinson.

Hermitage Index (Missouri)

Hernando, Matthew J. *Faces Like Devils: The Bald Knobber Vigilantes in the Ozarks* Vol. 1.
Columbia: University of Missouri Press, 2015.

History of Dade County and Her People Volume II. Greenfield, Missouri: Pioneer Historical
Company, November 1, 1917.

"History of Hollister," City of Hollister, Missouri (website). http://cityofhollister.com/visitors
/history_of_hollister/index.php.

Howell County Gazette (Missouri)

Houston (TX) Post

Hulston, John K. "Daniel Boone's Sons in Missouri." *Missouri Historical Review* 041, no. 4
(July 1947): 61–72.

———. Interview by Neil M. Johnson. Oral History Collection, Harry S. Truman Library,
Independence, Missouri. https://www.trumanlibrary.gov/library/oral-histories/hulstonj.

———. *Lester E. Cox 1895–1968: He Found Needs and Filled Them.* Cassville, Missouri:
Litho Printers, 1992.

———. *A Look at Dade County Missouri, 1905–1985.* Greenfield, Missouri: Citizens Home
Bank, 1985.

———. *An Ozark Boy's Story 1915–1945.* Point Lookout: School of the Ozarks Press, 1971.

Hurt, Douglas. *Nathan Boone and the American Frontier.* Columbia: University of Missouri
Press, 1998.

Jablow, Joseph. "Carl Withers (James West) 1900–1970." *American Anthropologist* 74, no. 3
(1972): 764–69. http://www.jstor.org/stable/671555.

James, George Wharton. *New Mexico, the Land of the Delight Makers.* Boston: Page
Company, 1920.

Janney, Caroline E. *Remembering the Civil War.* Chapel Hill: University of North Carolina
Press, 2013.

Jefferson City (MO) Post Tribune

Jefferson City (MO) Daily Capitol News

John K. and Ruth Hulston Civil War Research Library. Wilson's Creek National Battlefield,
National Park Service. https://www.nps.gov/wicr/learn/historyculture/hulston-civil
-war-research-library.htm.

Johnson, Glenn. "The Bull Shoals Dam." Chap. 18 in *The History of Marion County,
Arkansas.* https://www.argenweb.net/marion/history/history-marion-co-ar-18-bull
-shoals-dam.html.

Kansas City (MO) Post

Kansas City (MO) Star

Kansas City (MO) Times

Keefe, James F. *The First Fifty Years, Missouri Department of Conservation*. Jefferson City: Missouri Department of Conservation, 1987.

Kelly, Susan Croce. *Father of Route 66: The Story of Cy Avery*. Norman: University of Oklahoma Press, 2014.

———. "May Kennedy McCord, Hillbilly Sweetheart." *OzarksWatch Magazine*, Spring/Summer 2020.

Kenney, Anne R. " 'She Got to Berlin': Virginia Irwin, *St. Louis Post-Dispatch* War Correspondent." *Missouri Historical Review* 079, no. 4 (July 1985): 456–89.

Langum, Connie. "The Battle for Wilson's Creek." American Battlefield Trust (website). https://www.battlefields.org/learn/articles/battle-wilsons-creek.

———. "The Ray House at Wilson's Creek." American Battlefield Trust (website). https://www.battlefields.org/learn/articles/ray-house-wilsons-creek.

Long, Grace. "The Anglo-American Occupation of the El Paso District." MA thesis, University of Texas at Austin, 1931. https://repositories.lib.utexas.edu/handle/2152/73742.

Lucas, C. L. *The Milton Lott Tragedy: a history of the first white death in Boone County . . . together with a sketch of the life of Colonel Nathan Boone, the man that Explored the Upper Des Moines Valley*. Published under the auspices of the Madrid Historical Society, Madrid, Iowa, 1906.

"Lucile Morris Upton." Interview by Carolyn Gerdes, March 1978. *Spotlight on Women*, KOZK-TV, Springfield, Missouri. Lucile Morris Upton Papers (C3869), State Historical Society of Missouri.

"Lucile Morris Upton." Interview by Marilyn Prosser, November 1982. Oral History Interviews, Christian County Historical Society, Christian County Library, Ozark, Missouri.

"Lucile Morris Upton." Interview, May 26, 1981. *Springfield Profiles*, KOZK-TV. Gordon McCann Ozarks Music Collection, Missouri State University Digital Collections. Special Collections and Archives, Meyer Library, Missouri State University.

Lutes, Jean Marie. *Front-Page Girls, Women Journalists in American Culture and Fiction, 1880–1930*. Ithaca: Cornell University Press, 2006.

———. "Into the Madhouse with Nellie Bly: Girl Stunt Reporting in Late Nineteenth-Century America." *American Quarterly* 54, no. 2 (2002): 217–53. http://www.jstor.org/stable/30041927.

"Maud Duncan's Linotype Machine." *OzarksWatch Magazine*, Spring/Summer 2020, 48.

Mahnkey, Douglas. *Bright Glowed My Hills*. Point Lookout: School of the Ozarks Press, 1968.

———. "The Mahnkey and Prather Families." *White River Valley Historical Quarterly* 4, no. 2 (Winter 1970–71): 4–5.

"Mary Paxton Keeley." *Historic Missourians*. State Historical Society of Missouri (website). https://historicmissourians.shsmo.org/historicmissourians/name/k/keeley/.

Maryville Republican (Missouri)

Massey, Ellen Gray. *A Candle Within Her Soul, Mary Elizabeth Mahnkey and Her Ozarks, 1877–1948.* Lebanon, Missouri: Bittersweet, Inc., 1996.

———, ed. *Bittersweet Country.* Garden City: Anchor Press/Doubleday, 1978.

McConnell, Kaitlyn. "Behind the Byline: Generations Who Grew Up with the Newspaper." *Ozarks Alive!,* February 4, 2016. https://ozarksalive.com/behind-the-byline-generations -who-grew-up-with-the-newspaper/.

———. "Mary Scott Hair Lives on at the Crane County Museum." *OzarksAlive!,* May 21, 2018. https://ozarksalive.com/mary-scott-hair-lives-on-at-stone-county-museum/.

McCord, May Kennedy. "Hillbilly Heartbeats." *Ozark Life,* August 1929.

McIntyre, Douglas A. "Over 2000 American Newspapers Have Closed in Past 15 Years." *24/7 WALL ST,* January 6, 2020. https://247wallst.com/media/2019/07/23/over -2000-american-newspapers-have-closed-in-past-15-years/.

McIntyre, Stephen L., ed. *Springfield's Urban Histories: Essays on the Queen City of the Missouri Ozarks.* Springfield: Moon City Press, 2012.

Meador, Lewis E., Papers, 1904–1982 (R0674), State Historical Society of Missouri.

Menendez, Albert J. *The Geography of Presidential Elections in the United States, 1868– 2004.* Jefferson, North Carolina: McFarland, 2009.

Meredith, Owen. *Lucile.* New York: Frederick A. Stokes and Brother, 1888.

Meyer, Annie Nathan, ed. *Woman's Work in America.* New York: Henry Holt and Company, 1891.

Miller, John E. *Becoming Laura Ingalls Wilder: The Woman Behind the Legend.* Columbia: University of Missouri Press, 1998.

———. "Laura Ingalls Wilder: A Perspective from 1932, the Year of Publication of Her First 'Little House Novel." Southeast Missouri University Press (website). http://www .semopress.com/laura-ingalls-wilder-a-perspective-from-1932-the-year-of -publication-of-her-first-little-house-novel/.

Miller, Joseph and Henry G. Alsberg, eds. *New Mexico: A Guide to the Colorful State.* American Guide Series. New York: Hastings House, 1940.

"Minnie Reynolds Scalabrino," *Colorado Encyclopedia* (website). https:// coloradoencyclopedia.org/article/minnie-reynolds-scalabrino.

Minutes, Springfield City Council, January 26, 1970 and March 9, 1970. Busch Municipal Building, 840 Boonville Avenue, Springfield, Missouri.

Moberly Monitor-Index (Missouri)

Moore v. Moore. 337 S.W.2d 781 (Mo. Ct. App. 1960) Casetext. Appeal from the Circuit Court, Stone County, William R. Collinson, Judge. https://casetext.com/case/moore -v-moore-221.

Morrow, Lynn. "Boone's Lick in Western Expansion: James Mackay, the Boones, and the Morrisons." *Boonslick Historical Society Quarterly* 13, no. 3 and 4 (Fall–Winter 2014): 4–34.

———. "A Surveyor's Challenges: P. K. Robbins in Missouri." *Big Muddy, a Journal of the Mississippi River Valley* 7.2 (Fall 2007): 1–21.

———. Papers (R1000), State Historical Society of Missouri, Columbia, Missouri.

Morrow, Lynn and Linda Myers-Phinney. *Shepherd of the Hills Country, Tourism Transforms the Ozarks, 1880s–1930s*. Fayetteville: University of Arkansas Press, 1999.

Nashville Banner

"Nathan Boone House." National Register of Historic Places Inventory nomination form, US Department of the Interior National Park Service. December 1968. http://dnr.mo .gov/shpo/nps-nr/69000103.pdf.

National Park Service. "15th Regiment, Missouri Cavalry," Union Missouri Volunteers, Battle Unit Details, Civil War. https://www.nps.gov/civilwar/search-battle-units-detail .htm?battleUnitCode=UMO0015RC.

New Mexico Military Institute. https://www.nmmi.edu.

New York Daily News

Nugent, Walter. *Into the West*. New York: Alfred A. Knopf, 1899.

O'Brien, Mike. "Betty Love, Photojournalist." *OzarksWatch Magazine*, Fall 2017.

———. "Radio Signals to Rocket Engines: Camp Crowder." In *TechnOzarks: Essays in Technology, Regional Economy and Culture*, edited by Tom Peters and Paul L. Durham, 99–112. Springfield: Ozarks Studies Institute of Missouri State University, 2019.

———. "Ted Richmond and the Wilderness Library." *OzarksWatch Magazine*, Fall 2020.

"Our First National Military Park." *Hallowed Ground Magazine*. American Battlefield Trust (website), Fall 2010. https://www.battlefields.org/learn/articles/our-first-national -military-park.

"Our History." Branson.com. https://www.branson.com/branson/shepherd/history.htm.

"Ozark Folklore Society." *Encyclopedia of Arkansas* (website). https://encyclopediaofarkansas .net/entries/ozark-folklore-society-6239/.

Ozarkiana Collection. Lyons Memorial Library, College of the Ozarks, Point Lookout, Missouri.

"Ozarks Voices." Oral history interviews, Ozarks Studies Institute. Missouri State University Library Special Collections, Missouri State University.

Padgett.blogspot.com (blog). "Captain Joseph C. Lea, the Father of Roswell." http://padgitt .blogspot.com/2012/11/captain-joseph-c-lea-father-of-roswell.html.

Parsons Daily Sun (Kansas)

Payton, Crystal. *Handcrafted at Silver Dollar City*. Springfield: Lens and Pen Press, 2001.

———. *The Story of Silver Dollar City*. Springfield: Lens and Pen Press, 1997.

Perkins, J. Blake. *Hillbilly Hellraisers, Federal Power and Populist Defiance in the Ozarks*. Urbana: University of Illinois Press, 2017.

Perry, Douglas. *The Girls of Murder City: Fame, Lust and the Beautiful Killers Who Inspired "Chicago."* New York: Penguin Books, 2010.

Peters, Thomas A. *John T. Woodruff of Springfield, Missouri, in the Ozarks: An Encyclopedic Biography*. Springfield: Pie Supper Press, 2016.

Phillips, Christopher. *Damned Yankee: The Life of General Nathaniel Lyon*. Columbia: University of Missouri Press, 1990, reissued by Louisiana State University Press, 1996.

Piston, William Garrett and Richard W. Hatcher III. *Wilson's Creek, the Second Battle of the Civil War and the Men Who Fought It*. Chapel Hill: University of North Carolina Press, 2000.

Piston, William Garrett and John C. Rutherford. *We Gave Them Thunder: Marmaduke's Raid and the Civil War in Missouri and Arkansas*. Springfield: Ozarks Studies Institute of Missouri State University, 2021.

Powell, William H. *List of Officers of the Army of the US from 1779–1900*, compiled from official records. New York: L. R. Hamersly and Company, 1900.

Rafferty, Milton D. *The Ozarks: Land and Life*. Fayetteville: University of Arkansas Press, 2001.

Randolph, Vance. "A Word List from the Ozarks." *Dialect Notes* 5 (1926): 397–401. (New Haven: Tuttle, Morehouse & Taylor Company, Publication of the American Dialect Society). https://books.google.com/books?id=wbImAQAAIAAJ&source =gbs_book_other_versions.

———. *The Ozarks: An American Survival of Primitive Society*. Fayetteville: University of Arkansas Press, 2017.

———. *Ozark Folksongs*. Columbia: State Historical Society of Missouri, 1946.

———. *Ozark Superstitions*. New York: Columbia University Press, 1947.

———. *Pissing in the Snow and Other Ozark Folktales*. Urbana: University of Illinois Press, 1986.

———. *Stiff as a Poker, a Collection of Ozark Folk Tales*. New York: Columbia University Press, 1955.

Randolph, Vance and George P. Wilson. *Down in the Holler, a Gallery of Ozark Folk Speech*. Norman: University of Oklahoma, 1953.

Rayburn, Otto Ernest. *Forty Years in the Ozarks*. Eureka Springs: Ozarks Guide Press, 1957.

Riley, Glenda. ""Wimmin Is Everywhere": Conserving and Feminizing Western Landscapes, 1870 to 1940." *Western Historical Quarterly* 29, no. 1 (1998): 5–23. https://www.jstor.org/stable/i239747.

Ritchie, Donald A. *Reporting from Washington: The History of the Washington Press Corps*. New York: Oxford University Press, 2005.

Roberts, Larry. "The History of Fort Leonard Wood." *Maneuver Support Magazine*, Summer 2008. https://web.archive.org/web/20091229132642/http://www.wood .army.mil/engrmag/Maneuver%20Support%20Magazine/PDFs%20for%20 Summer%202008/Roberts.pdf.

Roggensees, David. "A Cherokee Thanksgiving: The Role of Nathan Boone in the Cherokee Crisis of 1845 and 1846." *Missouri Historical Review* 108, no. 4 (July 2014): 221–35.

Rutherford, John. "O'Reilly General Hospital of Springfield, Missouri: Springfield's Hospital with a Soul." Local History Collection, Springfield-Greene County Library Center. https://Thelibrary.Org/Lochist/Oreilly/Fiftyplus.Cfm.

St. Joseph News-Press (Missouri)

St. Louis Globe-Democrat

St. Louis Post-Dispatch

St. Louis Star and Times

Schudson, Michael. *Discovering the News*. New York: Basic Books, Inc., 1978.

Sedalia Weekly Democrat (Missouri)

Sigel, Jerry, Los Angeles, to *TIME* magazine, letter-to-the-editor, May 30, 1988.

"Significant Weather Events of the Century for Missouri." Climate Center, University of Missouri College of Agriculture, Food, and Natural Resources. http://climate.missouri. edu/sigwxmo.php.

Simpson, Ethel C. "Otto Ernest Rayburn, an Early Promoter of the Ozarks." *Arkansas Historical Quarterly* 58 (Summer 1999): 160–79.

Smith, Wilda M. and Eleanor A. Bogart. *The Wars of Peggy Hull: The Life and Times of a War Correspondent.* El Paso: Texas Western Press, 1991.

Springfield Daily News

Springfield Leader

Springfield Leader-Democrat

Springfield Leader and Press

Springfield News and Leader

Springfield News-Leader

Springfield Press

Springfield Republican

Sunday News and Leader

"The Status of Women in the U.S. Media 2019," Women's Media Center. https:// womensmediacenter.com/reports/the-status-of-women-in-u-s-media-2019.

Stebbins, Chad. *All the News Is Fit to Print: Profile of a Country Editor.* Columbia: University of Missouri Press, 1998.

Stewart, Kenneth. *News Is What We Make It, a Running Story of the Working Press.* Boston: Houghton Mifflin, 1943.

Stuck, Dorothy D. and Nan Snow. *Roberta, A Most Remarkable Fulbright.* Fayetteville: University of Arkansas Press, 1997.

Taft, William H. *Show-Me Journalists: The First 200 Years.* Marceline, Missouri: Heritage House Publishing, 2003.

Thayer News (Missouri)

Todd, Kim. *Sensational: The Hidden History of America's "Girl Stunt Reporters."* New York: Harper-Collins, 2021.

Truman, Harry S. "Address in Bolivar, Missouri, at the Dedication of the Simon Bolivar Memorial Statue, July 5, 1948." Gerhard Peters and John T. Woolley, American Presidency Project (website). https://www.presidency.ucsb.edu/node/232646.

Uhlenbrock, Tom. "Rare Historic Photos Show CCC Crew." *Daily Journal* online, February 24, 2016, updated March 2, 2017. https://dailyjournalonline.com/news/local/rare-historic -photos-show-ccc-crew/article_5072b85b-a9cf-5e26–8378–92dfd23b1370.html.

"Uncle George Stories." *Family History.* Sarah Morris Riddick interview with George Morris. Lucile Morris Upton Collection, Local History Department, Springfield- Greene County Library Center.

United States Census Bureau. 1910 Census: Volume 4. Population, Occupation Statistics (pub 1914). https://www.census.gov/library/publications/1914/dec/vol-4-occupations .html.

United States Census Bureau. 1920 Census: Volume 4. "Population, Occupations" (pub 1923). https://www.census.gov/library/publications/1923/dec/vol-04-occupations.html.

———. "A Comparison of the Census Occupation and Industry Classifications and Statistics of 1930 and 1940." https://www2.census.gov/library/publications/decennial/1940 /population-occupation/00312147ch1.pdf.

———. "1950 Census of Population: Volume 4. Special Reports, Table 2–Detailed Occupation of Employed Persons, by Detailed Industry and Sex, for the United States: 1950." https://www2.census.gov/library/publications/decennial/1950/population -volume-4/41601751v4p1ch6.pdf.

———. US Decennial Census. "Census of Population and Housing." https://www.census .gov/programs-surveys/decennial-census.html.

Upton, Lucile Morris. *Bald Knobbers*. Caldwell, Idaho: Caxton Press, 1939. Reprinted by the School of the Ozarks, 1971.

———. *Battle of Wilson's Creek*. Booklet reprinted from articles by LMU. Printed and distributed by Wilson's Creek Battlefield Foundation, Inc., Springfield, Missouri, 1950.

———. "Battle That Saved Missouri for the Union." *Civil War Times*, November 1959.

———. Collection. Local History Collection, Springfield-Greene County Library Center.

———. "Good Ol' Hillbilly . . ." *The University Review, Journal of the University of Kansas City* 4, no. 2 (1937): 188–90.

———. Interview by National Park Historian Richard Hatcher and Gus Klapp. Wilson's Creek National Battlefield, October 23, 1984.

———. Papers. (C3869) State Historical Society of Missouri.

———. *Three Morris Young-Uns*. Spiral-bound booklet compiled by Pam Morris Jones, 1990.

———. *Wilson's Creek Story*. *Springfield Leader-Press*, August 8, 1961. Sixteen-page newspaper supplement.

———. "Woodsaw Charlie's Wife." *Capper's Farmer*, October 1926.

———. "Writing Historical Articles for Local Newspapers." *Missouri Historical Review* (January 1960): 145–47.

Upton, Lucile Morris and John K. Hulston. *Nathan Boone, the Neglected Hero, From Writings by Lucile Morris Upton and John K. Hulston*. Edited by Carole Bills. Republic, Missouri: Western Printing Company, 1984.

Wahl-Jorgensen, Karin. "News Production, Ethnography, and Power on the Challenges of Newsroom-Centricity." In *The Anthropology of News and Journalism*, edited by S. E. Bird, 21–35. Bloomington: Indiana University Press, 2009.

Walker, Mason. "U.S. Newsroom Employment Has Fallen 26% since 2008." Pew Research Center. July 13, 2021. https://www.pewresearch.org/fact-tank/2021/07/13/u-s -newsroom-employment-has-fallen-26-since-2008/.

Way, Megan McDonald. *Family Economics and Public Policy, 1800–Present*. New York: Palgrave MacMillan, 2018.

Weinberg, Steve. *A Journalism of Humanity*. Columbia: University of Missouri Press, 2008.

Wendt, Diane. "Surviving Rabies 100 Years Ago." In *O Say Can You See? Stories from the Museum*. National Museum of American History, October 28, 1913. https://americanhistory.si.edu/blog/2013/10/surviving-rabies-100-years-ago.html.

West, James (Carl Withers). *Plainville U.S.A.* New York: Columbia University Press, 1945.

West Plains Journal-Gazette (Missouri)

White, Owen P. *The Autobiography of a Durable Sinner*. New York: G. P. Putnam's Sons, 1942.

Whitt, Jan. *Women in American Journalism, A New History*. Urbana: University of Illinois Press, 2008.

Wilson's Creek National Battlefield Collection. Wilson's Creek National Battlefield, Republic, Missouri.

Wilson's Creek National Battlefield Cultural Landscape Report, Volume 1. Prepared for National Park Service Midwest Regional Office, Omaha, Nebraska, by John Milner Associates, Inc., Charlottesville, Virginia, September 2004.

Wiley, Robert S. *Dewey Short, Orator of the Ozarks* Volume 1. Cassville: Litho Printers and Bindery, 1985.

Winfield, Betty Houchin. *Journalism 1908, Birth of a Profession*. Columbia: University of Missouri Press, 2008.

Winslow, Helen M. "Some Newspaper Women." In *The Arena* 17. no. 1, edited by John Clark Ridpath, 127. Boston: Arena Publishing Company, 1897. https://www.google.com/books/edition/The_Arena/jkVBAAAAYAAJ?hl=en&gbpv=1&dq=Helen+M.+Winslow+"Some+Newspaper+Women'&pg=PA127&printsec=frontcover.

Woloch, Nancy. "Eleanor Roosevelt's White House Press Conferences," National Women's History Museum. September 22, 2017. https://www.womenshistory.org/articles/eleanor-roosevelts-white-house-press-conferences.

Woman's Club of El Paso records, 1857, 1895—2016, MS 576, C. L. Sonnichsen Special Collections Department, University of Texas at El Paso Library. https://www.utep.edu/library/_Files/docs/special-collections/finding-aids/MS576_womens.pdf.

Wood, Larry. "The Barker Gang and the Murder of Sheriff Kelly." *Daily Journal* online, October 23, 2016. https://dailyjournalonline.com/news/the-barker-gang-and-the-murder-of-sheriff-kelly/article_19b62a7f-f301-52d1-bcab-a2d5d9bcc561.html.

———. "Lucile Morris Upton." *Missouri and Ozarks History* (blog), March 13, 2012. http://ozarks-history.blogspot.com/2012/03/lucille-morris-upton.html.

Workers of the Writers' Program of the Work Projects Administration in the State of Arkansas. *Arkansas, a Guide to the State*. New York: Hastings House, 1941.

INDEX

Page numbers in italics indicate a photograph
Lucile Morris Upton is referred to as LMU